Figure 1. Drainage map of the world

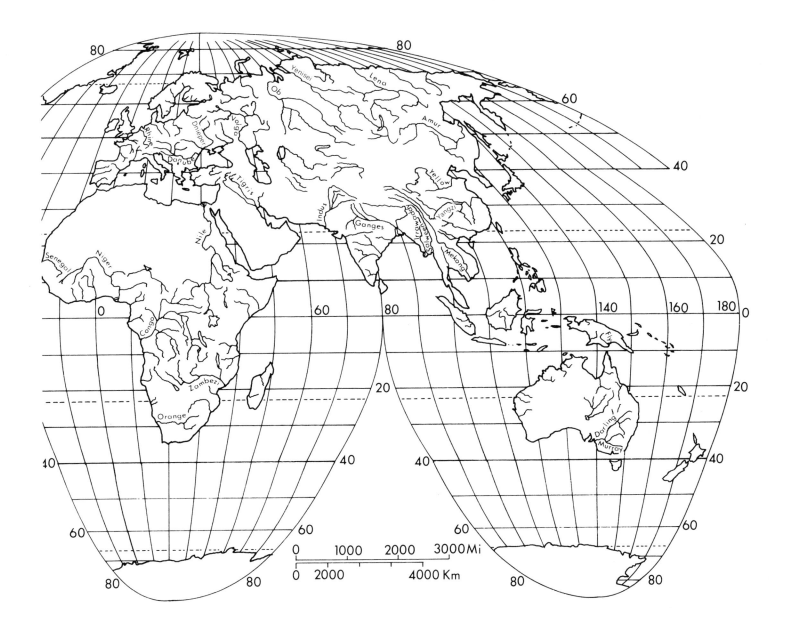

80   80

Yenisei   Lena

Ob   Amur   60

Rhine   Volga   40

Dnieper

Danube   Yellow

Tigris   Yangzi

Indus   20

Nile   Ganges   Mekong

Senegal   Niger

0   60   80   140   160   180   0

Congo

Zambezi   20   20

Orange   Darling

Murray

40   40   40   40

60   60   60   60

0   1000   2000   3000Mi

80   80   80   80

0   2000   4000 Km

An Atlas of Distribution of the Freshwater Fish Families of the World

An Atlas
of Distribution of the
Freshwater Fish Families
of the World

TIM M. BERRA

FOREWORD BY
R. M. McDowall

UNIVERSITY OF NEBRASKA PRESS
Lincoln and London

Library of Congress Cataloging in Publication Data

Berra, Tim M   1943–
   An atlas of distribution of the freshwater fish families of the
world.

   Bibliography: p.
   Includes index.
   1. Fishes, Fresh-water—Geographical distribution—
Atlases.   2. Fishes—Geographical distribution—
Atlases.   I. Title.
QL619.B47   597.092'9   80–24666
ISBN 0–8032–1411–1
ISBN 0–8032–6059–8 (pbk.)

Dedicated to
Gerald E. Gunning
and
Royal D. Suttkus,
Tulane University,
who stimulated and encouraged
my interest in fishes

ERRATA

As this book was going to press, I learned that the joint committee on Names of Fishes of the American Fisheries Society and the American Society of Ichthyologists and Herpetologists had decided on the spelling Petromyzontidae for the family referred to in this book as Petromyzonidae. In addition, Reeve M. Bailey, past chairman of that committee, informed me that the correct spelling of the family name that appears here as Pimelodontidae is Pimelodidae.

On p. 34, second column, lines 12 and 15, the correct date for Bell et al. is 1981.

Contents

Illustrations and Tables

Foreword

Freshwater fishes are among the most interesting and, for many decades, controversial animal groups in their distribution patterns and the ways these patterns have developed over space and through time. There are "freshwater fishes" almost everywhere. Antarctica lacks them, as do some of the smallest islands, but even deserts may have freshwater fishes, though they be sparse in number, intermittent in occurrence, and low in diversity. Species are found from cold, high alpine torrents, lakes, and tarns to warm coastal lagoons and estuaries. Great river systems in the larger continental masses, like the Nile, the Mississippi, and the Amazon, have large and highly diverse freshwater faunas, with hundreds of species of a wide array of types occupying a range of habitats. Smaller rivers, particularly those of the smaller and more geographically isolated land masses, have much less diverse faunas. Of the larger continents (apart from Antarctica), Australia has the least diverse and spectacular freshwater fish fauna—a product presumably of its geographical isolation, past climatic instability, and present low precipitation—the last of these largely limiting fish to coastal river systems and the moister southeast.

Freshwater fishes have always been a fruitful field for biogeographers. Having assumed that freshwater fish are strictly confined to freshwaters, many early biogeographers affirmed the need for continuity of freshwater (and thus of land) to explain the very obviously disjunct distribution patterns exhibited by some families—like characids in Africa and South America, cyprinids in Africa, Eurasia, and North America (but *not* South America), esocoids in northern, circumpolar cool-temperate waters or galaxiids in southern circumpolar cool-temperate waters.

Early biogeographers beginning with Darwin himself focused on the biogeographic problems that freshwater fishes pose. Explanations offered to cover highly disjunct distributions often involved the "erection" of land bridges in diverse places and across unlikely oceans. Some workers recognized that some of the "freshwater" species were actually diadromous, and turned to transoceanic dispersal as a mechanism for explaining distributions—for example, a brief paper by G. A. Boulenger in 1902 ("The explanation of a remarkable case of geographical distribution in fishes," *Nature* 67 : 84). Some workers who followed noticed, but disagreed with Boulenger that, for instance, galaxiid fishes could disperse through the sea; others seem not to have noticed or to have ignored his hypothesis. And while Boulenger's approach may have been helpful for diadromous species tolerant of sea water, it was of no help for the more strictly freshwater species—families that G. S. Myers was later to categorize as "primary freshwater fishes."

Debates about how freshwater fish distributions have developed continue to the present day. Widespread acceptance, until the 1960s, of a stable conformation of the earth's continents encouraged biogeographers to look for land connections and / or faunal migration routes whereby existing patterns could have developed. These, although often ingenious, were never widely satisfying. With the more general acceptance, initially among geologists and subsequently among biologists, of continental drift and plate tectonics, a whole new approach has developed, such that for some, continental drift has become the explanation for everything—giving seemingly simple answers to what are, in essence, often very complex questions.

The advent of plate tectonics has generated the viewpoint that freshwater fish distributions may be explained by "vicariance"—essentially the movement of biotas resident on shifting land masses. Much controversy relates to these various divergent yet not inconsistent viewpoints, and these simple answers, in my view, ignore some of the very real complexities of the historical development of fish distribution patterns during the last 100 million or so years.

FOREWORD

Essentially, biogeography comprises two activities: (1) identifying the patterns and (2) explaining the processes that produced these patterns.

The first of these is relatively simple, and disagreement occurs largely at the level of alpha taxonomy: are disjunct populations conspecific or not? Such disagreements have little or no real impact on the development of biogeographic hypotheses. It is at the stage of explaining the processes that significant controversy has occurred and continues to occur.

Most freshwater fish groups have left us very meagre fossil records, giving very few hints of their ancestral distributions, diversity, or morphology. Thus we have to deal primarily with existing distributions to explain a long history of past occurrences.

While these freshwater-restricted groups seem certain to have required "land" routes to spread and enlarge distributions, it is not necessarily so for the diadromous groups, some of which may be found hundreds of kilometers out to sea at any stage from newly hatched larvae to large adults. It is the role of these marine stages of supposedly freshwater fish species that is one of the centres of controversy in fish biogeography, a controversy that seems to have no logical solution.

Controversy, or no controversy, the resource materials for such discussions are the fish distributions themselves. With more than 8,000 species of freshwater fish, it is a mammoth task to attain a broad understanding of their distribution patterns. This book is a useful beginning in assisting workers interested in understanding and explaining freshwater fish distributions. By describing family distributions it highlights the distribution patterns that exist. It enables the identification of congruent distribution patterns. It suggests questions that can be asked about these congruent patterns. And it provides some of the resources by means of which investigators can find entry into the voluminous literature pertaining to these fish, thereby obtaining the more detailed distributional data that assist in answering the questions that the more simple "family distributions" provoke.

It is becoming increasingly evident and more widely accepted that sound historical biogeography has to be anchored in detailed phylogenetic analyses of fish groups.

No book and no one author can provide the data necessary or the answers to the many questions arising. In most instances, the work just hasn't been done—not even started. For *very few* groups are there detailed phylogenetic analyses.

This atlas, then, is the resource material for beginning biogeographical studies.

There is little doubt that ichthyologists and biogeographers will find this book an extremely useful basic resource for research purposes.

R. M. McDowall
Christchurch, New Zealand

Preface

The purpose of this book is to provide a visual synopsis of the approximate native distributions of the freshwater fish families of the world. The maps are not intended to pinpoint the exact range of each family, as, in many cases, this is not known and ranges are not static, since they are made up of living populations that may be in the process of expansion or contraction. This book is intended as a supplemental text for college level courses in ichthyology, zoogeography, and vertebrate natural history. Fishermen and aquarists will also find it informative.

The idea for the book occurred to me in 1965, when I was a graduate student in zoogeography class at Tulane University. I found that making rough maps of the distribution of each family of vertebrates was an effective way to study. I have since been gathering published maps and descriptions of the distribution of each fish family found in fresh water. I accumulated maps and descriptions in folders. When the time came to write the book in earnest, the information in each folder was spread out on my desk, and a composite distribution based on the references for each family was penciled on a blank map. The result is a sort of "visual Darlington."

The fishes of some areas of the world are better known than others; consequently, more reliability can be placed on the North American distributions than, say, those from South America or Africa, whose faunas and rivers are still relatively poorly known. In areas where data are incomplete a certain generalization is unavoidable.

I have tried to include all the primary and secondary division freshwater fish families and all the zoogeographically important peripheral ones as well as a sampling of marine families having some members that make incursions into coastal rivers. The range of these marine families is shown by shading from the continents into the sea, which implies that the particular family is found along the coast and may enter estuaries or ascend rivers, given their presence, the right temperature, salinity, and other factors. It does not necessarily mean that they are found in all coastal rivers. Likewise, the possible presence of a few families in scattered oases is indicated by shading across the Sahara. Nonnative distributions, such as trout in the Southern Hemisphere, are not included.

One of the biggest problems in studying for my zoogeography class was remembering which family was which. I have attempted to include in this book little tidbits of interesting natural history which, I hope, will make the families easier to remember. The pronunciation guide should help students and professionals alike. I have also included information on size, diet, and habitat for many families. The characteristics given for each group are designed to present an impression of a generalized representative and are not meant to be taxonomically diagnostic. In many cases the reader is referred to revisions of groups or major papers on family members. These references are intended as an entrance into the literature for students who desire further information. The classification and line drawings of most family members basically follow Greenwood et al. (1966) with a few changes. Fossil representatives are dated after Andrews et al. (1967) unless otherwise stated, and sizes mentioned are total lengths. An asterisk (*) after a reference means that a map is given in that publication.

The end matter includes useful handouts, such as geologic time scale, list of rivers and lakes, drainage map, guides to freshwater fishes of the United States and Canada, reading lists, *National Geographic* and *Scientific American* articles on fishes, and a glossary.

How the patterns of distribution indicated on the maps came about is a complicated problem, and I shall not presume to more than touch on it. Many explanations are needed to take into account such diverse information as continental drift, dispersal, vagility, age and area, centers of origin, ancestral versus derived characters, reliable phylogenies, and many other things. It is hoped that the visual impressions created by the maps in this book will be helpful to biogeographers grappling with these and related problems.

Acknowledgments

I owe a great debt of gratitude to the eminent ichthyogeographer, George S. Myers, for his interest and help with this project. He examined each map, wrote voluminous criticisms, then reexamined the corrected maps. He generously provided his pronunciations of family names, pointed out references, and suggested additional families to be included. He saved me from numerous, embarrassing errors. However, I do not want his help or that of anyone listed below to be construed as an imprimatur. The errors that remain, and undoubtedly there are some, are my own. I am confident my colleagues will point them out to me, along with new information, so that the distribution maps can be improved in the future.

Carter R. Gilbert, of the Florida State Museum, devoted a great deal of time to a careful review of the manuscript and provided factual material as well as many suggestions for improvement. P. H. Greenwood, curator of fishes at the British Museum (Natural History), reviewed the maps and made many helpful comments, especially on the African distributions. Donn E. Rosen, of the American Museum of Natural History, reviewed the manuscript and made numerous useful suggestions. Bruce B. Collette, of the National Marine Fisheries Service, provided detailed help on the Hemiramphidae and Belonidae. Tyson Roberts supplied some published and unpublished information that was useful in mapping the distribution of several families. Jack Garrick commented on the shark section, and Robert McDowall examined the Australian and New Zealand families. The following ichthyologists briefly commented upon various maps during the course of the 1977 and 1978 meetings of the American Society of Ichthyologists and Herpetologists: Clyde Barbour, John Briggs, Barry Chernoff, John Fitch, Garrett Glodek, Janet Gomon, Clark Hubbs, Robert Johnson, Robert Lavenberg, Bruce Menzel, Robert R. Miller, Lynne Parenti, K. V. Rama Rao, and Jamie Thomerson. Robert Behnke and George Van Dyke supplied some information via correspondence. Ross Feltes helped with the Polynemidae.

David Dennis drew the base map from the Goode Base Map Series, the drainage map, and Figures 2 and 3. Lisa Gassin plotted the distributions from my rough maps and drew the fish outlines. Ray-Jean Au made numerous Xerox copies of rough drafts. Linda Linn was a cheerful, speedy, and accurate typist. Revisions were retyped by Babette Mullet and Yolanda Allen. My wife, Rita, typed file cards for my growing reprint collection. Lynn Murphy Dominick ceaselessly rounded up odd interlibrary loans. I am very grateful for all of this help.

The College of Biological Sciences of Ohio State University provided a grant-in-aid which covered many of the expenses of this project. The Research Committee of the Mansfield Campus of Ohio State University provided additional funding. I would like to thank the chairman of the Department of Zoology of Ohio State University, Tony J. Peterle, for his overall support of my research efforts. I am also indebted to the former dean of the Mansfield Campus, James B. Heck, the current dean, David Kramer, and the associate dean, Richard Wink, for providing the kind of climate in which research can flourish.

Introduction

What is a Fish?

This question is not as simple as it sounds at first reading. What makes it a difficult question is that there are many exceptions for each character used to define "fish." For example: Character: fishes swim in water. Exceptions: the mudskipper, *Periophthalmus*, skips about on mangrove flats completely out of water; grunions, *Leuresthes*, spawn on beaches above the low tide mark; the walking catfish, *Clarias*, ambles overland from pond to pond. Character: fishes respire by means of gills. Exceptions: lungfish, *Protopterus*, can breathe atmospheric air via lungs and can even remain encysted in a dry mud cocoon; anabantids have a labyrinth organ in their head that provides a large, highly vascularized surface for oxygen uptake. Character: fishes have scales. Exceptions: catfishes lack scales; some sticklebacks have an armour plating of modified scales; some fishes are only partially scaled, and some (eels) have such tiny, embedded scales that they are easily overlooked. Character: fishes have fins. Exceptions: *Gymnarchus* lacks pelvic, anal, and caudal fins, while *Gymnotus* lacks dorsal and pelvic fins. The swamp eels (Synbranchidae) lack both pectoral and pelvic fins, and the anal and dorsal fins exist only as ridges. Character: fishes are cold-blooded. Exceptions: many fast-swimming species such as tunas and their relatives develop muscle temperatures in excess of ambient.

If we allow room for these and other exceptions, we can define a fish as a poikilothermic, aquatic chordate with appendages (when present) developed as fins, whose chief respiratory organs are gills and whose body is usually covered with scales. This broad definition makes no mention of skeletal material and therefore includes the cartilaginous lampreys and elasmobranchs as well as the bony fishes.

Primary, Secondary and Peripheral Division Fish Families

Myers (1938, 1949, 1951) developed a widely used classification of fishes in fresh water based on their tolerance to salt water. This system is, of course, ecological rather than taxonomic. As modified by Darlington (1957) the three divisions are primary, secondary, and peripheral. Primary division freshwater fish families are those whose members have little salt tolerance and are confined to fresh waters. Salt water is a major barrier for them, and their distribution has not depended upon passage through the sea. The salt tolerance of individual species within a family does vary, however.

Secondary division freshwater fish families are those whose members are usually confined to fresh water, but they have some salt tolerance, and their distribution may reflect dispersal through coastal waters or across short distances of salt water. Some peripheral family members may be confined to fresh water, and others may spend a considerable portion of their life cycle in fresh water, but they both are derived from marine ancestors who used the oceans as dispersal routes. Other peripheral division families are basically marine groups, some of whom enter fresh water. The ecological designation followed in this book is taken from Darlington (1957), who wrote, "We may, if we wish, doubt the 'reality' of Myers' divisions, but how can we doubt their usefulness in zoogeography?" On the other hand, Rosen (1974) has challenged the usefulness of such a salt tolerance classification scheme, and he views fishes as being either continental or oceanic. In the family accounts here given, 1st, 2d and Per refer to primary, secondary, and peripheral divisions respectively.

How Many Kinds of Fishes are There?

Cohen (1970) attempted an analysis of this problem by surveying ichthyologists who were experts in the various taxonomic groups. His results indicated about 50 species of Agnatha (lampreys and hagfishes), 535 species of Chondrichthyes (sharks, skates, rays, chimaerids), and about 20,000 species of Osteichthyes (bony fishes), excluding fossil forms. A similar estimate, 18,300, was made by Bailey (1971). Of the 20,000 bony fishes, approximately 33 percent (6,650) are primary division freshwater species, and 93 percent of these are ostariophysan fishes. Secondary division freshwater fishes accounted for about 8 percent (1,625) of the total Osteichthyes, and most of these are cichlids and cyprinodontoids. Thus freshwater fishes make up about 41 percent (8,275) of all bony fishes, and as Cohen (1970) pointed out, this surprisingly high percentage is a reflection of the degree of isolation and diversity of niches possible in the freshwater environment. The large numbers of species in fresh water becomes even more amazing if the volume of fresh water on earth is compared to the volume of the oceans. The oceans account for 97 percent of all the water on earth, whereas the fresh water in lakes and rivers is an almost negligible percentage, 0.0093 percent (Horn 1972). (The rest of the water is tied up as ice, groundwater, atmospheric water, and so forth.) Therefore 41 percent of all fish species live in less than 0.01 percent of the world's water (Horn 1972). Further data on productivity of marine and freshwater environments and calculations—which show that there are about 113,000 km^3 of water for each marine species while only 15 km^3 for each freshwater species—an approximate 7,500-fold difference—can be found in Horn (1972).

The rate at which new species have been named is interesting. The tenth edition of Linnaeus's *Systema naturae* (1758) listed 478 species in 50 teleost genera. By 1870 Gunther put the total number of known teleosts at about 8,700. An analysis of new names proposed for teleosts from 1869 to 1970 (Berra and Berra 1977) yielded an estimate of 15,370 new names for the 100-year period. If this figure is added to Gunther's calculation, we arrive at a total of 24,070 teleost names, which, when synonymies are taken into account, agrees well with Cohen's data derived independently.

Berra and Berra (1977) found that the families receiving the most new names were the cyprinids, gobiids, characins, and cichlids. They also reported that of the newly named freshwater species 35 percent were from South America, 30 percent from Africa, and 23 percent from Asia. This agrees well with the diversity and endemism data shown in tables 1 and 2 and with the figures given by Gilbert (1976).

Wallace's Line

The foundations of biogeography can be traced to the writings of Georges Louis Leclerc, comte de Buffon and Augustin Pyramus de Candolle (Nelson 1978). However, it was Alfred Russel Wallace (1823–1913), a British naturalist and codiscoverer with Charles Darwin of evolution via natural selection, who elaborated the concept of zoogeographic regions with the publication of his classic work, *The Geographical Distribution of Animals*, in 1876. He recognized 6 zoogeographical realms, which he called Nearctic (North America except tropical Mexico), Neotropical (South and Central America with tropical Mexico), Palearctic (nontropical Eurasia and north tip of Africa), Ethiopian (Africa and southern Arabia), Oriental (tropical Asia and nearby islands), and Australian (Australia, New Guinea, New Zealand) (fig. 2). Darlington (1957) gave a detailed discussion of continental patterns of the distribution of vertebrates.

In 1860 Wallace proposed a hypothetical boundary between the Oriental and Australian faunas. This line passes between Bali and Lombok, through the Makasar Strait between Borneo and the Celebes, and south of the Philippines (fig. 3). A few years later T. H. Huxley named the boundary Wallace's line. He also modified it on the basis of bird studies to place the Philippines east of the line within the Australian realm. Mayr (1944) treated this controversy in depth. As the fauna of this region (Wallacea) became better known, many examples of animal groups crossing Wallace's line were noted, and most zoogeographers today do not take Wallace's line literally as an exact boundary between the Oriental and Australian faunas. However, the line does suggest a major faunal break separating the rich Oriental continental fauna from the depauperate Australian island fauna.

Of the vertebrate groups, the freshwater fishes are most inhibited by a saltwater barrier and, therefore, most closely follow Wallace's line. There are 23 families of primary division freshwater fishes on Borneo. Only 1 family, Osteoglossidae, has managed to cross Wallace's line naturally. There are 3 species in 3 genera (*Anabas*, *Ophicephalus*, *Clarias*) that man likely transported across the Makasar Strait to the Celebes. A few salt-tolerant oryziatids have reached the Celebes, Lombok, and Timor, and the endemic secondary division Adrianichthyidae occur in the Celebes. Only 2 cyprinid genera, *Puntius* and *Rasbora*, occur on both Bali and Lombok, with *Rasbora* reaching Sumbawa. These 2 cyprinid genera and a few others also occur in the Philippines along with an endemic silurid and clariid catfish (Darlington 1957). With these few exceptions, the Asian and Australian freshwater fish faunas do not mix but, rather, end abruptly, which is unlike the situation in the New World, where the faunas of North and South America mingle in a Central American transitional zone.

A second line, Weber's line, was proposed by Pelseneer in 1904. Weber's line represents the "line of faunal balance" that separates the islands with a majority of Oriental groups from those with an Australian majority. Mayr (1944) favored this line and provided more details. Weber's line (fig. 3) is closer to Australia and reflects the fact that the Oriental fauna has made more of an intrusion to the east than has the Australian fauna to the west.

Which line, if any, one chooses to defend really depends upon the taxonomic group in question and how many exceptions one is willing to tolerate. Furthermore, these lines are irrelevant to plant geographers, whose subject is much more directly influenced by climate.

Distribution Patterns

Freshwater fishes are one of the most important groups zoogeographically because they are more or less confined to drainage systems which can be thought of as dendritic islands of water surrounded by land, which is in turn bordered by a saltwater barrier. The freshwater fishes provide a relatively conservative system for examining patterns of distribution that may reflect continental changes. The family is the taxon that best reflects the evolution and dispersal of a group, and, in fact, zoogeographic patterns are one of the evidences of evolution cited in introductory zoology texts.

The distribution of 128 primary, secondary, and peripheral division families is given in table 2. The Neotropical realm has the largest number (32) of primary division families (table 1), whereas the Oriental and Ethiopian regions are close behind with 28 and 27 primary division families each. The Nearctic and Palearctic regions have 14 primary division families each. The only primary division freshwater fishes in Australia are the lungfish, *Neoceratodus forsteri*, and 2 species of osteoglossids, *Scleropages*.

The Neotropical realm also has the greatest number of secondary division freshwater families (6), while the Nearctic and Oriental regions have 5 apiece, most of which are cyprinodontoids (table 1). The Ethiopian region has only 2 secondary families, the Cyprinodontidae and the Cichlidae; however, the cichlids are represented by an enormous number of endemic species with a great diversity of forms and habits. In Australia and New Guinea, the Melanotaeniidae occupy many cyprinodont and cyprinid niches. Oryziatids and cyprinodontids make up the secondary freshwater fish fauna of the Palearctic (table 2).

The Neotropical and Oriental realms have the largest number of families, with 46 and 43 respectively (table 1). The Ethiopian, Palearctic, and Nearctic have totals of 32, 29, and 27 families. The Australian freshwater fauna is depauperate, as expected of an island, and is dominated by peripheral groups. If the other marine families with freshwater representatives included in this book were taken into account, the proportion of peripheral representatives in Australian fresh waters would be even more lopsided.

By far the greatest number of endemic primary division families (29) is found in the Neotropical zone (table 1). In fact, all but 3 primary families are endemic. This is a reflection of the extensive radiation of the ostariophysan characoids and siluriforms. The Ethiopian and Oriental regions are a distant second and third place in the endemism race, with 15 and 14 families respectively. The Nearctic region has only 7 endemic primary division families. The only endemic primary division family in Australia is the Ceratodontidae.

The Oriental and Neotropical regions each have 2 endemic secondary division families, the Adrianichthyidae and Horaichthyidae, and the Anablepidae and Jenynsiidae, respectively. The Goodeidae of the Nearctic and the Melanotaeniidae of Australia are the only endemic secondary division families of those regions.

The highest percentage of endemism of freshwater fish families is in the Neotropical area, with 70 percent of the families found nowhere else (table 1). About half (44 percent and 47 percent, respectively) of the families found in the freshwaters of the Oriental and Ethiopian realms are endemic to those areas. The fish faunas, at the family level, are about 39 percent endemic in the fresh waters of the Australian realm and 30 percent endemic in the Nearctic realm. The endemic families of the Palearctic region comprise only 10 percent of the freshwater fish families (table 1). Several families share a Nearctic and Palearctic distribution which may be considered a Holarctic pattern. It should be noted that some of the peripheral families excluded from tables 1 and 2 have endemic

Table 1
Number of Fish Families and Percent Endemism in Each Biogeographical Realm, Based upon 128 Families
(widely distributed peripheral families excluded)

	Nearctic	Neotropical	Palearctic	Ethiopian	Oriental	Australian
No. Primary Families	14	32	14	27	28	2
No. Secondary Families	5	6	2	2	5	1
No. Peripheral Families	8	8	13	3	10	15
Total No. Families	27	46	29	32	43	18˙
No. Endemic Primary	7	29	0	15	14	1
No. Endemic Secondary	1	2	0	0	2	1
No. Endemic Peripheral	0	1	3	0	3	4
Total Endemic Families	8	32	3	15	19	7˙
Percent Endemic Primary	26	63	0	47	33	6
Percent Endemic Secondary	4	4	0	0	5	6
Percent Endemic Peripheral	0	2	10	0	7	22
Percent Endemic Total	30	70	10	47	44	39˙

˙The Lepidogalaxiidae is included in the total.

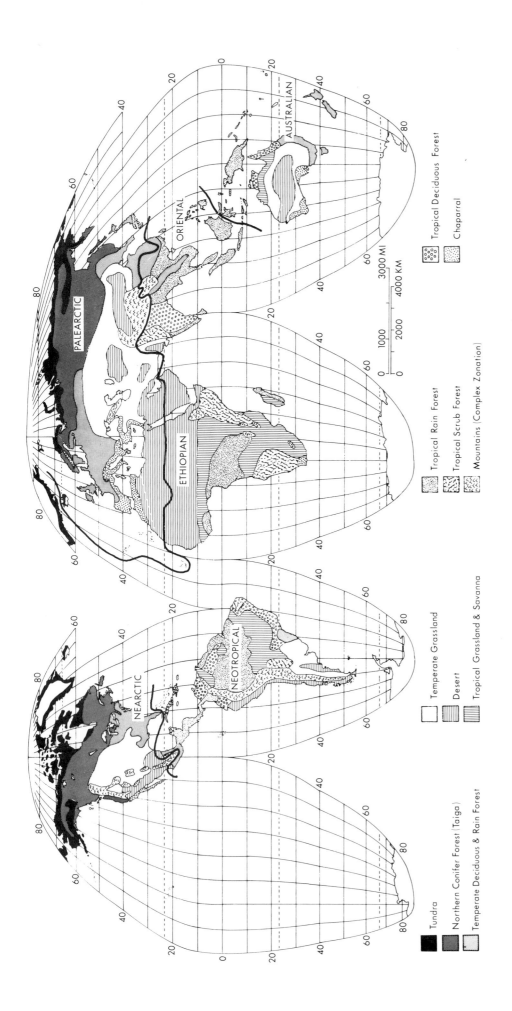

Figure 2. Wallace's six zoogeographic realms and the major biomes of the world

Tundra

Northern Conifer Forest (Taiga)

Temperate Deciduous & Rain Forest

Temperate Grassland

Desert

Tropical Grassland & Savanna

Tropical Rain Forest

Tropical Scrub Forest

Mountains (Complex Zonation)

Tropical Deciduous Forest

Chaparral

NEARCTIC

NEOTROPICAL

PALEARCTIC

ETHIOPIAN

ORIENTAL

AUSTRALIAN

0 1000 2000 3000 MI

0 2000 4000 KM

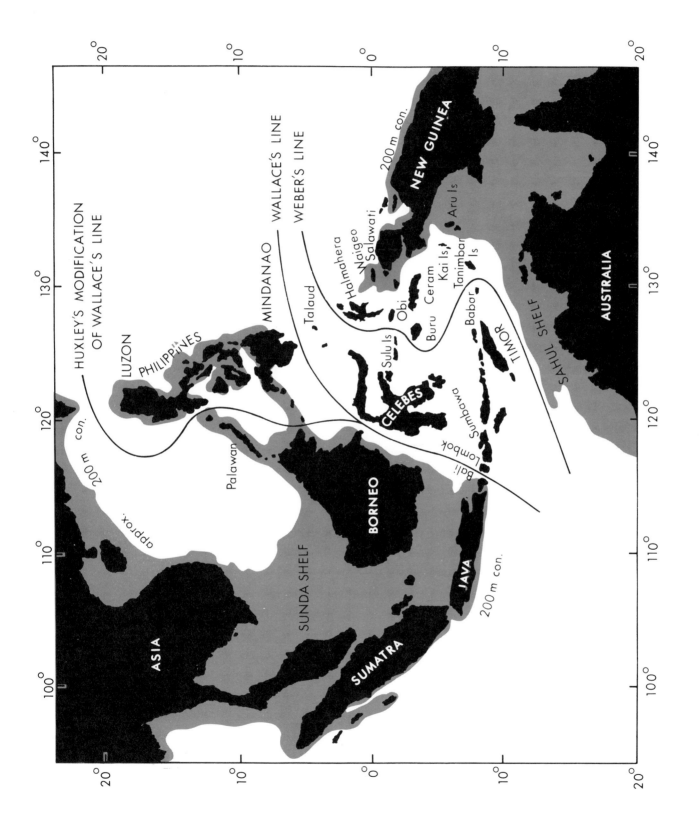

Figure 3. Lines of zoogeographic importance in the Malay Archipelago. *Redrawn from Mayr (1944)*

freshwater species in the various biogeographical realms. This is not reflected in an analysis based on families.

Continental Drift

One of the most exciting areas of zoogeography today is the idea that the distribution of certain fish groups can be explained by the past movement of the continents. In 1915 Alfred Wegener published the first edition of *Die Entstehung der Kontinente und Ozeane* (*The Origin of Continents and Oceans*), in which he called attention to the similarity of the east coast of South America and the west coast of Africa and suggested that they fit together like the pieces of a giant jigsaw puzzle. This concept was slow to be accepted, but in light of the modern geophysical evidences of plate tectonics and paleomagnetics, this hypothesis has become elevated to one of the basic theories in nature.

Continental drift theory states that all the continents were once part of a large land mass, Pangaea. This supercontinent became divided about 180 million years ago (Jurassic) into a northern portion, Laurasia (North America and Eurasia), and a southern portion, Gondwanaland (South America, Africa, India, Antarctica, Australia and New Zealand). About 90 million years ago (Cretaceous), Gondwanaland broke apart into the separate southern continents (see references cited by Novacek and Marshall [1976] for the geologic timing of these events). The propulsive forces for these movements, which are still going on today, are convection currents in the earth's mantle generated by the heat of radioactivity within the interior. These currents move the 6 major plates which make up the earth's surface and which float on the mantle. (Further reading on this subject should include: Mayr [1952], Wegener [1966], Runcorn [1962], Dietz and Holden [1970], Colbert [1973], Berggren and Hollister [1974], Cox [1974], Cracraft [1974, 1975], Howden [1974], Glen [1975], Brundin [1975], Tarling [1975], the Scientific American book *Continents Adrift* [1973], and Smith and Briden [1977].)

Dispersal

How the present patterns of fish distribution evolved is beyond the scope of this atlas and requires a knowledge of the factors mentioned in the preface. (A few attempts at explaining various aspects of ichthyogeography include Darlington [1957], Miller [1958], Myers [1966, 1967], Rosen and Bailey [1963], Chardon [1967], Nelson [1969], Croizat, Nelson, and Rosen [1974], Briggs [1974, 1979], Rosen [1974, 1975, 1978], Novacek and Marshall [1976], Gilbert [1976], Platnick and Nelson [1978], McDowall [1978], and Vari [1978]. A lively discussion of the relationship between vicariance and dispersal as related to the distribution patterns of freshwater fishes can be found in 1974–79 issues of *Systematic Zoology* and *Copeia*. The bibliographies of the papers cited above extend the discussion.)

Naturally, major vicariant events such as the movement of land masses will affect worldwide fish distribution. In addition to these rather dramatic movements, freshwater fishes may also disperse over a continent in a variety of ways. During times of flooding, drainage systems may overlap on a flood plain, allowing fishes access to other drainages. Stream capture, whether by headwater piracy or lowland meanders, may allow fishes to move from one river system to another and thereby spread across large continental areas. Freshwater fishes with some salt tolerance may swim from one river mouth through brackish or marine waters into another river mouth and then move upstream. During periods of glacial melt, drainage systems may be connected by overflow streams. Conversely, streams may be isolated in times of glacial advance because of lowered sea levels. Some fishes such as eels can actually wiggle across grassy areas from one stream to another. Other fishes may survive dispersal in the egg or other stages on mud attached to aquatic birds' feet, or by waterspouts. The uplifting of mountain ranges may separate river systems, which can result in a similar fauna on both sides of a divide, which may then diverge. These are just a few of the considerations necessary for the understanding of the patterns of freshwater fish distribution.

Table 2

PRIMARY, SECONDARY, AND SELECTED PERIPHERAL FRESHWATER FISH FAMILIES AND THE GEOGRAPHICAL AREAS WHERE THEY OCCUR

FAMILY	DIVISION	NEARCTIC	NEOTROPICAL	PALEARCTIC	ETHIOPIAN	ORIENTAL	AUSTRALIAN
Petromyzonidae	per	X		X			
Geotriidae	per		X				X
Mordaciidae	per		X				X
Potamotrygonidae	per		X				
Ceratodontidae	1st						X
Lepidosirenidae	1st		X				
Protopteridae	1st				X		
Polypteridae	1st				X		
Acipenseridae	per	X		X		X	
Polyodontidae	1st	X		X			
Lepisosteidae	2nd	X	X				
Amiidae	1st	X					
Denticipitidae	1st				X		
Osteoglossidae	1st		X		X	X	X

Family	Division	Nearctic	Neotropical	Palearctic	Ethiopian	Oriental	Australian
Pantodontidae	1st				X		
Hiodontidae	1st	X					
Notopteridae	1st				X	X	
Mormyridae	1st				X		
Gymnarchidae	1st				X		
Salmonidae	per	X		X			
Plecoglossidae	per			X			
Osmeridae	per	X		X			
Salangidae	per			X		X	
Retropinnidae	per						X
Prototroctidae	per						X
Galaxiidae	per		X		X		X
Aplochitonidae	per		X				X
Lepidogalaxiidae	?						X
Esocidae	1st	X		X			
Umbridae	1st	X		X			
Kneriidae	1st				X		
Phractolaemidae	1st				X		
Characidae	1st	X	X		X		
Erythrinidae	1st		X				
Ctenoluciidae	1st		X				
Hepsetidae	1st				X		
Cynodontidae	1st		X				
Lebiasinidae	1st		X				
Parodontidae	1st		X				
Gasteropelecidae	1st		X				
Prochilodontidae	1st		X				
Curimatidae	1st		X				
Anostomidae	1st		X				
Hemiodontidae	1st		X				
Chilodontidae	1st		X				
Distichodontidae	1st				X		
Citharinidae	1st				X		
Ichthyboridae	1st				X		
Gymnotidae	1st		X				
Electrophoridae	1st		X				
Apteronotidae	1st		X				
Rhamphichthyidae	1st		X				
Cyprinidae	1st	X		X	X	X	
Gyrinocheilidae	1st					X	
Psilorhynchidae	1st					X	
Catostomidae	1st	X		X			
Homalopteridae	1st					X	
Cobitidae	1st			X	X	X	
Diplomystidae	1st		X				
Ictaluridae	1st	X					
Bagridae	1st			X	X	X	
Cranoglanididae	1st					X	
Siluridae	1st			X		X	
Schilbeidae	1st				X	X	
Pangasiidae	1st					X	
Amblycipitidae	1st					X	
Amphiliidae	1st				X		
Akysidae	1st					X	
Sisoridae	1st			X		X	
Clariidae	1st			X	X	X	
Heteropneustidae	1st					X	
Chacidae	1st					X	
Olyridae	1st					X	
Malapteruridae	1st				X		
Mochokidae	1st				X		
Doradidae	1st		X				
Auchenipteridae	1st		X				
Aspredinidae	1st		X				
Pimelodontidae	1st		X				

Family	Division	Nearctic	Neotropical	Palearctic	Ethiopian	Oriental	Australian
Ageneiosidae	1st		X				
Hypophthalmidae	1st		X				
Helogeneidae	1st		X				
Cetopsidae	1st		X				
Trichomycteridae	1st		X				
Callichthyidae	1st		X				
Loricariidae	1st		X				
Astroblepidae	1st		X				
Amblyopsidae	1st	X					
Aphredoderidae	1st	X					
Percopsidae	1st	X					
Oryziatidae	2nd			X		X	
Adrianichthyidae	2nd					X	
Horaichthyidae	2nd					X	
Cyprinodontidae	2nd	X	X	X	X	X	
Goodeidae	2nd	X					
Anablepidae	2nd		X				
Jenynsiidae	2nd		X				
Poeciliidae	2nd	X	X				
Melanotaeniidae	2nd						X
Neostethidae	per					X	
Phallostethidae	per					X	
Gasterosteidae	per	X		X			
Indostomidae	per					X	
Channidae	1st			X	X	X	
Synbranchidae	per		X	X	X	X	X
Cottidae	per	X		X			
Cottocomephoridae	per			X			
Comephoridae	per			X			
Percichthyidae	per	X	X	X			X
Centrarchidae	1st	X					
Percidae	1st	X		X			
Toxotidae	per					X	X
Scatophagidae	per				X	X	X
Enoplosidae	per						X
Nandidae	1st		X		X	X	
Embiotocidae	per	X		X			
Cichlidae	2nd	X	X		X	X	
Gadopsidae	per						X
Bovichthyidae	per		X				X
Rhyacichthyidae	per					X	X
Kurtidae	per					X	X
Anabantidae	1st				X	X	
Belontiidae	1st			X		X	
Helostomatidae	1st					X	
Osphronemidae	1st					X	
Luciocephalidae	1st					X	
Mastacembelidae	1st			X	X	X	
Chaudhuriidae	1st					X	

The following widely distributed peripheral families (mostly marine) are omitted from this analysis although they are included in the text: Carcharhinidae, Elopidae, Megalopidae, Anguillidae, Clupeidae, Engraulidae, Chanidae, Ariidae, Plotosidae, Batrachoididae, Gadidae, Ophidiidae, Hemiramphidae, Belonidae, Atherinidae, Sygnathidae, Alabetidae, Centropomidae, Ambassidae, Teraponidae, Kuhliidae, Sparidae, Sciaenidae, Monodactylidae, Mugilidae, Polynemidae, Gobiidae, Soleidae, Tetraodontidae.

Pronunciation of Family Names

The names of zoological families are, for the most part, derived from Latin and Greek roots and always end in -idae. There are, of course, rules for the pronunciation of these names derived from the original language. A sampling of some of these rules follows:

1. All vowels are pronounced.
2. Diphthongs (two vowels written together) are pronounced as a single vowel.
3. *Ch* is pronounced as *k* if it is derived from a Greek word.
4. When *c* is followed by *ae, e, oe, i,* or *y,* it is pronounced as a soft *s;* but when followed by *a, o, oi,* or *u,* it has the hard *k* sound.
5. *G,* when followed by *ae, e, i, oe,* or *y,* has the soft *j* sound, yet when followed by *a, o, oi,* or *u* is pronounced as in *go.*
6. Scientific names beginning with *ps, pt, ct, cn, gn,* or *mn* are pronounced as if the first letter were not there; however, the first letter is sounded if these combinations appear in the middle of a word.
7. *X* is pronounced as *z* in the beginning of a word, but as *ks* elsewhere.
8. In family names the major accent is on the antepenult (the third syllable from the end of the word)—the syllable before *-idae.* There may be a secondary accent on a syllable near the beginning of a very long word.
9. The vowel of the antepenult is short where it is followed by a consonant except when the vowel is *u.*
10. The vowel of the antepenult is long where it is followed by another vowel.

For a detailed exposition of these and other rules and for a source of word roots, consult Borror (1960).

These rules are not inflexible, however, and due consideration should be given to accepted usage as well as to the classically correct way. For example, most ichthyologists I have heard would pronounce the Amiidae as "ā'-mī-ĭ-dē" which is closer to the generic name upon which it is based, yet *Webster's New International Dictionary* (2d ed.) lists "à-mī'-ĭ-dē." The accent and the *a* and *i* sounds are different in the two pronunciations. Likewise with the Galaxiidae and most other family names which have an *i* before the *-idae* ending.

George S. Myers was kind enough to send me his pronunciations of the families included in this book. He explained that his usage, as well as that of Carl L. Hubbs, is derived from David Starr Jordan, who was a noted classicist. Jordan, in turn, based his pronunciations upon botanists who used an Americanized pronunciation. In the text I have given the classical pronunciation and syllabification in parentheses if listed in Webster's. If it is substantially the same as the Jordan-Hubbs-Myers version, only one pronunciation is listed. If there are significant differences in pronunciation, I have listed both, with the latter in brackets. If the family name or its root is not in Webster's, I have given just the Jordan-Hubbs-Myers method in brackets. Where the Jordan-Hubbs-Myers pronunciation is different, it is usually an attempt to make the family name sound more like its generic base by placing the major accent on the fourth syllable from the end rather than on the antepenult.

Families and Maps

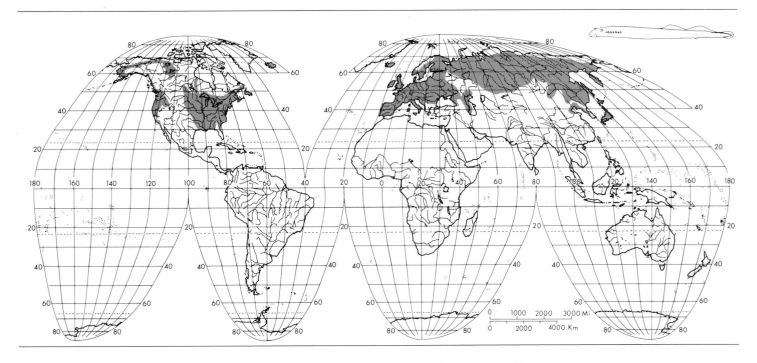

CLASS: Agnatha
    SUBCLASS: Cyclostomata

ORDER: Petromyzoniformes
    (Per) FAMILY: **PETROMYZONIDAE**—lampreys
    (pĕt'-rō-mī-zŏn'-ĭ-dē)

These eellike, jawless fishes have a holarctic distribution in temperate marine and fresh waters. There are 7 genera and 27 species. Temperature appears to be the factor limiting distribution. The relict populations of *Tetrapleurodon spadiceus* and *T. geminis* in Mexico occur at high altitude and are not exposed to the higher temperatures of the surrounding area. Adult lampreys have a suckerlike mouth with rasping teeth on the tongue and oral disc. Some freshwater species are free-living, others are external parasites of bony fishes and feed on blood and tissue fluids. This primitive group lacks scales, paired fins, and bone. Adults have 7 gill openings. All lampreys undergo a metamorphosis in fresh water, in which a blind, toothless larva called an ammocoete is transformed into an adult over a period of 1–4 years. Ammocoetes burrow in soft mud on the bottom of streams and lakes. Sea-dwelling adults may enter fresh water to spawn (anadromous). Adult nonparasitic forms do not feed, but migrate immediately upstream to spawn and then die. The loss of a parasitic existence is thought to be a specialization derived from parasitic ancestors. One species, the parasitic sea lamprey, *Petromyzon marinus*, has done much damage to fish populations since its man-caused entrance into the Great Lakes via the Welland Canal. Many of the small stream-dwelling lampreys in the United States are endangered because of siltation and pollution. Fossil lampreys date to the mid-Pennsylvanian of Illinois. All aspects of lamprey biology are dealt with in Hardisty and Potter (1971), and individual species accounts can be found in Trautman (1957) and Scott and Crossman (1973).

Map references: Berg 1949, Darlington 1957, Eigenmann 1909a*, Grzimek 1973*, Hubbs and Potter 1971*, Meek 1916*, Nelson 1976*, Pflieger 1971*, Rostlund 1952*, Scott and Crossman 1973*, Trautman 1957*, Whitaker 1968*.

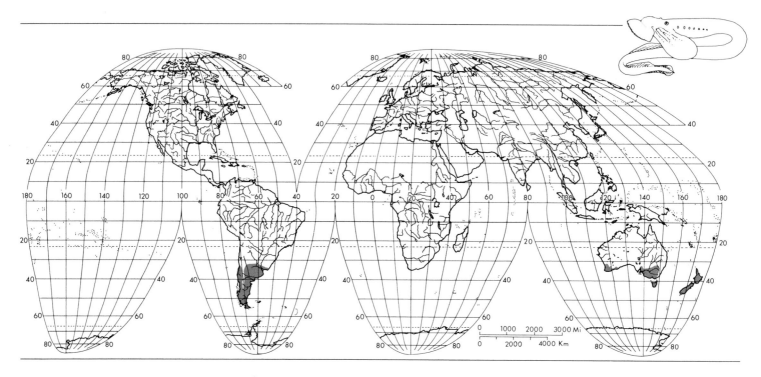

CLASS: Agnatha
   SUBCLASS: Cyclostomata

ORDER: Petromyzoniformes
   (Per) FAMILY: **GEOTRIIDAE**—pouched lamprey
   [jē-ō′-trĭ-ĭ-dē]

This monotypic family, composed of *Geotria australis*, is confined to southern regions of South America, Australia, and New Zealand. The common name is derived from the large gular sac developed by sexually mature males, the function of which is obscure. *G. australis* is an anadromous, parasitic species and is thought to be more specialized than its Northern Hemisphere distant relatives with which it was formerly classified. Adults may reach a length of 51 cm. Further information on taxonomy and biology of this species can be found in Hardisty and Potter (1971) and McDowall (1978b, 1980).

Map references: Eigenmann 1927, Hubbs and Potter 1971*, Lake 1971, Scott, Glover, and Southcott 1974.

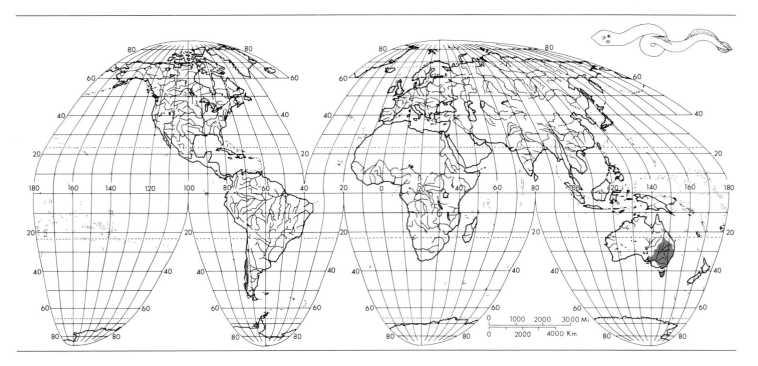

CLASS: Agnatha
  SUBCLASS: Cyclostomata

ORDER: Petromyzoniformes
  (Per) FAMILY: MORDACIIDAE—Southern
  Hemisphere lampreys [mōr-dā′-sē-ī-dē]

This small family of 3 species is found in Chile and southeast Australia. *Mordacia mordax* and *M. praecox* are Australian, and *M. lapicida* is Chilean. *M. praecox* is free-living in fresh water, while *M. mordax* is parasitic and anadromous. The Mordaciidae and Geotriidae have previously been included in the Petromyzonidae, but differences in dentition and the long period of isolation seem sufficient to separate the Northern and Southern Hemisphere forms. The Petromyzonidae appear to be ancestral, but the Southern lampreys probably descended at different times from ancestral stocks. *M. mordax* reaches 56 cm in length. For more information consult Hardisty and Potter (1971) and McDowall (1980).

Map references: Eigenmann 1927, Hubbs and Potter 1971*, Lake 1971, Scott, Glover, and Southcott 1974.

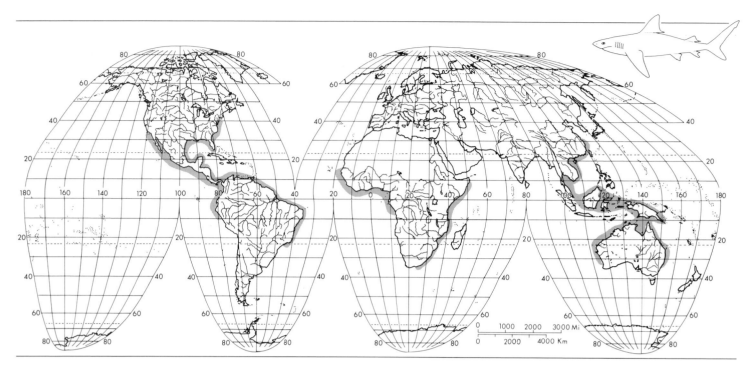

CLASS: Chondrichthyes
SUBCLASS: Elasmobranchii
SUPERORDER: Selachimorpha

ORDER: Lamniformes
(Per) FAMILY: **CARCHARHINIDAE**—requiem sharks
(kăr'-kă-rī'-nĭ-dē)

This family of typical sharks is worldwide in tropical and temperate seas. It is included in this account because of the propensity of at least one of its members, the bull shark, *Carcharhinus leucas*, for brackish and fresh waters. The bull shark has been reported from rivers and lakes far from the sea throughout the world. There is a well-known population in Lake Nicaragua (Thorson 1976a, b), and the Ganges River of India and the Zambezi River of Africa are famous as shark rivers. The bull shark has been reported from Lake Jamoer in New Guinea (Boeseman 1956, 1964); 3,500–4,000 km up the Amazon River in Colombia and Peru (Myers 1952); the Miraflores Locks, Panama Canal; Lake Izabul, Guatemala (Bigelow and Schroeder 1948). In the United States, *C. leucas* has been found 440 km up the Atchafalaya River in Louisiana (Gunter 1938) and 2,800 km up the Mississippi River at Alton Locks and Dam (Thomerson and Thorson 1977).

The carcharhinid sharks are a very difficult group to work with taxonomically because of their overall similarities. There are over 100 nominal species, but probably only about one-quarter of these will be found to be valid. The Lake Nicaragua and Zambezi River sharks have been described as different species, but are most likely *C. leucas* (Garrick and Schultz 1963).

The bull shark is an archetypical carcharhinid with no outstanding morphological features that immediately compel recognition of this species. It has a short, broadly rounded snout, and its back lacks a dorsal ridge. The second dorsal fin is much smaller than the first, and its teeth have serrate cusps (Bigelow and Schroeder 1948). The pectoral fins are short and broad, and the fin tips are usually the same grayish color as the rest of the upper surface. Often specimens will have trematode parasites or scars between the 2 dorsal fins (Ellis 1975). This species grows to at least 3.1 meters and 182 kg. It is an opportunistic and indiscriminate feeder which will pursue living prey or scavenge.

The studies of Thorson, Watson, and Cowan (1966) and Thorson (1971) have shown that the bull sharks in Lake Nicaragua move freely between the Caribbean Sea and the lake. This movement is apparently not related to the life history (Thorson 1976a), but is probably a matter of exploitation of an ecological opportunity by a species physiologically equipped to deal with a freshwater existence. Jensen (1976) concluded that *C. leucas* does not use the lake for reproduction, and parturition normally occurs near river mouths. Thorson and Gerst (1972) showed that fetal pups have the full range of urea tolerance for a euryhaline life. Their body fluids, which reflect the maternal condition, range from the hyperuremic condition of sea-dwelling sharks to the reduced urea levels of sharks inhabiting fresh water. Near-term young taken from pregnant females and neonatal bull sharks can tolerate either fresh or salt water.

Only about 27 species of the 250 odd species of sharks are definitely known to have been responsible for unprovoked attacks on man or boats (Garrick and Schultz 1963). Of the 1,165 case histories in the Shark Attack File at the Mote Marine Laboratory, some level of identification was possible in 267 cases (Baldridge 1974). The bull shark had 21 attacks attributed to it (Baldridge 1974). This species has a nasty reputation as a man-eater and is well equipped to do damage with large serrated teeth and powerful jaws. *C. leucas* has been implicated in attacks in Lake Nicaragua, Florida, South Africa, and India (Garrick and Schultz 1963). This species seems most dangerous off the Natal coast of Africa (Davies 1963, 1964). Thorson (1976a) reported that although there are documented instances of loss of human life to *C. leucas* in the Lake Nicaragua–San Juan river system, this is very rare, and the statements that bull sharks are more ferocious and dangerous in fresh water than in the sea are unsupported by evidence. Randall (1963) suggested that bull sharks had more contact with man because of their occurrence in shallow coastal regions and in fresh water. Thorson (1976b) provided reprints of all articles relating to Lake Nicaragua and its sharks.

For further information on the biology, taxonomy, and behavior of sharks, consult the following references: American Zoologist (1977), Baldridge (1974), Bigelow and Schroeder (1948), Brown (1973), Budker (1971), Casey (1964), Coppleson (1958), Cousteau and Cousteau (1970), Davis (1964), Edwards (1975), Ellis (1975), Gilbert (1963), Gilbert, Mathewson, and Rall (1967), Lineaweaver and Backus (1973), McCormick, Allen, and Young (1963), Pope (1973), Stead (1963), and Young (1934).

Map references: Bigelow and Schroeder 1948, Boeseman 1956, 1964, Budker 1971*, Garrick 1967, Garrick and Schultz 1963, Gunter 1938, Lake 1971, Miller and Lea 1972, Myers 1952, Thomerson and Thorson 1977, Thorson 1976a, b*.

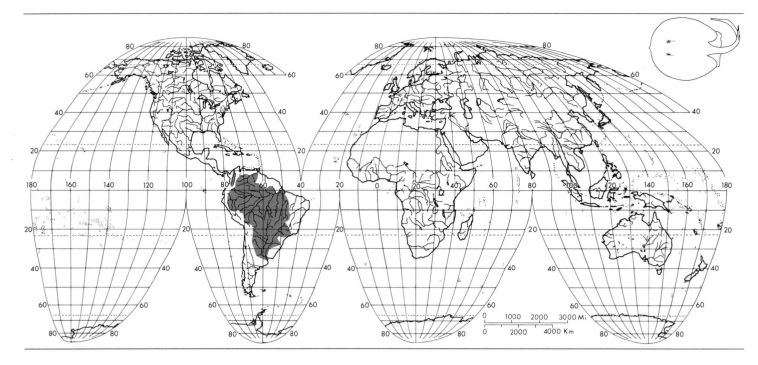

CLASS: Chondrichthyes
   SUBCLASS: Elasmobranchii
      SUPERORDER: Batoidimorpha

ORDER: Rajiformes
(Per) FAMILY: **POTAMOTRYGONIDAE**—freshwater stingrays (pŏt'-ă-mō-trī-gŏn'-ĭ-dē)

Freshwater stingrays are found in the Magdalena, Orinoco, Amazon, and Paraná river systems of South America, where they have undergone extensive radiation into about 18 species. Most are placed in the genus *Potamotrygon*, but one Amazonian species is *Disceus thayeri* (Castex 1967). This family was defined by Garman (1913) and is similar to the Dasyatidae. The major difference between the 2 families is that the Potamotrygonidae has an extended median pelvic process directed anteriorly, whereas this process is absent in the Dasyatidae. In addition, the potamotrygonids have very little urea in their body fluids (Thorson, Cowan, and Watson 1967), whereas dasyatids have a high level of urea as an osmoregulatory agent. The freshwater stingrays osmoregulate in the same way as freshwater bony fishes, by producing copious quantities of dilute urine and by actively transporting sodium into the body across the gills. Other features of the freshwater stingrays include the absence of a caudal and dorsal fin, and a tail longer than the width of the flattened body.

An African species of freshwater stingray from the Benue River of the Niger River system has been reassigned to the Dasyatidae because it did not possess the prepelvic process, and it did have high urea values (Thorson and Watson 1975). Castex (1967) mentioned the occurrence of rays in the Mekong River of Laos, but their relationship remains to be determined.

Thorson and Watson (1975) pointed out that the absence of urea retention does not necessarily mean that potamotrygonids lost this ability. If elasmobranchs originated in freshwater, then urea retention is a derived character in response to the invasion of the marine environment.

Like marine stingrays, these animals bury themselves in sandy bottoms. If an unwary wader treads on its dorsal surface, the ray lashes back with its tail, driving its spine into the victim, which causes great pain. The venomous sting of freshwater stingrays produces a predominantly local symptomology with a torpid and chronic involvement of the affected parts, according to Castex (1967), whereas marine rays cause less local symptoms and more general response.

Map reference: Castex 1967*

8

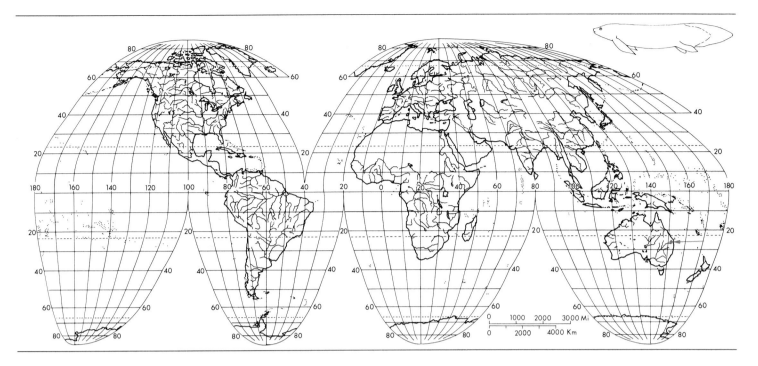

CLASS: Osteichthyes
  SUBCLASS: Sarcopterygii, Dipnoi, or Dipneusti

ORDER: Dipteriformes
  (1st) FAMILY: **CERATODONTIDAE**—Australian lungfish (sĕr'-ă-tō-dŏn'-tī-dē)

This single species, *Neoceratodus fosteri*, is native to the Mary and Burnett rivers in southeastern Queensland; however, it has been introduced to other Australian rivers. The Australian lungfish has 1 lung and does not require air to survive, but can utilize atmospheric oxygen when the dissolved oxygen level of its habitat decreases. It does not aestivate, as do the other lungfishes. The body is covered with large scales, and the paired fins are paddlelike. The caudal fin is pointed and extends dorsally and ventrally. This species is probably the most primitive of the living lungfishes. *Neoceratodus* deposites large eggs among aquatic plants in shallow waters and can grow to 180 cm and 45 kg. See Roughley (1966) and Lake (1971) for more details. An extinct genus, *Ceratodus*, is very similar and was widely distributed around the world in the Triassic, 200 million years ago. See Miles (1977) for a discussion of Devonian fossils and for a review of dipnoan skulls.

Map references: Bartholomew, Clarke, and Grimshaw 1911*, Darlington 1957, Grzimek 1974*, Lake 1971, Meek 1916*, Nelson 1976*, Sterba 1966*.

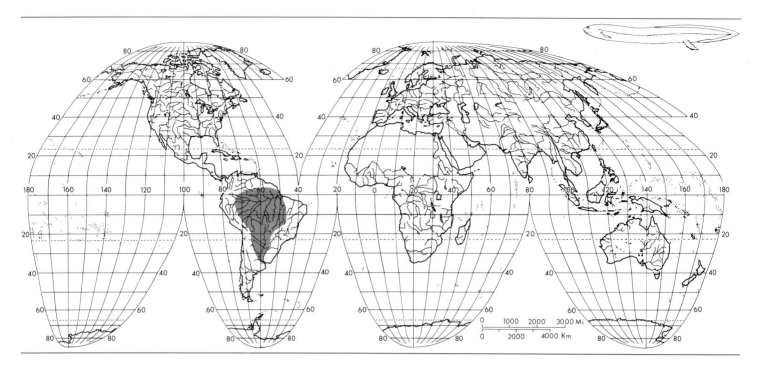

CLASS: Osteichthyes
  SUBCLASS: Sarcopterygii, Dipnoi, or Dipneusti

ORDER: Dipteriformes
  (1st) FAMILY: LEPIDOSIRENIDAE—South American lungfish (lĕp'-ĭ-dō-sī-rĕn'-ĭ-dē)

Lepidosiren paradoxa is the only species in this family, and it is found in tropical South America in the Amazon and Paraná river systems. It has an elongate, eellike body with reduced paired fins that serve as tactile organs. The pelvic fins of the males bear accessory respiratory capillaries during the spawning season that may release oxygen from the blood to the water surrounding the young during brooding. These lungfish have 2 lungs, modified from the swim bladder, that allow them to tolerate very low oxygen habitats such as

swamps. The South American lungfish may burrow into the mud during drought, but it does not form a protective cocoon. Maximum size is about 1.2 m.

Map references: Bartholomew, Clarke, and Grimshaw 1911*, Bertin and Arambourg 1958*, Darlington 1957, Eigenmann 1909a*, Gery 1969, Grzimek 1974*, Meek 1916*, Nelson 1976*, Norman and Greenwood 1975*, Sterba 1966*.

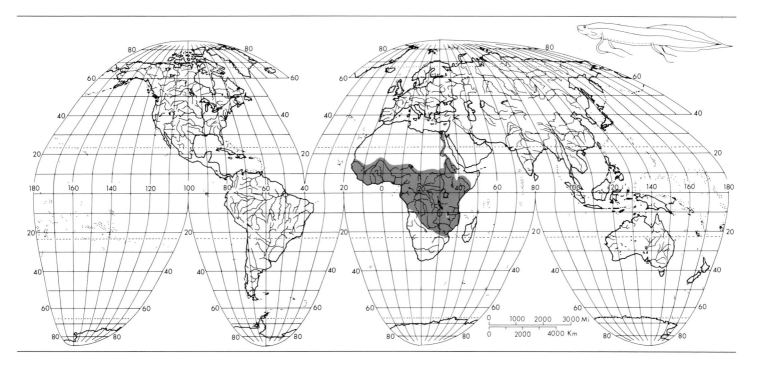

CLASS: Osteichthyes
    SUBCLASS: Sarcopterygii, Dipnoi, or Dipneusti

ORDER: Dipteriformes
    (1st) FAMILY: **PROTOPTERIDAE**—African lungfishes
    [prō-tŏp-tĕr'-ĭ-dē)

The 4 species of African lungfishes are found in tropical Africa in the Senegal, Niger, Congo, Nile, and Zambezi rivers. The single genus, *Protopterus*, is often classified with the South American lungfish in the Lepidosirenidae. *P. dolloi* most closely resembles *Lepidosiren*, and the distribution of these 2 families may lend support to a former land connection between South America and Africa. *Protopterus* is not as elongate as *Lepidosiren*, has longer, more threadlike paired fins; and the 2 genera have different arrangements of gill arches. These fishes have 2 lungs and seem to be obligatory air breathers even in the presence of sufficient dissolved oxygen. They possess the ability to aestivate in the bottom mud during drought and remain for many months (even years) utilizing

their own muscle tissue and storing waste products as urea. The largest member of the family, *P. aethiopicus*, may reach 210 cm. Fossil lungfishes date to the Devonian. Consult Herald (1962), Sterba (1966), and Grzimek (1974) for life history information and illustrations. Luling (1974) summarized the order, and Jarvik (1968) and Bertmar (1969) discussed lungfish phylogeny.

Map references: Bartholomew, Clarke, and Grimshaw 1911*, Bertin and Arambourg 1958*, Darlington 1957, Grzimek 1974*, Meek 1916*, Nelson 1976*, Norman and Greenwood 1975*, Poll 1973*, Roberts 1975, Sterba 1966*.

11

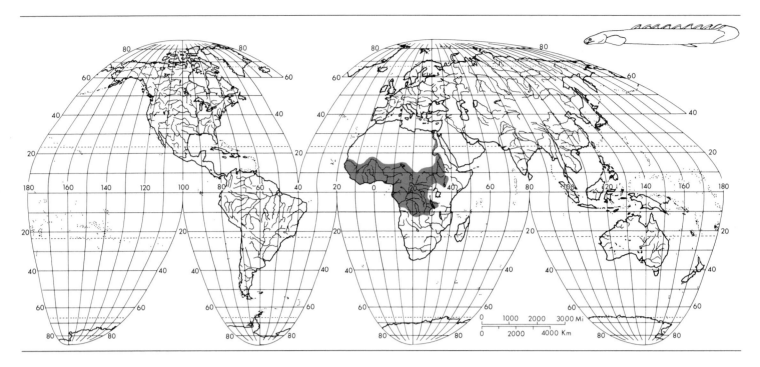

CLASS: Osteichthyes
  SUBCLASS: Brachiopterygii

ORDER: Polypteriformes
  (1st) FAMILY: **POLYPTERIDAE**—Bichirs
  (pŏl'-ĭp-tĕr'-ĭ-dē)

Bichirs inhabit shores and flood plains of rivers and lakes of central and west tropical Africa, including the Nile, but are absent from south and east Africa. There are 2 genera: *Polypterus* (10 species) and the eellike reedfish, *Erpetoichthys calabaricus*, which lacks pelvic fins. *Polypterus* means "many fins" and refers to the numerous flaglike dorsal finlets set atop the elongate body. Bichirs can remain out of the water for several hours; however, their small left lung and larger right lung are less efficient than those of lungfish. Bichirs may drown if prevented from gulping air at the surface. This family has numerous other primitive characteristics, such as heterocercal tail, spiral valve, gular plates, spiracles, diamond shaped ganoid scales, and pectoral fins with fleshy lobes. They are carnivorous egg layers, and the young have external gills until metamorphosis several weeks after hatching. Some species may reach 120 cm. Fossils date to the mid-Cretaceous—Lower Eocene of Egypt (Greenwood 1974*b*).

Map references: Bartholomew, Clarke, and Grimshaw 1911*, Darlington 1957, Grzimek 1973*, Nelson 1976*, Poll 1973*, Roberts 1975, Sterba 1966*.

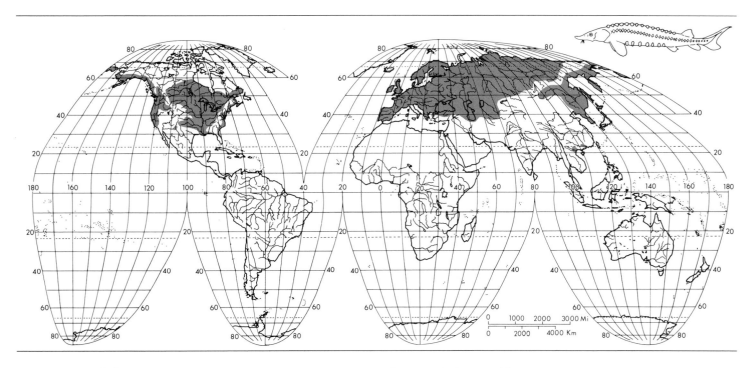

CLASS: Osteichthyes
SUBCLASS: Actinopterygii

ORDER: Acipenseriformes
(Per) FAMILY: ACIPENSERIDAE—sturgeons
(ăs-ĭ-pĕn-sĕr'-ĭ-dē)

Sturgeons are very large, ancient fishes with a holarctic distribution. There are approximately two dozen species in 4 genera (*Acipenser*, *Huso*, *Pseudoscaplirhynchus*, and *Scaphirhynchus*), with the largest concentration of species in central and eastern Europe and lesser numbers in North America. Some species are marine, but all spawn in fresh water. Primitive features include cartilaginous skeleton, heterocercal tail, spiral valve, spiracle, and heavy plates along the sides and dorsum. Sturgeons feed on bottom invertebrates and fishes detected with the help of external taste buds and fleshy barbels located around a ventrally positioned mouth. From a larva just 13 mm may grow a giant beluga, *Huso huso*, of the Black and Caspian seas weighing 1,300 kg and reaching a length of 8 m in at least 80 years. This qualifies the beluga as the largest fish living in fresh water. Various other size records may be found in Wood (1972). Large oviparous females contribute millions of eggs each to the caviar industry, which, along with increasing pollution, may be responsible for the diminished sizes now showing up in the fishery. Fossils date to Upper Cretaceous of Montana. Taxonomic and life history information along with further references can be found in Berg (1949), Vladykov and Greeley (1963), and Scott and Crossman (1973).

Map references: Bartholomew, Clarke, and Grimshaw 1911*, Berg 1949, Darlington 1957, Meek 1916*, Nelson 1976*, Nicholas 1943, Pflieger 1971*, Rostlund 1952*, Scott and Crossman 1973*, Trautman 1957*, Vladykov and Greeley 1963, Whitaker 1968*.

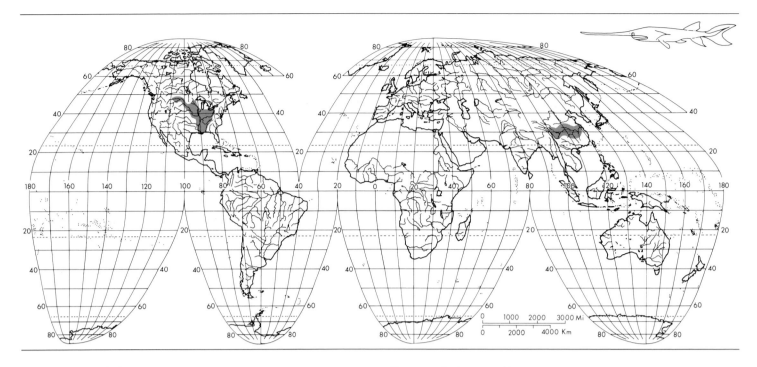

CLASS: Osteichthyes
  SUBCLASS: Actinopterygii

ORDER: Acipenseriformes
  (1st) FAMILY: **POLYODONTIDAE**—paddlefishes
  (pŏl′-ĭ-ō-dŏn′-tĭ-dē)

This odd and archaic family of 2 species is presently disjunctly distributed in the Mississippi River system (*Polyodon spathula*) and in the Yangzi River system of eastern China (*Psephurus gladius*), although Upper Cretaceous fossils indicate that the family was formerly holarctic. Paddlefishes and sturgeons are considered to be in the same taxonomic order (either Acipenseriformes or Chondrostei) because of a similarity of structural features such as cartilaginous skeleton, presence of barbels, spiral valve, and the resemblance of both larval forms. The function of the paddle is obscure, and the animal feeds on plankton, which it collects by swimming with its mouth open wide. The planktonic organisms are strained by numerous slender gill rakers. American paddlefish fry lack the paddle until about 35 mm and then grow rapidly

to a maximum size of 75 kg and 1.8 m, of which the paddle is about one-third. The Chinese species is piscivorous, grows to be much larger (Nichols [1943] mentions 7 m), and has a swordlike snout. Dam building has seriously reduced the habitat and prevented spawning migrations, hence the decline in their commercial importance as a source of caviar. See Eddy and Underhill (1974) and Herald (1962) for further information. Graham and Bonislawsky (1978) have compiled a useful indexed bibliography of the paddlefish.

Map references: Bartholomew, Clarke, and Grimshaw 1911*, Darlington 1957, Nelson 1976*, Nichols 1943, Pflieger 1971*, Rostlund 1952*, Trautman 1957*, Whitaker 1968*.

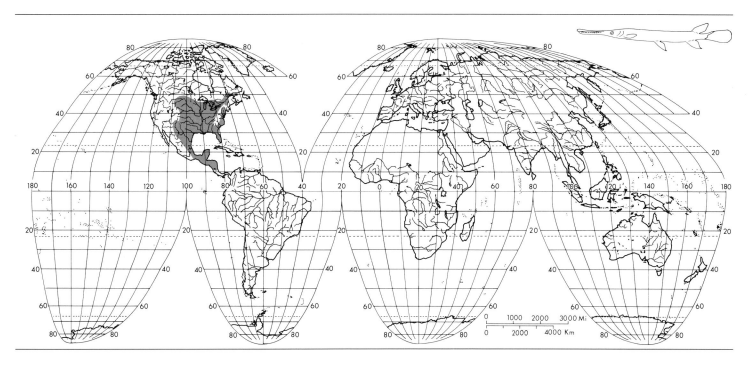

CLASS: Osteichthyes
SUBCLASS: Actinopterygii

ORDER: Lepisosteiformes
(2d) FAMILY: **LEPISOSTEIDAE**—gars
(lĕp'-ĭ-sŏs'-tē-ĭ-dē) [lĕ-pĭ-sŏ-stĕ'-ĭ-dē]

These primitive cylindrical fishes with needle-sharp teeth in a slender snout are found in eastern North America from the Rocky Mountains eastward to the Atlantic coast and from southern Quebec to Costa Rica and Cuba. There are 7 living species in 2 genera, *Lepisosteus* and *Atractosteus*. Most are found in fresh water, but a few species may tolerate brackish or even marine conditions. Gars and bowfins have been classified together in the category Holostei, which some authors variously consider as a subclass, infraclass, or superorder. Gars are distinct from all other fishes in having ball-and-socket vertebral articulations (opisthocoelous), whereas most fishes have biconcave vertebrae. Gars have such primitive characteristics as heterocercal tail; rudimentary spiral valve; lunglike swim bladder that assists respiration; and hinged,

rhombic, nonoverlapping ganoid scales. Although the alligator gar, *A. spatula*, may reach 3 m and 135 kg and is a voracious feeder, there is no authenticated report of an attack on man. Fossils are found in Europe and west Africa (Upper Cretaceous) and Indian (Eocene). Suttkus (1963) and Wiley (1976) presented a wealth of information on the taxonomy and biology of this family.

Map references: Bartholomew, Clarke, and Grimshaw 1911*, Darlington 1957, Meek 1916*, Miller 1966*, Nelson 1976*, Pflieger 1971*, Rosen 1975*, Rostlund 1952*, Trautman 1957*, Scott and Crossman 1973*, Suttkus 1963, Sterba 1966*, Whitaker 1968*, Wiley 1976*.

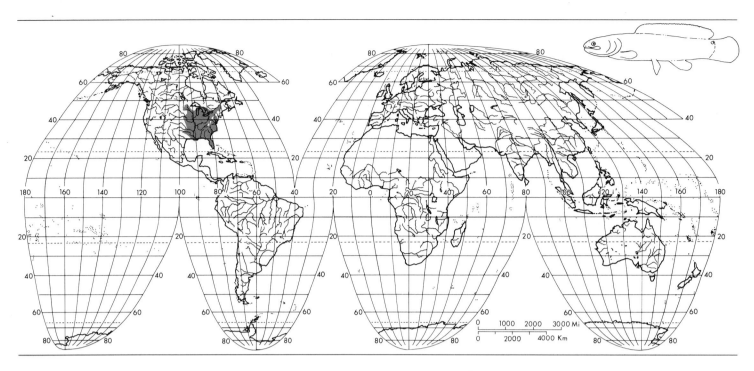

CLASS: Osteichthyes
    SUBCLASS: Actinopterygii

ORDER: Amiiformes
    (1st) FAMILY: AMIIDAE—bowfin (ă-mī'-ĭ-dē)
    [ā'-mī-ĭ-dē]

This ancient and highly predacious family was once widespread in European fresh waters (Eocene-Miocene) but is now restricted to 1 species, *Amia calva*, in the eastern half of North America. Bowfins are somewhat more advanced than the Acipenseriformes in possessing a bony skeleton, but they have a trace of a spiral valve, heterocercal tail, and a lunglike swim bladder which enables them to live in stagnant waters of very low oxygen content. Bony head plates, gular plates, cycloid scales reinforced with ganoin, and a long, flowing, spineless dorsal fin make this species easy to recognize. Large

bowfins may reach 90 cm and weigh 3.8 kg. They are egg layers, and the male guards the young, which swim under him in a dense school. See Scott and Crossman (1973) for more information on their biology.

Map references: Bartholomew, Clarke, and Grimshaw 1911*, Darlington 1957, Grzimek 1973*, Hubbs and Lagler 1958, Nelson 1976*, Pflieger 1971*, Rostlund 1952*, Scott and Crossman 1973*, Sterba 1966*, Trautman 1957*, Whitaker 1968*.

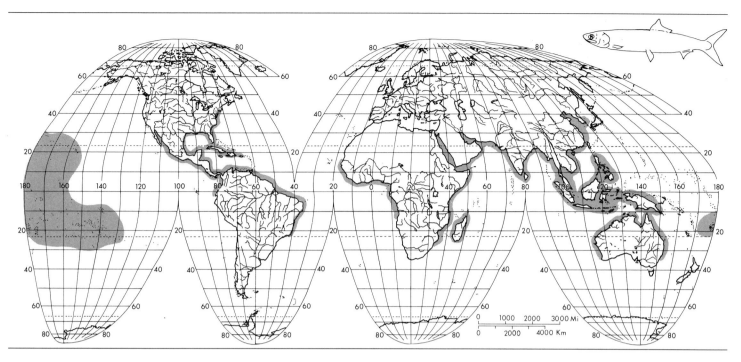

CLASS: Osteichthyes
  SUBCLASS: Actinopterygii
    SUPERORDER: Elopomorpha

ORDER: Elopiformes
  SUBORDER: Elopoidei
    (Per) FAMILY: **ELOPIDAE**—ladyfishes (ē-lŏp'-ĭ-dē)

These primitive, herringlike fishes are primarily a coastal, marine group in the tropical and subtropical waters of the world; however, they may ascend rivers and are therefore included in this account. The machete, *Elops affinis*, may be taken in the lower Colorado River. *E. saurus* is very widely distributed and accounts for most of the distribution shown on the map. There may be about 5 or 6 species in the genus. The Elopidae share a gular plate with their near relative, the tarpons, as an indication of their primitiveness. A leptocephalus larval stage is present, which shrinks to produce a miniature adult at metamorphosis. The mutual presence of leptocephalus larvae links the elopiform and anguilliform fishes. Ladyfishes travel in schools, frequently leap above the surface, and feed on fish

and invertebrates. Although *E. saurus* is sometimes called the tenpounder, its weight probably does not exceed half that. Maximum length is 90 cm. Fossils date to the Upper Jurassic. Consult Regan (1909), Gehringer (1959), Whitehead (1962), Hildebrand (1963a), and Forey (1973) for further details. Greenwood (1977) has recently reviewed the anatomy and classification of elopomorph fishes.

Map references: Boulenger 1909, Day 1878, Fowler 1959, Grzimek 1973*, Herre 1953, Hildebrand 1963a, Kiener and Richard-Vindard 1972, La Monte 1952, McCulloch 1929, Miller 1966, Moore 1968, Smith 1965, Tinker 1978.

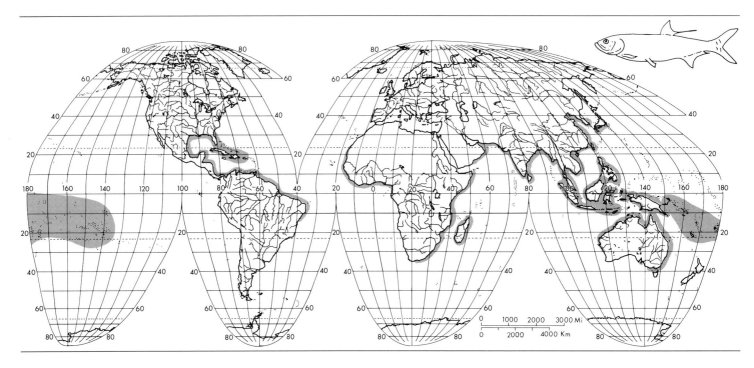

CLASS: Osteichthyes
   SUBCLASS: Actinopterygii
      SUPERORDER: Elopomorpha

ORDER: Elopiformes
   SUBORDER: Elopoidei
      (Per) FAMILY: **MEGALOPIDAE**—tarpons
      (mĕg′-ă-lŏp′-ĭ-dē) [mĕ-gă-lō′-pĭ-dē]

Tarpons are distributed in tropical and subtropical waters around the coastlines of the world and frequently enter fresh water, especially as young. They are very closely related to the Elopidae and many authors place both the ladyfish and tarpons in the Elopidae. Tarpons have an elongated dorsal filament that ladyfish lack. There are 2 species, the Atlantic tarpon, *Megalops atlantica*, and the Pacific tarpon, or ox-eyed herring, *M. cyprinoides*, which can be found in tropical rivers far above tidal influence. Tarpons, like ladyfishes, have a gular plate and a leptocephalus larval stage. They probably represent the most primitive suborder of teleosts. Both species are carnivorous egg layers. *M. atlantica* grows to a much greater size than either ladyfish or *M. cyprinoides*, reaching 2.5 m and 158 kg. As anglers know, tarpons are tremendous fighters, attempting to dislodge the hook with fantastic leaps. They have great strength, as witnessed by Hildebrand's report of a 67.5 kg man being tossed 5 m by one stroke of a tarpon tail. See Hildebrand (1963a) for further information on the Atlantic species, Smith (1945) for the Pacific species, and Wade (1962) for both species.

Map references: Fowler 1959, Grzimek 1973*, Herre 1953*, Hildebrand 1963a, Kiener and Richard-Vindard 1972, Lake 1971, La Monte 1952, Smith 1965.

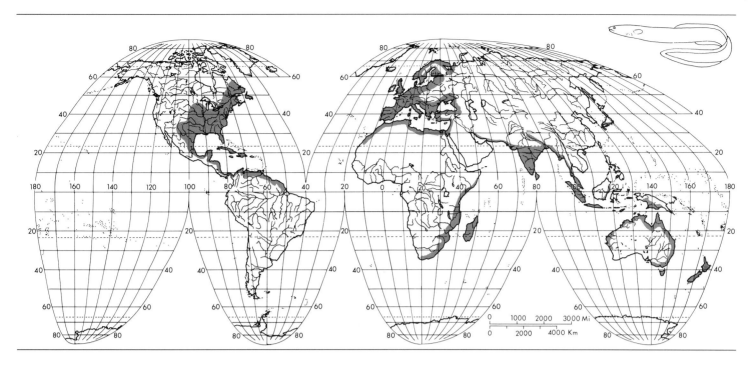

CLASS: Osteichthyes
  SUBCLASS: Actinopterygii
    SUPERORDER: Elopomorpha

ORDER: Anguilliformes
  SUBORDER: Anguilloidei
    (Per) FAMILY: **ANGUILLIDAE**—freshwater eels
    (ăng-gwĭl′-ĭ-dē)

This family of eels, composed of 1 genus, *Anguilla*, and about 16 species, is widespread but disjunctly distributed throughout inland eastern North America and coastally from Greenland to Brazil, throughout European fresh waters, coastal North Africa and the east coast of Africa from Kenya to the Cape of Good Hope, from India through the East Indies and coastal Australia northward to Japan. The absence of eels from other areas may be due to lack of the required high temperature and lack of high salinity at the specific spawning depth or lack of proper current to facilitate distribution of the leptocephalus larvae (Herald 1962). The European eel, *A. anguilla*, has been taken in the Red Sea but probably arrived within the last hundred years via the Suez Canal from the Mediterranean (Fowler 1956).

The females of this catadromous species may spend a good deal of time far upstream growing in fresh water before embarking upon an oceanic spawning migration. The males, which are smaller, seem to remain near river mouths. Johannes Schmidt, a Danish ichthyologist, patiently searched for the spawning grounds from 1904 to 1922 and finally discovered them between Bermuda and the West Indies. Both the American eel, *A. rostrata*, and the European eel spawn in the depths of the Sargasso Sea. The spawning grounds of other species are unknown. The adults die after spawning, and the newly hatched, transparent, leaflike leptocephali then undertake a tremendous migration back to their respective continents. The journey takes 1 year to America and 3 years to Europe. Upon arrival the leptocephalus transforms into a glass eel, then an elver, and moves upstream. The European and American eel are very similar, the major difference being vertebral number (European, 110–19; American, 103–11). Tucker (1959) has suggested that there is only 1 species, that the American stocks repopulate European waters, and that the longer migration time to Europe results in a greater vertebral count.

This family of eels has tiny, embedded cycloid scales, lacks pelvic fins, and feeds on fishes and invertebrates while in fresh water. They apparently do not feed while migrating to the Sargasso Sea. In Europe the eel is considered a delicacy and is important commercially; however, the blood of *Anguilla* is neurotoxic and can cause infection in humans (Herald 1962). The European eels may spend 12–15 years in fresh water, growing to 1.5 m and 6 kg, before they begin their 4,800 km downstream migration. The males migrate when much smaller (50 cm) and after only 4–8 years. Fossils of this suborder date back to the Cretaceous of Lebanon. For more information on eels, consult Schmidt (1922, 1925), Ege (1939), Bertin (1956), Tucker (1959), Bruun (1963), Vladykov (1964), Tesch (1977), Moriarty (1978), and McDowall (1978b, 1980).

Map references: Berg 1949, Boulenger 1915, Darlington 1957, Grzimek 1973*, Jubb 1967, Kiener and Richard-Vindard 1972, Lake 1971, Meek 1916*, Miller 1966, Nelson 1976*, Pflieger 1971*, Rostlund 1952*, Scott and Crossman 1973*, Tesch 1977*, Trautman 1957*, Wheeler 1969*, Whitaker 1968*, Whitley 1968.

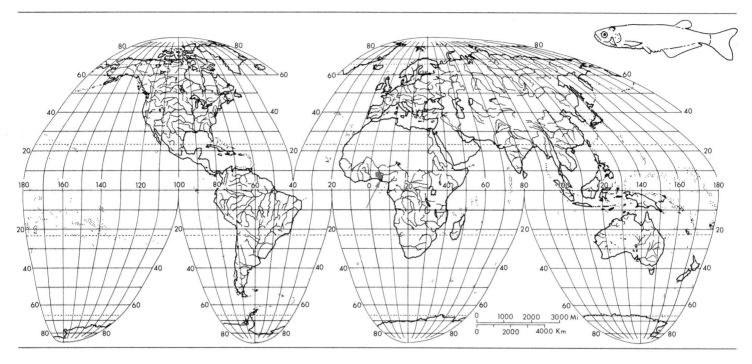

CLASS: Osteichthyes
   SUBCLASS: Actinopterygii
      SUPERORDER: Clupeomorpha

ORDER: Clupeiformes
   SUBORDER: Denticipitoidei
      (1st) FAMILY: **DENTICIPITIDAE** [dĕn-tĭ-cĭ-pĭ′-tĭ-dē]

This monotypic family, described in 1959 and composed of *Denticeps clupeoides*, is known only from a few clear, fast-flowing coastal rivers in Benin (Dahomey) and Nigeria. It is the most primitive herringlike fish. *Denticeps* may reach 5 cm and possesses a peculiar series of toothlike projections on the head, pectoral girdle, and anterior lateral line scales. The paired fins are small, and the anal fin is long. Caudal skeleton differences and a lateral line that is well developed on the trunk distinguish this fish from all other Clupeiformes. Fossils date to the Miocene of Tanzania (Greenwood 1974*b*). See Clausen (1959) and Greenwood (1968) for further details.

Map references: Clausen 1959, Roberts 1975.

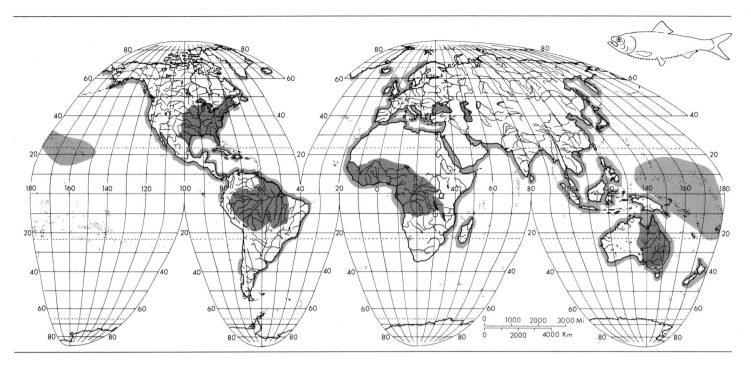

CLASS: Osteichthyes
  SUBCLASS: Actinopterygii
    SUPERORDER: Clupeomorpha

ORDER: Clupeiformes
  SUBORDER: Clupeoidei
    (Per) FAMILY: **CLUPEIDAE**—herrings
    (klōō-pē′-ĭ-dē)

The herrings, sardines, menhaden, shad, and others are a large (approximately 200 species in 50 genera), marine, cosmopolitan family with a few representatives living in fresh waters, such as *Alosa* and *Dorosoma* in eastern North America, *Pristigaster* in the Amazon, *Pellonula* in tropical west Africa, and *Nematulosa* and *Potamolosa* in eastern Australia. Herrings have a saw-toothed belly, naked head, easily shed (deciduous) cycloid scales, lack an adipose fin, and are missing a lateral line on the body. In older classifications, tarpons, herrings, salmons, pikes, and other soft-rayed fishes are placed in the order Isospondylii ("equal vertebrae"), which refers to the fact that these fishes have similar vertebrae at their anterior and posterior ends. Clupeids, even though of relatively small size, are probably the most economically important fishes in the world either as food, fish protein concentrate, fertilizer, or oil source. Herrings feed on plankton, which they extract via long, thin gill rakers. Aside from their commercial importance this group is extremely valuable in the food web as converters of minute food items into a size suitable for larger predatory fishes, birds, and marine mammals. Fossil clupeids date back to the Cretaceous of Switzerland. An extended discussion of herring life history can be found in Schubert (1973). Taxonomy is treated in Hildebrand, Rivas, and Miller (1963), Whitehead (1963), Berry (1964), Greenwood (1968), and Nelson and Rothman (1973).

Map references: Berg 1949, Boulenger 1909, Cooper 1971*, Eigenmann and Allen 1942, Fowler 1959, Gery 1969, Grzimek 1973*, Kiener and Richard-Vindard 1972, Lake 1971, Maitland 1977*, Meek 1916*, Miller 1966, Norman 1963*, Pfleiger 1971*, Rostlund 1952*, Scott and Crossman 1973*, Tinker 1978, Trautman 1957*, Whitaker 1968*, Whitley 1968.

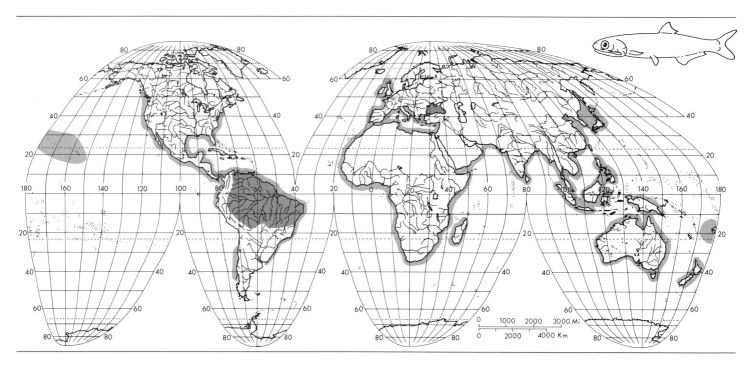

CLASS: Osteichthyes
    SUBCLASS: Actinopterygii
        SUPERORDER: Clupeomorpha

ORDER: Clupeiformes
    SUBORDER: Clupeoidei
        (Per) FAMILY: **ENGRAULIDAE**—anchovies
        (ĕn-graw'-lĭ-dē)

The greatest abundance of the worldwide anchovies is in tropical marine waters; however, some occur in fresh and brackish waters, especially in South America and Southeast Asia. Anchovies have an unusually large mouth and an overhanging snout. They lack an adipose fin and lateral line, and the cycloid scales are easily lost. These small silvery fishes are usually always found in schools. New World anchovies lack abdominal scutes, which, as a rule, are present in Old World species. There are approximately 20 genera with over 100 species. Most of these plankton-straining species are less than 13 cm, but some may reach 25 cm in length. Anchovies are of commercial significance as food, fish meal, and bait and are of ecological importance as forage species in the food chain of fishes and sea birds.

The genera *Anchoviella* and *Coilia* inhabit fresh and brackish waters of South America and Southeast Asia respectively. *Coilia* has a tiny, pointed caudal fin joined to a very long anal fin. *Anchoa mitchilli*, the bay anchovy, may enter streams of the Atlantic and Gulf coasts from Maine to Yucatan. See Jordan and Seale (1926), Hildebrand (1943, 1963b), and Nelson (1970) for further taxonomic information.

Map references: Day 1876, Eigenmann and Allen 1942, Fowler 1959, Moore 1968, Nichols 1943, Smith 1945, Tinker 1978.

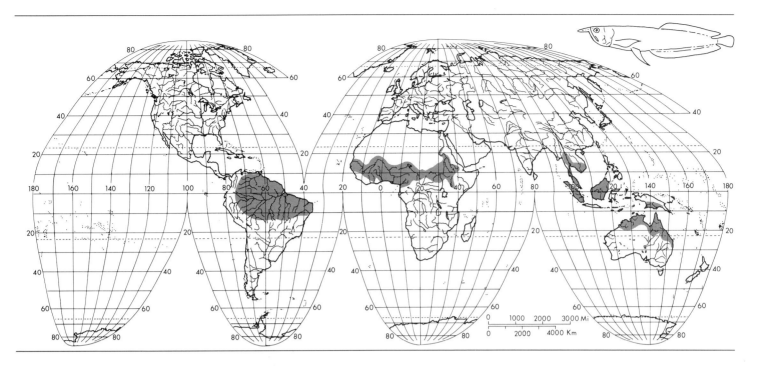

CLASS: Osteichthyes
  SUBCLASS: Actinopterygii
    SUPERORDER: Osteoglossomorpha

ORDER: Osteoglossiformes
  SUBORDER: Osteoglossoidei
    (1st) FAMILY: **OSTEOGLOSSIDAE**—bonytongues
    (ŏs'-tē-ō-glŏs'-ĭ-dē)

This family of 4 genera and 6 species is distributed in the fresh waters of tropical South America (*Arapaima*, 1 species; *Osteoglossum*, 2 species); Africa (*Heterotis*, 1 species); Malay Archipelago, Borneo, southern New Guinea, and northern Australia (*Scleropages*, 2 species). It is the only family of primary division freshwater fishes that crosses the line between the Asian and Australian realms to a major extent. This Southern Hemisphere distribution, similar to the Dipteriformes (lungfishes), may reflect a previous Gondwanian pattern with subsequent breakup and drifting of the supercontinent. Fossil osteoglossids date to the Eocene of North America and Sumatra and the Tertiary of Australia and India.

Most osteoglossids feed on fish and crustaceans, but *Heterotis* can extract plankton with a helical organ above the gill arches. Most bonytongues possess upturned large mouths, posteriorly positioned, long, unpaired fins, and large heavy scales. They have a highly vascularized swim bladder that can function as a lung. *Arapaima* and *Heterotis* are nest builders, whereas *Scleropages* and *Osteoglossum* are buccal incubators. *A. gigas* from South America is one of the largest freshwater fishes in the world, reaching at least 3 m and perhaps 4.5 m. The other species may grow to 1 m, and all are locally important as food fishes. Greenwood (1974c) summarized the order. Consult Herald (1962), Ladiges (1973), Lake (1971), and Nelson (1969) for further details and references.

Map references: Bartholomew, Clarke, and Grimshaw 1911*, Bertin and Arambourg 1958*, Darlington 1957, Eigenmann 1909a*, Eigenmann and Allen 1942, Gery 1969, Hoedeman 1974*, Grzimek 1973*, Lake 1971, Meek 1916*, Nelson 1976*, Norman and Greenwood 1975*, Poll 1973*, Roberts 1975, Sterba 1966*.

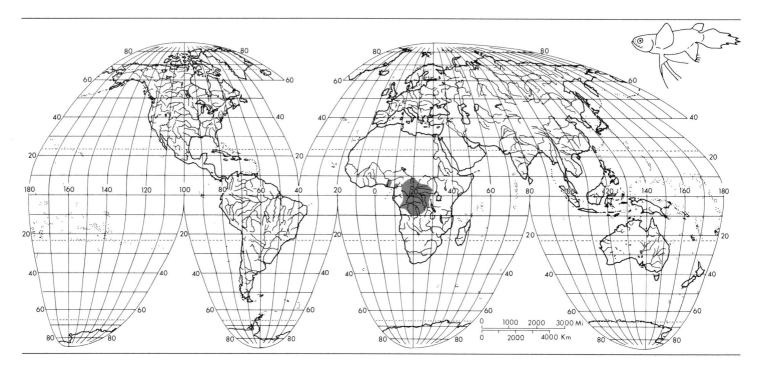

CLASS: Osteichthyes
    SUBCLASS: Actinopterygii
        SUPERORDER: Osteoglossomorpha

ORDER: Osteoglossiformes
    SUBORDER: Osteoglossoidei
        (1st) FAMILY: **PANTODONTIDAE**—butterflyfish
        (păn'-tō-dŏn'-tĭ-dē)

The family Pantodontidae is monotypic and restricted to the sluggish fresh waters of tropical west Africa. *Pantodon bucholzi* may reach 13 cm and can leap a meter or more out of the water, gliding with the help of enlarged pectoral fins. Its pelvic fins have elongate rays which may serve a tactile function. *Pantodon* is a surface-feeding insect eater, which lays floating eggs and can utilize atmospheric oxygen with the help of a highly vascularized swim bladder. The anal fin shows some sexual dimorphism, but little is known about the biology of this species. Consult Breder and Rosen (1966) for references to reproduction, and Greenwood and Thompson (1960) for anatomy and flight potential. Fossils date to the Paleocene (Patterson 1975).

Map references: Bartholomew, Clarke, and Grimshaw 1911*, Hoedeman 1974*, Poll 1973*, Roberts 1975, Sterba 1966*.

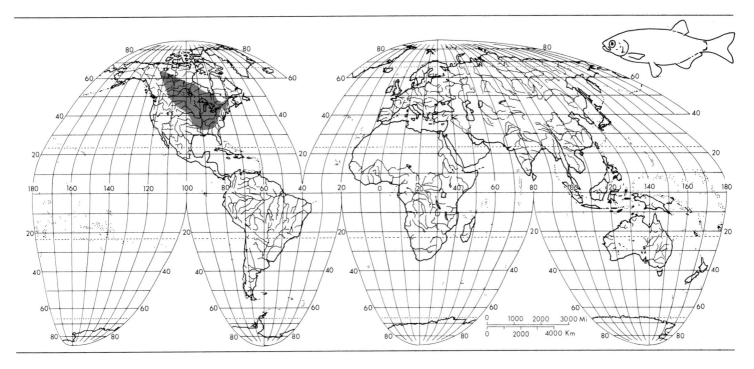

CLASS: Osteichthys
  SUBCLASS: Actinopterygii
    SUPERORDER: Osteoglossomorpha

ORDER: Osteoglossiformes
  SUBORDER: Notopteroidei
    (1st) FAMILY: **HIODONTIDAE**—mooneyes
    (hī'-ō-dŏn'-tĭ-dē)

The mooneye, *Hiodon tergisus*, and the goldeneye, *H. alosoides*, are autochthonous to northeastern and north central North America. This is the only osteoglossiform family not found in the tropics. These large-eyed, thin-bodied, egg-laying, herringlike fishes possess a ventral keel, but not a serrated abdomen as do the clupeids. The keel extends more anteriorly in *H. alosoides* than in *H. tergisus*. The goldeneye may reach 50 cm and, when smoked, is of commercial importance in Canada. Goldeneyes seem to prefer, or at least tolerate, turbid waters, whereas mooneyes are found in clearer rivers. Both feed upon aquatic insects, small fishes, and other invertebrates. Fossil hiodontids date to the Eocene of Canada, and superfamily fossils date to the Upper Jurassic of China (Patterson and Rosen 1977). Consult Scott and Crossman (1973) for details of their life history and references.

Map references: Bartholomew, Clarke, and Grimshaw 1911*, Hubbs and Lagler 1958, McPhail and Lindsey 1970*, Meek 1916*, Moore 1968, Nelson 1976*, Pflieger 1971*, Rostlund 1952*, Scott and Crossman 1973*, Trautman 1957*, Whitaker 1968*.

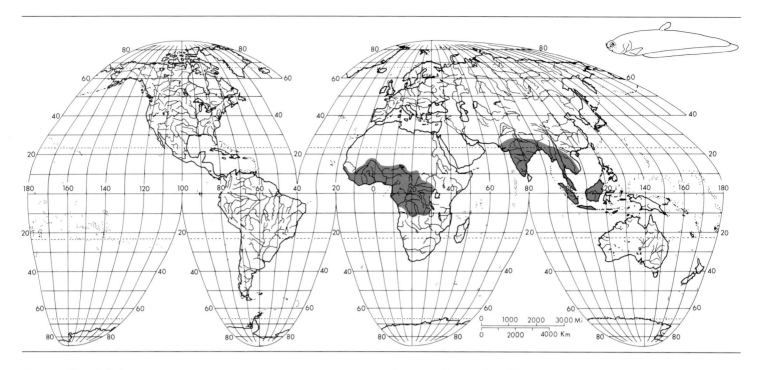

CLASS: Osteichthyes
  SUBCLASS: Actinopterygii
    SUPERORDER: Osteoglossomorpha

ORDER: Osteoglossiformes
  SUBORDER: Notopteroidei
    (1st) FAMILY: **NOTOPTERIDAE**—featherbacks
    (nō'-tŏp-tĕr'-ĭ-dē)

The featherbacks, so called because of the single, featherlike dorsal fin, are found in the fresh and brackish waters of west and central tropical Africa, India, and the Malay Archipelago. There are 3 genera and 6 species. *Notopterus*, with 4 species, is found in Asia, and the monotypic *Xenomystus* and *Papyrocranus* are confined to Africa. *Xenomystus* lacks a dorsal fin, and all species have a long flowing anal fin which joins the reduced caudal fin and provides propulsion. The body of notopterids is not bent during swimming, perhaps because the long swim bladder extends to the posterior end of the body cavity. Featherbacks can live in oxygen-poor habitats and gulp air at the surface. They are also known to make un-derwater noises with their swim bladders. The oriental species *N. chitala* is the largest, growing to a meter in length in India and is an important food fish in Thailand. *Notopterus* is an egg layer, and the males guard the eggs and drive off intruders. Diet includes small fishes and invertebrates. Fossils date to the Upper Eocene of Sumatra. See Smith (1945) for further life history details.

Map references: Bartholomew, Clarke, and Grimshaw 1911*, Darlington 1957, Meek 1916*, Nelson 1976*, Poll 1973*, Roberts 1975, Sterba 1966*.

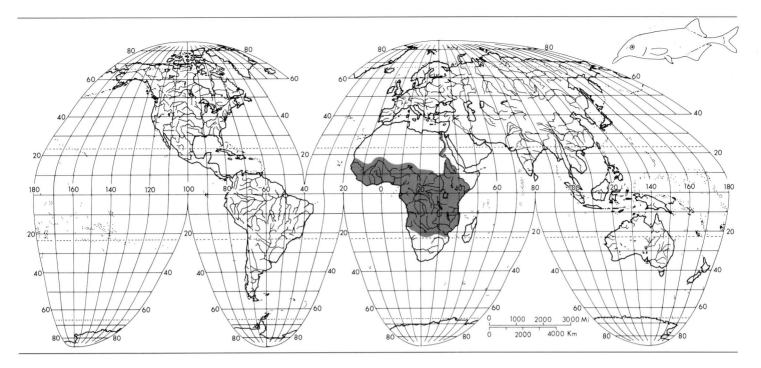

CLASS: Osteichthyes
  SUBCLASS: Actinopterygii
    SUPERORDER: Osteoglossomorpha

ORDER: Mormyriformes
  (1st) FAMILY: **MORMYRIDAE**—elephant fishes
  (mŏr-mĭr′-ĭ-dē) [mōr-mȳ′-rĭ-dē]

The mormyrids are found in the fresh waters of tropical Africa and the Nile system. There are over 100 species in about 10 genera, many of peculiar shape, such as the elephant-nosed *Campylomormyus numenius*, which has a trunklike snout. Other genera include *Gnathonemus*, *Mormyrus*, and *Mormyrops*. In addition to the many unusual mouth and snout modifications, mormyrids have a very narrow caudal peduncle and a deeply forked tail. Most are small, 20–50 cm, but the elongate snout may add to the total length. These fishes possess an electrical system derived from muscle tissue which sends out constant, weak impulses that function something like radar in the detection of obstacles, food, and mates in the turbid waters which they inhabit. It is not an offensive electrical shocking system, such as is found in the electric eel and electric catfish. The impulse-generating tissue is coupled with an unusually large cerebellum which coordinates the system. See Lissmann (1958) and Bennett (1971a, b) for a review of electric organs. Fossils of related fishes date to the Lower Cretaceous of Asia (Patterson 1975). Gery (1973a) should be consulted for a general account of mormyrid life history.

Map references: Bartholomew, Clarke, and Grimshaw 1911*, Boulenger 1909, Grzimek 1973*, Jubb 1967, Meek 1916*, Nelson 1976*, Roberts 1975, Sterba 1966*.

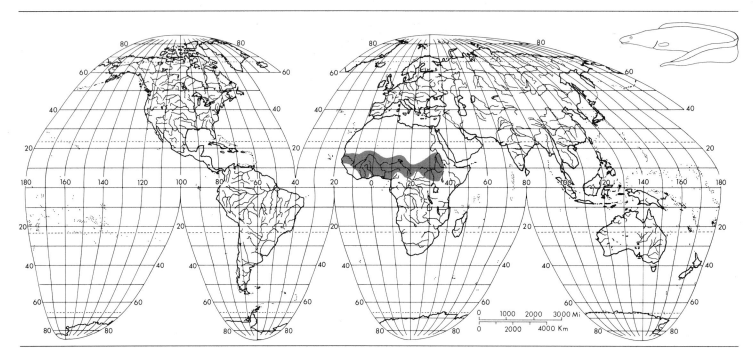

CLASS: Osteichthyes
    SUBCLASS: Actinopterygii
        SUPERORDER: Osteoglossomorpha

ORDER: Mormyriformes
    (1st) FAMILY: GYMNARCHIDAE—gymnarchid eel
    (jĭm-năr′-kĭ-dē)

This monotypic family, composed of the elongate species *Gymnarchus niloticus*, is found in the fresh waters of west and central Africa, including the upper Nile. *Gymnarchus* is related to the mormyrids but has lost its pelvic, anal, and caudal fins and has an elongate dorsal fin stretching from head to tail. The total length may reach 1.6 m, but most are half this size. *G. niloticus* emits a weak electrical field like the mormyrids, builds a floating nest, guards its territory, and feeds on fishes and crustaceans.

Map references: Boulenger 1909, Grzimek 1973*, Roberts 1975.

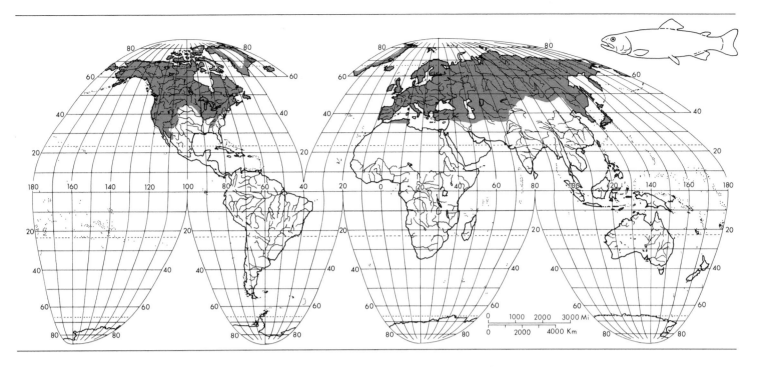

CLASS: Osteichthyes
    SUBCLASS: Actinopterygii
        SUPERORDER: Protacanthopterygii

ORDER: Salmoniformes
    SUBORDER: Salmonoidei
        (Per) FAMILY: SALMONIDAE—trouts, salmons
        (săl-mŏn'-ĭ-dē)

The 70 or so species of salmonids are distributed in a typical holarctic pattern in cool and cold waters of the north temperate zone, including Africa north of the Atlas Mountains, northwest Mexico, and Taiwan. The family is composed of Pacific salmons (*Oncorhynchus*), trouts (*Salmo*), charrs (*Salvelinus*), whitefishes (*Coregonus*), graylings (*Thymallus*), and at least 3 other genera. The last 2 named genera have previously been considered as comprising distinct but related families that are now treated as subfamilies. The Salmonidae contains both freshwater and anadromous forms, which make long spawning migrations into freshwater streams to lay their eggs and die. The young then migrate to the sea, where they grow for several years before mysteriously reappearing at their natal stream to complete the cycle. See Harden-Jones (1968), Hasler (1966), and Netboy (1974) for information on salmon navigation and migration. This family is one of the dominant families in holarctic waters, and the arctic charr, *Salvelinus alpinus*, occurs further north than any other freshwater fish. The chinook salmon, *Oncorhynchus tshawytscha*, is one of the largest salmonids and may weigh 50 kg. A Eurasian species, *Hucho taimen*, may reach 80 kg.

Salmonids are extremely important sport and commercial fishes and have been introduced into cool waters of Australia, New Zealand, Africa, and South America. One can even fish for trout in the highlands of New Guinea (Glucksman, West, and Berra 1976). One of the classic studies in fisheries biology was done on trout in New Zealand (Allen 1951).

Salmonids possess an adipose fin, cycloid scales, pelvic axillary process, and the males of some species develop an upturned lower jaw (kype) during their spawning migration. Some populations of normally anadromous species may be completely landlocked. The Great Lakes populations of lake trout, *Salvelinus namaycush*, and whitefishes, *Coregonus* species, have been badly depleted or, in some cases, exterminated by the parasitic sea lamprey. The Coregoninae is a very large and difficult group to work with taxonomically. The subfamily's distribution is similar to the Salmoninae, but the coregonids do not extend as far north and south. The Thymallinae, which is strictly a freshwater group, consists of 4 species, including the European *Thymallus thymallus* and the American *T. arcticus*, which have a large flaglike dorsal fin and a less extensive holarctic distribution than the Salmoninae. Fossils of this suborder date to the Lower Eocene of Denmark.

The Salmonidae has been very extensively studied because of its economic importance. Detailed life histories, taxonomic information, and references can be found in Lavender (1978), Morton (1980), Norden (1961), Scott and Crossman (1973), Dymond (1963), Vladykov (1963), Karbe (1973), and Berg (1949). Salmoniform taxonomy is in a state of flux and was recently reviewed by Rosen (1974), who presented a revised classification and phylogeny with zoogeographic implications. Behnke (1972, 1974) and Nelson (1976) gave an overview of the order, and Balon (1980) has edited a book on charrs (*Salvelinus*).

Map references: Bartholomew, Clarke, and Grimshaw 1911*, Berg 1949, Carl, Clemens, and Lindsey 1959*, Darlington 1957, Dymond 1963, Grzimek 1973*, Koelz 1929*, McPhail and Lindsey 1970*, Meek 1916*, Nelson 1976*, Netboy 1974*, Pflieger 1971*, Rostlund 1952*, Rosen 1974*, Scott and Crossman 1973*, Sterba 1966*, Trautman 1957*, Wheeler 1969*.

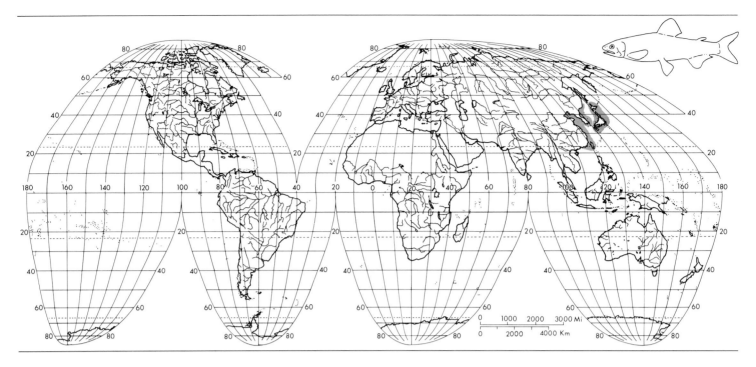

CLASS: Osteichthyes
   SUBCLASS: Actinopterygii
      SUPERORDER: Protacanthopterygii

ORDER: Salmoniformes
   SUBORDER: Salmonoidei
      (Per) FAMILY: **PLECOGLOSSIDAE**—ayu
      [plĕ-cō-glŏs′-sĭ-dē]

This monotypic, oriental family consists of the ayu, *Pleco-glossus altivelis*, and is distributed along the Pacific coast of north China, Japan, Korea, and Taiwan. This species is notable for the movable, small teeth seated in a fold of skin on the maxillary and mandible. The body form is typically salmonid with an adipose fin and very small scales; however, a pelvic axillary process is absent. Maximum size is 30 cm. This usually anadromous species can also be found in lakes and is unusual for a salmoniform fish in that it feeds on phytoplankton.

Plecoglossus is the object of the peculiar cormorant fisheries, whereby a trained cormorant, with a ring around its neck to prevent swallowing, scoops up many ayus on their spawning run. The bird's owner then turns the cormorant upside down and shakes out its catch. The long-suffering bird is rewarded with a piece of fish. Rosen (1974) classifies the Plecoglossidae with the superfamily Osmeroidea.

Map references: Grzimek 1973*, Nichols 1943, Rosen 1974*.

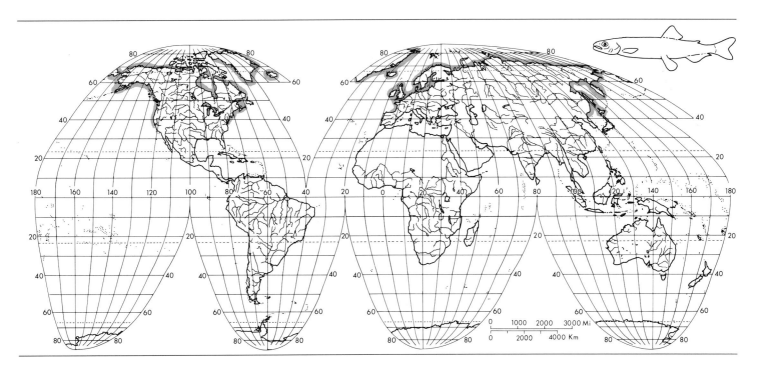

CLASS: Osteichthyes
  SUBCLASS: Actinopterygii
    SUPERORDER: Protacanthopterygii

ORDER: Salmoniformes
  SUBORDER: Salmonoidei
    (Per) FAMILY: **OSMERIDAE**—smelts (ŏs-mĕr′-ĭ-dē)

The smelts are a circumpolar family found in the cold and temperate coastal waters of the Northern Hemisphere. A few species such as the rainbow smelt, *Osmerus mordax*, which may be conspecific with the European *O. eperlanus*, live in inland waters. Some coastal species enter rivers during spawning runs. The presence of *O. mordax* in the Great Lakes, however, is the result of introduction by man in this century. Smelts are small, slender, carnivorous fishes with thin, easily shed, cycloid scales, large mouth, an adipose fin, and no pelvic axillary process. There are about 10 species in 6 genera, most of which are in the North Pacific. Smelts are important commercially as food and bait and as a link in the food chain because of their great numbers. See Scott and Crossman (1973), Bigelow and Schroeder (1963), and Berg (1949) for life histories and references, McAllister (1963) for a revision of the family, and Gruchy and McAllister (1972) for a bibliography.

Map references: Berg 1949, Bigelow and Schroeder 1963, Grzimek 1973*, McPhail and Lindsey 1970*, Meek 1916*, Nelson 1976*, Rosen 1974*, Scott and Crossman 1973*, Trautman 1957*, Whitaker 1968*.

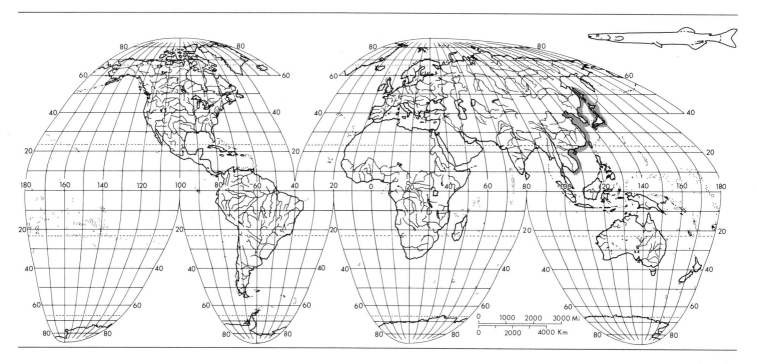

CLASS: Osteichthyes
  SUBCLASS: Actinopterygii
    SUPERORDER: Protacanthopterygii

ORDER: Salmoniformes
  SUBORDER: Galaxioidei or Salmonidei
    (Per) FAMILY: **SALANGIDAE**—ice fishes
    [să-lăn′-gĭ-dē]

This small family (6 genera and about 12 species) of little, translucent, elongate fishes is found in coastal and fresh waters from the Amur River south to Vietnam. Salangids have minute, deciduous scales, posteriorly placed dorsal and anal fins, and an adipose fin. *Salangichthys* is locally very abundant and is used as a food fish in China. See Berg (1949) and Nicholas (1943) for further details. Weitzman (1967) and McDowall (1969) do not think that the oriental salangids are part of the Southern Hemisphere galaxioid lineage as reflected by the Greenwood et al. (1966) classification. Rosen (1974) classifies the salangids within the superfamily Osmeroidea, which includes the Osmeridae, Plecoglossidae, Retropinnidae, and Salangidae and defines the salmonoids and osmeroids as sister groups.

Map references: Berg 1949, Nichols 1943, Rosen 1974*.

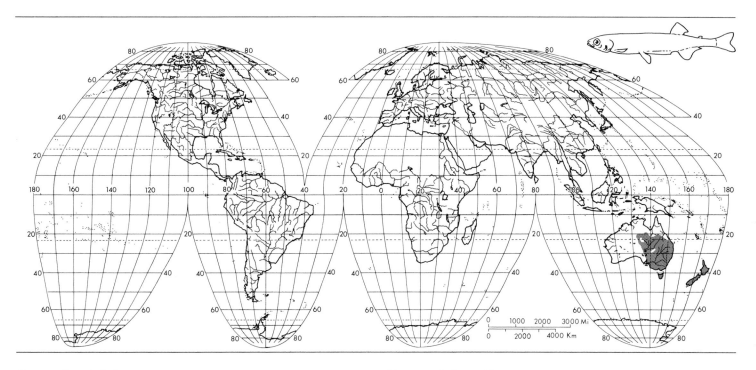

CLASS: Osteichthyes
   SUBCLASS: Actinopterygii
      SUPERORDER: Protacanthopterygii

ORDER: Salmoniformes
   SUBORDER: Galaxioidei
      (Per) **FAMILY: RETROPINNIDAE**—Southern
      Hemisphere smelts (rĕ-trō-pīn′-nĭ-dē)

This family is confined to southeastern Australia, Tasmania, and New Zealand. These small smeltlike fishes are grouped into 2 genera, *Retropinna* (3 species) and *Stokellia anisodon*. The latter is only found in New Zealand, as is *R. retropinna*, while *R. semoni* and *R. tasmanica* are the Australian species. Some complete their life cycle in fresh water, whereas others return to fresh water to spawn after a marine larval or juvenile stage. They rarely exceed 13 cm in length, and feed on plankton. There is some sexual dimorphism, with males having larger fins and developing more nuptial tubercles. The dorsal fin is above the anal fin. An adipose fin is present, scales are cycloid, there is no lateral line, and a right gonad is lacking. Some species are of limited commercial importance.

See Lake (1971), Woods (1963, 1968), and McDowall (1970*a*, 1978*b*, 1979, 1980) for more details.

McDowall (1969) felt that the Galaxioidei should contain only the Galaxiidae, Retropinnidae, Aplochitonidae, and Prototroctidae, thereby removing the Salangidae from the otherwise Southern Hemisphere assemblage of salmoniform fishes. Rosen (1974), on the other hand, put the Osmeridae, Plecoglossidae, Retropinnidae, and Salangidae in the superfamily Osmeroidea, while placing the galaxiids and salmonids in the superfamily Salmonoidea.

Map references: Darlington 1957, Frankenberg 1974*, Lake 1971, McDowall 1978*b**, 1979*, Rosen 1974*, Whitley 1968.

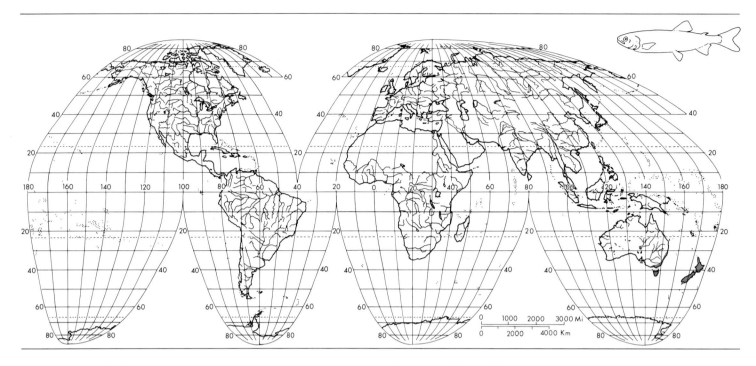

CLASS: Osteichthyes
  SUBCLASS: Actinopterygii
    SUPERORDER: Protacanthopterygii

ORDER: Salmoniformes
  SUBORDER: Galaxioidei
    (Per) FAMILY: **PROTOTROCTIDAE**—Southern
    Hemisphere graylings (prō'-tō-trŏk'-tī-dē)

The Southern Hemisphere graylings consist of 2 species, the New Zealand grayling, *Prototroctes oxyrhynchus*, which hasn't been collected since the mid-1920s and is probably extinct, and the Australian grayling, *P. maraena*. These attractive troutlike fishes are scaled and have an adipose fin. The lateral line is absent, and a horny sheath surrounds the lower jaw. A small mid-ventral keel is present, and only the left gonad is developed in both sexes. Males of the Australian species develop breeding tubercles. Their dentition consists of blunt, comblike teeth, and their looped alimentary canal is longer than other salmoniform fishes. Graylings are omnivorous, feeding on algae, cladocerans, and insects. *P. maraena* is found in clear, gravel-bottomed, coastal rivers from about the latitude of Sydney southward along the New South Wales, Victorian, and Tasmanian coasts. They spawn in fresh water in late April, and the young are presumably swept downstream to brackish water. The adults remain in fresh water. The juveniles return to fresh water about 6 months after

hatching. The Australian grayling grows to about 30 cm and has an odor like freshly cut cucumbers.

Graylings are closely related to the retropinnids, but differ in that their dorsal fin is much further forward than the anal fin. McDowall (1969) removed *Prototroctes* from the Aplochitonidae, which shows relationships to the Galaxiidae. Nelson (1972) placed the graylings in the Galaxiidae. Rosen (1974) considered the Aplochitonidae as a subfamily of the Galaxiidae and put *Prototroctes* with the Retropinnidae. See McDowall (1976) for a review of the family. For recent life history information see McDowall (1974, 1978b), Jackson (1976), Bishop and Bell (1978, 1979), and Bell et al. (1980). McDowall (1980) provided a color photograph of the Australian species.

Map references: Bell et al. 1980*, Lake 1971, McDowall 1976*, 1978b*.

34

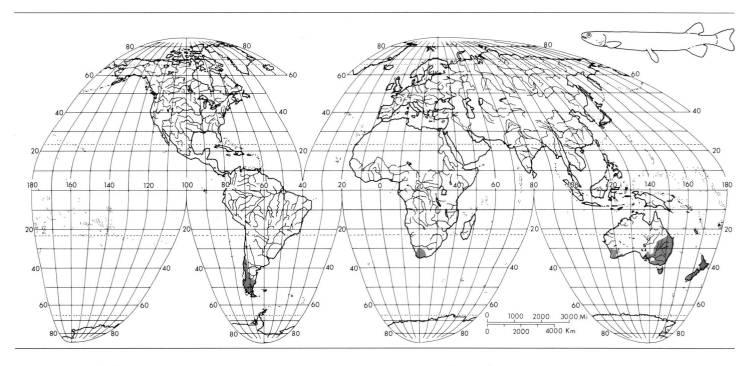

CLASS: Osteichthyes
   SUBCLASS: Actinopterygii
      SUPERORDER: Protacanthopterygii

ORDER: Salmoniformes
   SUBORDER: Galaxioidei
      (Per) FAMILY: **GALAXIIDAE**—galaxiids
      (găl'-ăk-sī'-ĭ-dē) [gă-lăx'-ĭ-ĭ-dē]

The galaxiids, consisting of about 35 species in 6 genera, show a very interesting Southern Hemisphere distribution pattern, occurring in South America from about lat. 33°S, the tip of South Africa, and southern Australia, New Zealand, Lord Howe Island, and New Caledonia. This family does not occur in the Northern Hemisphere in spite of Day's description of *Galaxias indicus*, which McDowall (1973b) regarded as a *nomen dubium*. One species, *Galaxias maculatus* (= *G. attenuatus*), is found in both South American and Australian–New Zealand waters. It is the only galaxiid to breed in brackish water; all others spawn in fresh water. Galaxiids can be distinguished from other salmoniform fishes by the absence of an adipose fin. These small, 4–30 cm (*G. argentus* may reach 58 cm), scaleless fishes appear to be the ecological equivalents of the Northern Hemisphere trouts and are found up to an altitude of 1 km. The New Zealand *Neochanna apoda* and *N. diversus* lack pelvic fins and can aestivate in mud during droughts for several weeks. The continental drift pattern presented by galaxiid distribution is striking in view of the fact that galaxiids are represented on each of the major continents originally making up Gondwanaland. However, McDowall (1978a, b) believes that dispersal could have been through the sea. Fossils of this suborder date to the Pliocene of New Zealand. See Rosen (1974) for an extended discussion, classification, phylogeny and distribution. Consult Andrews (1976), Frankenberg (1969), McDowall (1969, 1970b, 1971a, 1972, 1973a), McDowall and Frankenberg (in press), McDowall and Fulton (1978) for further taxonomic information and Lake (1971), Woods (1963), Berra (1973) and McDowall (1978b, 1980) for life history details.

Map references: Bartholomew, Clarke, and Grimshaw 1911*, Darlington 1957, Eigenmann 1909a*, Eigenmann 1927, Frankenberg 1974*, Gosztonyi and McDowall 1974*, Grzimek 1973*, Jubb 1967, Lake 1971, McDowall 1978b, Meek 1916*, Rosen 1974*, Whitley 1968.

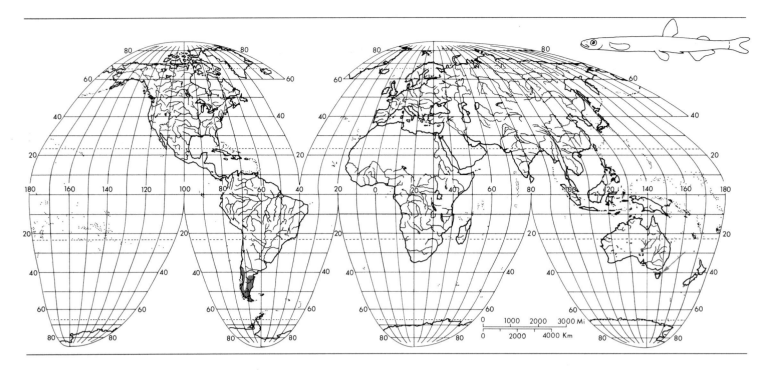

CLASS: Osteichthyes
  SUBCLASS: Actinopterygii
    SUPERORDER: Protacanthopterygii

ORDER: Salmoniformes
  SUBORDER: Galaxioidei
    (Per) FAMILY: **APLOCHITONIDAE**
    [ăp-lō-kī-tŏn'-ĭ-dē]

This small family consists of 2 genera, *Aplochiton* (2 species) in southern South America to lat. 38°S, and the larvalike *Lovettia sealii* found along the north and east coasts of Tasmania. These slender fishes possess an adipose fin and lack scales, but whether they belong in the same family needs further study. *Lovettia* is white with tiny black dots and a silvery band along the sides. Its dorsal fin is just behind the level of the pelvic fins. It can reach 77 mm and was once caught commercially for canning during its spawning migration up rivers. The larvae drift downstream to the sea, then return to fresh water to spawn 1 year later. Males have the genital papilla just behind the head, whereas females have it in front of the anal fin.

McDowall (1969) concluded that *Aplochiton* and *Lovettia* form a valid group, and removed *Prototroctes* to its own family. Rosen (1974) considered the Aplochitoninae as a subfamily of the Galaxiidae. See Blackburn (1950) for details of the biology of *Lovettia* and McDowall (1971*b*, 1980) for a review of the family.

Map references: Bartholomew, Clarke, and Grimshaw 1911*, Darlington 1957, Eigenmann 1909*a**, Eigenmann 1927, Frankenberg 1974*, Gery 1969, Lake 1971, Meek 1916*, McDowall 1971*b**.

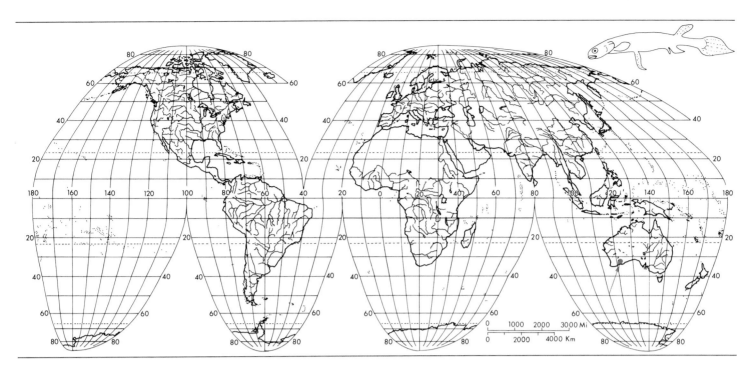

CLASS: Osteichthyes
  SUBCLASS: Actinopterygii
    SUPERORDER: Protacanthopterygii

ORDER: Salmoniformes
  SUBORDER: Galaxioidei
    (?) **FAMILY: LEPIDOGALAXIIDAE** (lĕp'-ĭ-dō-găl'-ăk-sī'-ĭ-dē) [lĕ-pī-dŏ-gă-lăx'-ĭ-ĭ-dē]

Lepidogalaxias salamandroides, the single species in this family, is known only from a small creek which flows into the Shannon River in southwest Western Australia. It leads a benthic existence in small streams and swamps. *Lepidogalaxias* is not an active swimmer and feeds on dipteran larvae and slow-swimming plankton. Maximum size is about 60 mm.

It was first described by Mees (1961) as a galaxiid, even though it has scales, probably because it lacks an adipose fin. McDowall (1969) expressed doubt of this galaxiid relationship. Frankenberg (1969) reported that evidence from otoliths and the size and position of the scapular foramen favored a galaxioid affinity over an esocoid one. He considered the caudal skeleton of *Lepidogalaxias* to be very similar to that of *Umbra limi*, but felt that this may represent convergence since both have a similar habitat and life style. Frankenberg (1969) wrote that this species should be regarded as a specialized form adapted for a benthic existence at an early stage in salmoniform evolution, and that it should be in its own superfamily, Lepidogalaxioidea, of the suborder Galaxioidea. A recent study of gill arches, caudal skeleton, and secondary sexual characters (Rosen 1974) indicated that this unusual fish could be a Southern Hemisphere esocoid, which, if correct, is the only Southern Hemisphere representative of the suborder and presents a very peculiar distribution pattern. Lake (1978) provided a color photograph of this strange fish.

Map references: Lake 1971, Rosen 1974*.

37

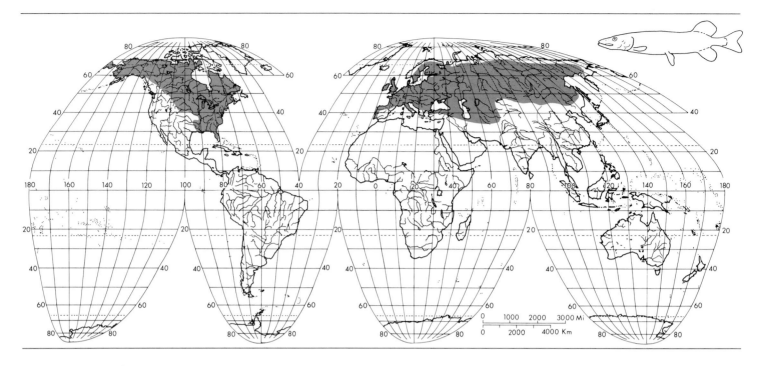

CLASS: Osteichthyes
  SUBCLASS: Actinopterygii
    SUPERORDER: Protacanthopterygii

ORDER: Salmoniformes
  SUBORDER: Esocoidei
    (1st) FAMILY: **ESOCIDAE**—pikes (ē-sŏs'-ĭ-dē) [ē-sō'-sĭ-dē]

The pikes are large, predacious fishes distributed holarctically in northern and eastern North America and Eurasia. There is 1 genus, *Esox*, with 4 species in North America, 1 of which, the northern pike *E. lucius*, is also widely distributed in Eurasia, and 1 endemic in the Amur River region of Siberia, *E. reicherti*. Although there are 3 American endemics, the group probably originated in Eurasia as reflected by Old World Oligocene fossils (Crossman 1978). This family of cylindrical, duckbilled fishes with posteriorly placed unpaired fins has representatives that may grow to great size. The muskellunge, *E. masquinongy*, may reach 2 m and 50 kg, whereas a large northern pike may be half that weight. Both are important

sport fishes. Pickerel, *E. niger* and *E. americanus*, may reach 70 cm and 38 cm respectively. See Scott and Crossman (1973) and Berg (1949) for life histories and references, and Crossman (1978) for a review of the taxonomy and distribution of North American species.

Map references: Bartholomew, Clarke, and Grimshaw 1911*, Berg 1949, Crossman 1966*, 1978*, Darlington 1957*, Grzimek 1973*, Lagler, Barbach, and Miller 1962*, McPhail and Lindsey 1970*, Maitland 1977*, Meek 1916*, Nelson 1976*, Pflieger 1971*, Rosen 1974*, Rostlund 1952*, Scott and Crossman 1973*, Sterba 1966*, Trautman 1957*, Whitaker 1968*.

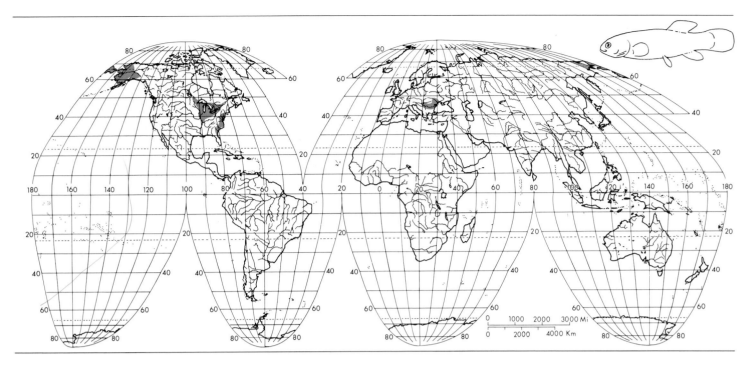

CLASS: Osteichthyes
   SUBCLASS: Actinopterygii
      SUPERORDER: Protacanthopterygii

ORDER: Salmoniformes
   SUBORDER: Escoidei
      (1st) FAMILY: **UMBRIDAE**—mudminnows
      (ŭm′-brĭ-dē)

This family of small fishes (7–18 cm) is disjunctly distributed as follows: Alaska blackfish, *Dallia pectoralis*, Alaska–Eastern Siberia; Olympic mudminnow, *Novumbra hubbsi*, Chehalis River, Washington; central mudminnow, *Umbra limi*, Great Lakes region and upper Mississippi Valley; eastern mudminnow, *U. pygmaea*, Atlantic coast of North America; and European mudminnow, *U. krameri*, in the Danube and Dniester rivers of eastern Europe. *U. pygmaea* has been introduced into Belgium, France, and Holland. Mudminnows have a rounded caudal fin, small pelvic fins, and are capable of utilizing atmospheric oxygen. They prefer vegetated, sluggish habitat and are very tolerant of cold, drought, and low oxygen levels. Umbrids are capable of aestivating in the bottom mud during unfavorable seasons. Insects and other invertebrates make up the diet of these egg layers. Each genus was placed in a separate family in older classifications, and there is still no general agreement on relationships, as pointed out by Cavender (1969) and Nelson (1972). The chromosome number varies widely (22–78) among the genera (Beamish, Merriles, and Crossman 1971), and *U. limi* has been found to be an ideal animal for experimental karyotype studies (Mong and Berra 1979). Fossils are from the Lower Eocene of Europe. See Scott and Crossman (1973), Wheeler (1969), and Berg (1949) for further details.

Map references: Berg 1949, Darlington 1957, Lagler, Bardach, and Miller 1962*, Maitland 1977*, McPhail and Lindsey 1970*, Miller 1958*, Nelson 1976*, Rostlund 1952*, Scott and Crossman 1973*, Sterba 1966*, Trautman 1957*, Wheeler 1969*, Whitaker 1968*.

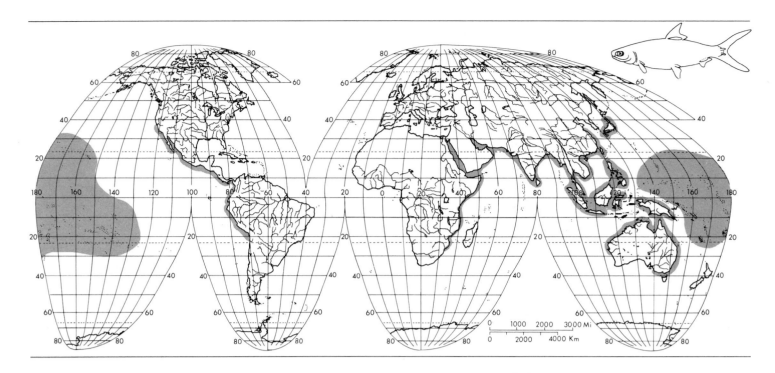

CLASS: Osteichthyes
  SUBCLASS: Actinopterygii
    SUPERORDER: Protacanthopterygii

ORDER: Gonorynchiformes
  SUBORDER: Chanoidei
    (Per) FAMILY: **CHANIDAE**—milkfish [kă'-nĭ-dē]

The milkfish, *Chanos chanos*, is the only member of this Indo-Pacific family. This toothless species resembles a herring with a deeply forked caudal fin. It has adipose eye lids, small cycloid scales, and lacks abdominal scutes. *Chanos* is an open-water species but spawns near shore and may enter rivers. It is an important food fish because of its excellent growth rate on a phytoplankton diet. It may reach 1 m, and is utilized in pond culture in southeast Asia. Fossils of the sub-order are from Lower Cretaceous of Africa, Brazil, and Italy (Patterson 1975). Peters (1973) discussed the biology of milk-fish and other members of the Gonorynchiformes.

Map references: Fowler 1959, Herre 1953, Kiener and Richard-Vindard 1972, La Monte 1952, Lake 1971, Miller 1966, Munro 1955, Tinker 1978, Weber and De Beaufort 1913.

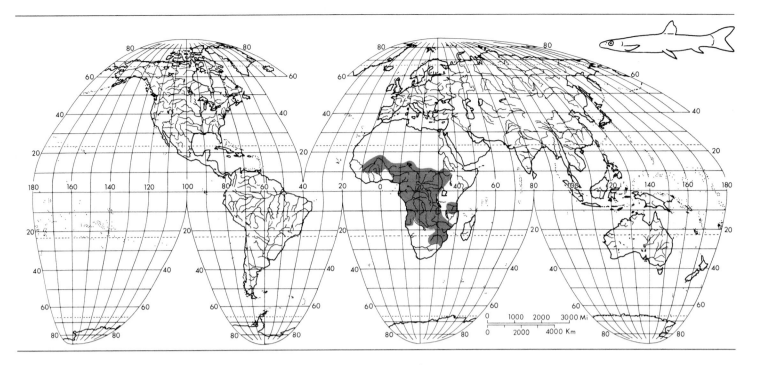

CLASS: Osteichthyes
   SUBCLASS: Actinopterygii
      SUPERORDER: Protacanthopterygii

ORDER: Gonorynchiformes
   SUBORDER: Chanoidei
      (1st) FAMILY: **KNERIIDAE**—kneriids [nĕ'-rĭ-ĭ-dē]

The kneriids are small (2–15 cm) minnowlike fishes of tropical Africa. There are about a dozen species. *Kneria* and *Parakneria* each contain several species of herbivorous fishes that prefer fast-flowing habitat. Male *Kneria* develop a peculiar horny rosette on each operculum, which they rub against the female as a sexual stimulant. The transparent, scaleless *Cromeria nilotica* and *Grasseichthys gabonensis* resemble lar-vae, even though they have a completely developed skeleton. The latter 2 species are sometimes put into separate families, Cromeriidae and Grasseichthyidae, respectively. See Peters (1973) for more details.

Map references: Bartholomew, Clarke, and Grimshaw 1911*, Jubb 1967, Poll 1973*, Roberts 1975.

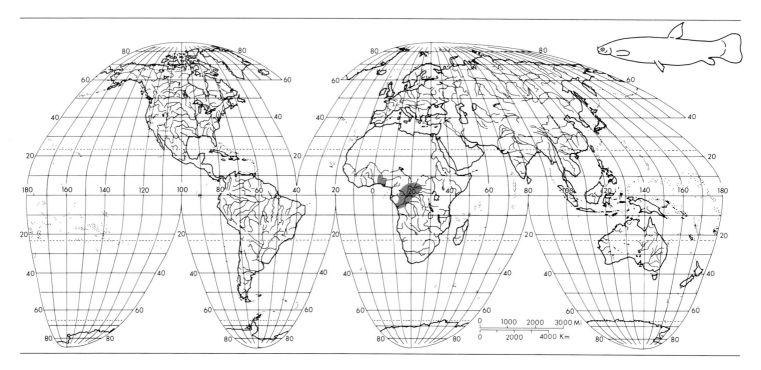

CLASS: Osteichthyes
  SUBCLASS: Actinopterygii
    SUPERORDER: Protacanthopterygii

ORDER: Gonorynchiformes
  SUBORDER: Chanoidei
    (1st) FAMILY: **PHRACTOLAEMIDAE**
    [frăk-tŏ-lē'-mĭ-dē]

The Phractolaemidae is a monotypic family distributed in tropical west Africa in the Niger and Congo river systems. *Phractolaemus ansorgi* has large cycloid scales and may reach about 18 cm. It is found in sluggish, swampy habitat and can breathe atmospheric air. It feeds on detritus and small food items that it can extract from bottom mud with its almost toothless tubular mouth. An unusual characteristic is a small projection in front of the single nasal opening on each side of the head. See Thys van den Audenaerde (1961) for an important paper on this family.

Map references: Peters 1973, Poll 1973*, Roberts 1975, Sterba 1966*.

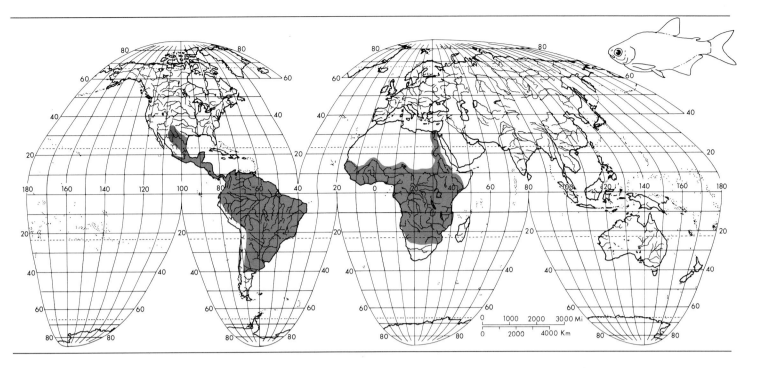

CLASS: Osteichthyes
  SUBCLASS: Actinopterygii
    SUPERORDER: Ostariophysi

ORDER: Cypriniformes
  SUBORDER: Characoidei
    (1st) FAMILY: **CHARACIDAE**—characins
    (kă-răs′-ĭ-dē)

The family Characidae (14 subfamilies and about 800 species) ranges from the Rio Grande in southern Texas (*Astyanax fasciatus*) through Central America to about lat. 41°S in Chile and Argentina (*Cheirodon*) and in tropical Africa and the Nile system. Note that they are absent from most of North America, all of Eurasia, the Orient, and Australia. In these areas, except Australia, characins are replaced by the Cyprinidae. Conversely, the cyprinids are absent from South America. These 2 families can be considered ecological equivalents.

Characoids, cyprinoids, and siluroids are ostariophysan fishes, which denotes the presence of 4 or 5 modified vertebrae that connect the swim bladder with the inner ear. Siluroids have 5 vertebrae in the Weberian apparatus, non-siluroids have 4. These ossicles, called the Weberian apparatus, confer an acute sense of hearing upon this group and may account for the dominance of ostariophysan fishes in the fresh waters of the world. Yerger (1974) estimated that about one-fourth the total number of fish species are ostariophysans. The swim bladder acts as a resonator and amplifier, so that gas-volume changes due to sound waves in the water are transmitted to the ear by the Weberian apparatus. The range of hearing is 16–10,000 hertz for ostariophysan fishes. See Rosen and Greenwood (1970) for a discussion of the origin of the Weberian apparatus. Myers (1967) placed the origin of the ostariophysan fishes in the late Triassic on a southern land mass, parts of which are now South America and Africa (Gondwana origin). Novacek and Marshall (1976) also favor a continental drift explanation with South America as the center of origin. Gery (1969) and Patterson (1975) favor Africa, while Briggs (1979) supplies reasons why the Orient should

be considered the center of origin for ostariophysan fishes. Briggs (1979) hypothesized that a characoid prototype evolved in the Upper Jurassic in the Oriental region from a gonorynchiform ancestor, and that siluriform fishes developed and dispersed from the same area shortly thereafter. The cyprinoids developed in the Oriental region of the Cretaceous. There are no characoid fossils from Southeast Asia, however. See Novacek and Marshall (1976) for another view, and Gosline (1973) for a phylogeny of cypriniform fishes based on feeding apparatus.

Gery (1973*b*) reported that about half of all freshwater fish species in South America belong to this suborder. He estimates that there are about 1,000 South American species and 200 African species of characoids. The characins are a very diverse group in morphology (2–160 cm), behavior (from vegetarians to the carnivorous piranhas), and ecological requirement. Most have 1 or both of the following 2 characteristics: jaw teeth and an adipose fin. These features distinguish characins from cyprinids. Most characins are adhesive egg scatterers. They are extremely important in the aquarium industry, as many species are small, colorful, and easily maintained. Fossils of this family date to the Eocene of Europe (Patterson 1975).

Yeger (1974) presented an overview of the superorder, and Gery (1973*b*) can be consulted for life history details. For information, illustrations, and references on piranhas see Myers (1972), Gery (1972) and Zahl (1970). Sterba (1966) and Hoedeman (1974) are good sources of aquarium information, and the following are just a few of the many important taxonomic papers on this group: Eigenmann and Myers (1917–

43

29), Gregory and Conrad (1938), Weitzman (1962), and Roberts (1969). Gery (1972) provided a bibliography of American characoid fishes. See Mitchell, Russell, and Elliott (1977) for a review of Mexican eyeless characins.

Map references: Bartholomew, Clarke, and Grimshaw 1911*, Bertin and Arambourg 1958*, Boulenger 1909, Darlington 1957, Eigenmann 1909a*, Eigenmann 1927, Eigenmann and Allen 1942, Gery 1969, Grzimek 1973*, Hoedeman 1974*, Innes 1966*, Jubb 1967, Meek 1916*, Miller 1966*, Nelson 1976*, Norman and Greenwood 1975*, Roberts 1975, Sterba 1966*.

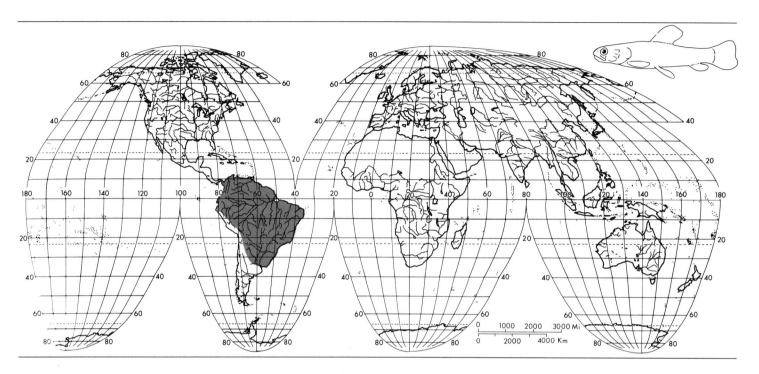

CLASS: Osteichthyes
  SUBCLASS: Actinopterygii
    SUPERORDER: Ostariophysi

ORDER: Cypriniformes
  SUBORDER: Characoidei
    (1st) FAMILY: **ERYTHRINIDAE** [ĕ-rĭ-thrī′-nĭ-dē]

The erythrinids are primitive characoid fishes widely distributed throughout north and central South America north to the Canal Zone. There are about 5 highly predacious species in 3 genera: *Erythrinus* (1 species), *Hoplias* (2 species), and *Hoplerythrinus* (2 species). They have an elongate body, rounded caudal fin, and no adipose fin, and the swim bladder is modified for air breathing. In some a capillary network may be present on the operculum. *Hoplias malabaricus* may reach 1 m in length. See Weitzman (1964) for a definition of the family.

Map references: Sterba 1966, Wheeler 1975.

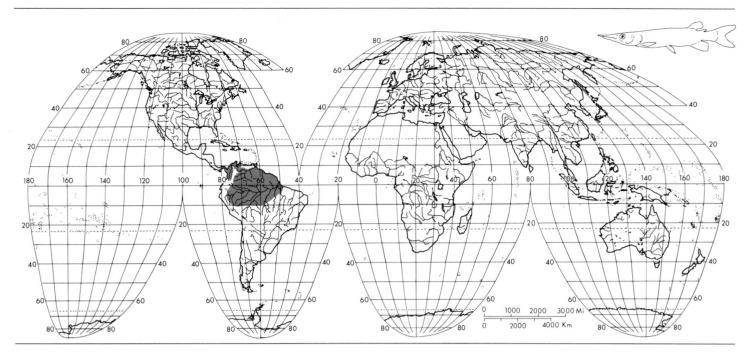

CLASS: Osteichthyes
    SUBCLASS: Actinopterygii
        SUPERORDER: Ostariophysi

ORDER: Cypriniformes
    SUBORDER: Characoidei
        (1st) FAMILY: **CTENOLUCIIDAE** [tē-nō-lŭ′-sĭ-ī-dē]

This family of small pikelike characoids is composed of 2 genera (*Ctenolucius* and *Boulengerella*) and 4 species, and is found in the Amazon, Orinoco, and Magdalena river systems of South America. These fishes grow to less than 30 cm, have ctenoid scales, and have a peculiar fleshy jaw flap of un-

known function. See Roberts (1969) for details of osteology and relationships.

Map references: Eigenmann 1922, Grzimek 1973*, Miller 1966.

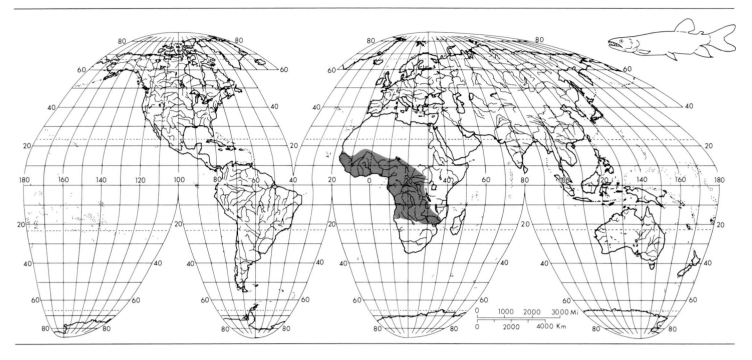

CLASS: Osteichthyes
   SUBCLASS: Actinopterygii
      SUPERORDER: Ostariophysi

ORDER: Cypriniformes
   SUBORDER: Characoidei
      (1st) FAMILY: **HEPSETIDAE**—African pike
      [hĕp-sē′-tĭ-dē]

This monotypic family consists of *Hepsetus odoe* and is found in tropical Africa from Senegal through Angola. It occurs in the rivers of west Africa: the Chari, Congo, Upper Zambesi, and Cunene. This species is pikelike, with a depressed head, large mouth, well-developed conical teeth, and long, slender gill rakers. They are voracious fish predators. The dorsal fin is set far back on the body, and they may reach 35 cm. They resemble the South American characin, *Acestrorhynchus*. See Roberts (1969) for details of osteology and relationships.

Map references: Bell-Cross 1968, Boulenger 1909, Roberts 1975, Sterba 1966.

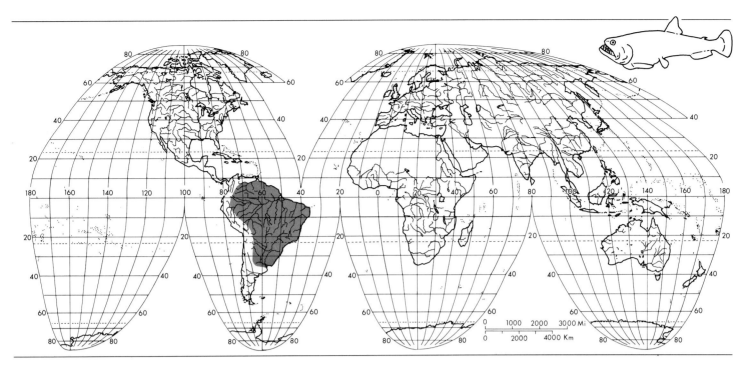

CLASS: Osteichthyes
  SUBCLASS: Actinopterygii
    SUPERORDER: Ostariophysi

ORDER: Cypriniformes
  SUBORDER: Characoidei
    (1st) FAMILY: **CYNODONTIDAE** [sī-nō-dŏn'-tĭ-dē]

The Cynodontidae is found from the Orinoco to Río de la Plata. The body is compressed, and the large oblique mouth contains many well-developed conical teeth, especially anteriorly. The scales are minute and the pectoral and anal fins are very long. The largest representative may be over 60 cm.

There are 3 genera: *Cynodon*, *Rhaphiodon*, and *Hydrolycus*. Some authorities place these fishes with the Characidae. Consult Howes (1976) for a study of musculature and taxonomy.

Map references: Gery 1973, Howes 1976, Wheeler 1975.

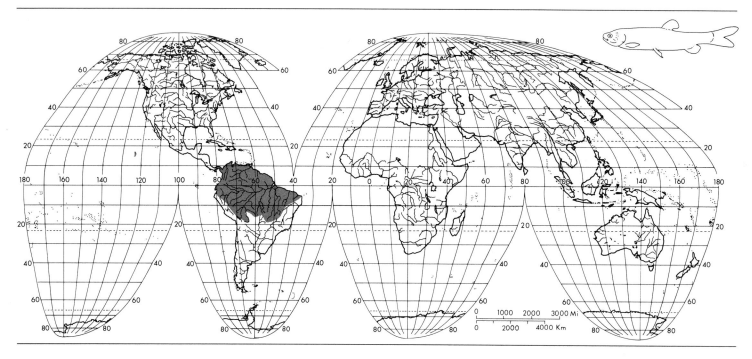

CLASS: Osteichthyes
  SUBCLASS: Actinopterygii
    SUPERORDER: Ostariophysi

ORDER: Cypriniformes
  SUBORDER: Characoidei
    (1st) **FAMILY: LEBIASINIDAE** [lē-bē-ă-sīn′-ĭ-dē]

This family of characoid fishes is found in tropical South America, mainly in the Amazon River system, and consists of about 35 species and 6 genera in 2 subfamilies. Some of these fishes have unusual behavior. For example, some species of *Nannostomus* (= *Poecilobrycon*) stand vertically on their tails in the water. *Copeina arnoldi* lays its eggs out of the water on overhanging vegetation by leaping and ejecting eggs in a gelatinous mass. The males splash the eggs with water to prevent dessication. When the young hatch in about 36 hours, they fall into the water. Family members are usually slender, with at least 1 lateral dark stripe and a maximum size of 6.5 cm. Most are much smaller. The adipose fin may be present, absent, or reduced, and the lateral line is usually absent. Lebiasinids are carnivorous and highly valued as aquarium specimens because of their attractive coloration and peculiar behavior. Consult Sterba (1966) and Hoedeman (1974) for aquarium information. Weitzman (1964, 1966, 1978) and Weitzman and Cobb (1975) have reviewed the taxonomy of this group. See Krekorian (1976) for information and references on the unusual behavior of *Copeina*.

Map references: Eigenmann 1922, Miller 1966, Weitzman 1964, 1966.

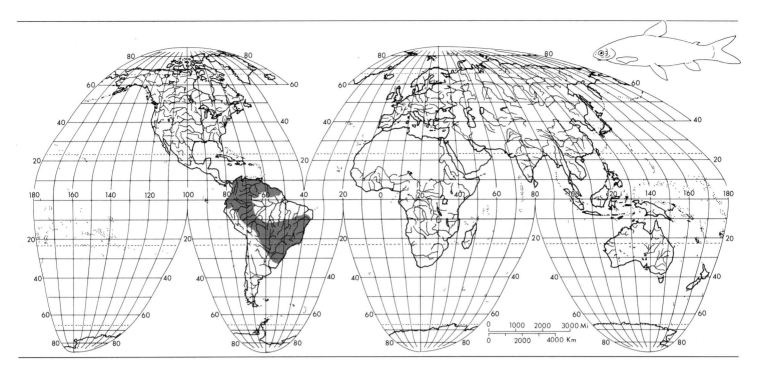

CLASS: Osteichthyes
    SUBCLASS: Actinopterygii
        SUPERORDER: Ostariophysi

ORDER: Cypriniformes
    SUBORDER: Characoidei
        (1st) FAMILY: **PARODONTIDAE** [pă-rō-dŏn'-tĭ-dē]

The Parodontidae is found in eastern Panama, on both the Pacific and Caribbean coasts of Colombia, the Pacific coast of Ecuador, in the Orinoco southward to the Guianas, and in the upper Amazon southward to Río de la Plata. They are fishes of swift mountain streams and, as such, have not been found in the middle and lower Amazon. There are about two dozen species in 3 genera: *Parodon*, *Apareiodon*, and *Saccodon*. Most adults range between 10 and 15 cm and feed on algae with the assistance of specialized premaxillary teeth. The adipose fin is small, the body is slender, and the pectoral fins are expanded probably as an adaptation to swift currents.

Many workers consider the Parodontidae and the Hemiodontidae to be closely related because of the striking similarity of their dentition and lower jaw; however, Roberts (1974b) has found many other differences. For further taxonomic information consult Regan (1911), Eigenmann (1912) and Roberts (1974a, b). Sazima (1980) provided information on feeding and spawning of *Apareiodon*.

Map references: Hoedeman 1974, Roberts 1974b, Wheeler 1975.

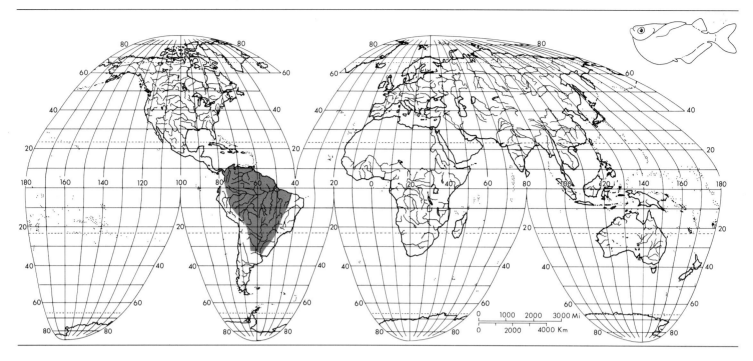

CLASS: Osteichthyes
   SUBCLASS: Actinopterygii
      SUPERORDER: Ostariophysi

ORDER: Cypriniformes
   SUBORDER: Characoidei
      (1st) FAMILY: **GASTEROPELECIDAE**—flying
      chararcins, hatchet fishes [gās-tĕ-rō-pĕ-lĕs'-ĭ-dē]

Hatchet fishes are found from Panama to the Río de la Plata. These fishes (3 genera, 9 species) are often cited as the only true flying fishes because they flap their enlarged pectoral fins during flight, as opposed to merely gliding, as do the marine flying fishes of the family Exocoetidae. The fin flapping actually creates an audible buzzing noise, but whether or not fin flapping increases the distance of the leap (up to several meters) is unknown. There is, however, a highly developed pectoral fin musculature attached to the sternum. This keel-like structure is a modification of broad coracoid bones of the pectoral girdle. The chest muscles and sternum may account for 25 percent of the animal's weight. These fishes grow to a maximum size of 8 cm and normally feed on insects at the surface. Flight is a mechanism for escaping predation and perhaps for catching airborne insects. Like the Characoidei in general, *Carnegiella*, *Gasteropelecus*, and *Thoracocharax* are used as aquarium animals (with a lid on the tank, of course). See Sterba (1966) and Hoedeman (1974) for aquarium information, and Fraser-Brunner (1950) and Weitzman (1954, 1960) for taxonomic revisions.

Map references: Darlington 1957, Eigenmann 1909*a**, Fraser-Brunner 1950, Grzimek 1973*, Hoedeman 1974*, Miller 1966, Sterba 1966*.

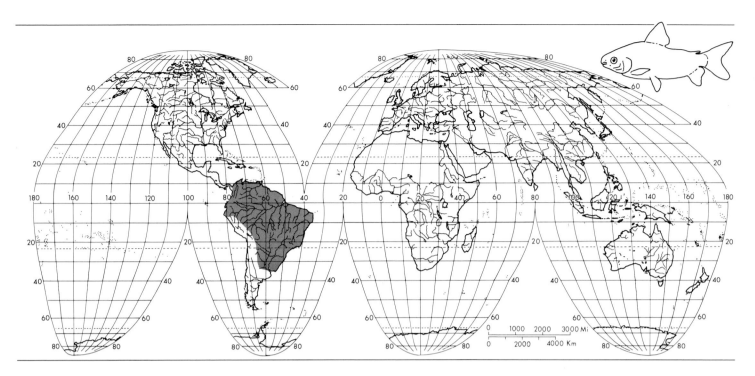

CLASS: Osteichthyes
   SUBCLASS: Actinopterygii
      SUPERORDER: Ostariophysi

ORDER: Cypriniformes
   SUBORDER: Characoidei
      (1st) FAMILY: **PROCHILODONTIDAE**
      [prō-kī-lō-dŏn'-tĭ-dē]

The Prochilodontidae is represented in the rivers of central South America by about 30 species in the following 3 genera: *Prochilodus*, *Ichthyoelephas*, and *Semaprochilodus*. The body is compressed, elongate, and deep anteriorly. Some species may exceed 64 cm. Prochilodontids superficially resemble the cyprinid genus *Labeo*. They have large fleshy lips with many tiny teeth, and they feed on organic detritus. Schools of *Prochilodus* in the Río de la Plata may be larger than the schools of any other South American freshwater fish. They are important food fishes. Some *Prochilodus* undertake an exten-sive spawning migration, and the migrating males emit a loud sound which can be heard above the surface. Roberts (1973) likens the sound to the noise of a motorcycle. The mechanics of sound production are not known. Roberts (1973) presented osteological evidence based on jaw suspension to show a relationship of this group with the Anostomidae rather than with the Curimatidae. See Regan (1911) and Eigenmann (1912, 1922) for early taxonomic work.

Map references: Roberts 1973, Sterba 1966, Wheeler 1975.

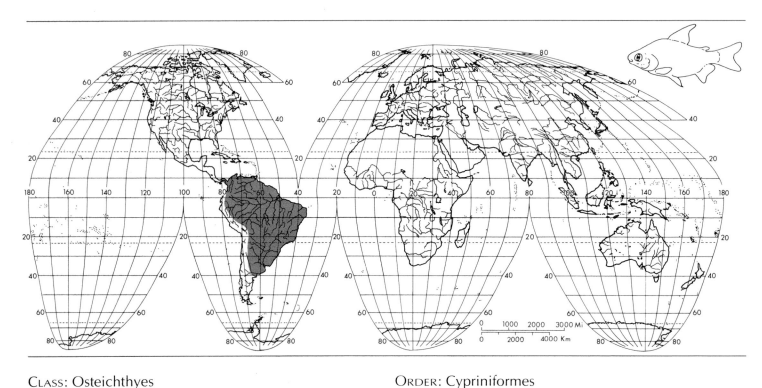

CLASS: Osteichthyes
    SUBCLASS: Actinopterygii
        SUPERORDER: Ostariophysi

ORDER: Cypriniformes
    SUBORDER: Characoidei
        (1st) FAMILY: **CURIMATIDAE** [cū-rē-mă'-tĭ-dē]

This family is widespread throughout most of South America and is composed of over 100 species in several genera, of which *Curimatus* is one of the largest. These carplike characoids, which may reach 20 cm, lack jaw teeth as adults and feed on bottom mud. An adipose fin is present. See Eigen-mann and Eigenmann (1889) for a revision of the family, and Roberts (1974*b*) for a list of characteristics.

Map references: Eigenmann 1922, Miller 1966, Sterba 1966.

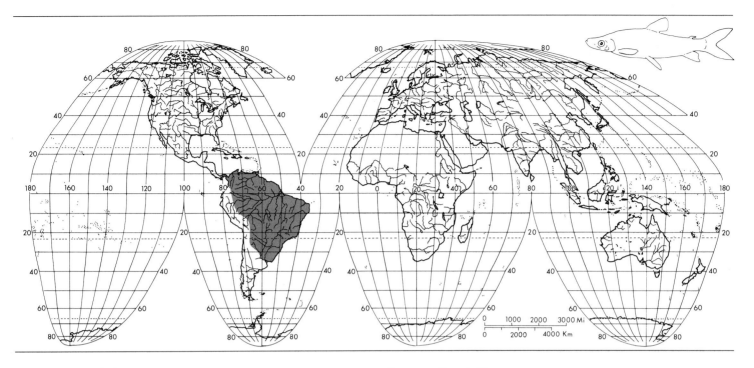

CLASS: Osteichthyes
    SUBCLASS: Actinopterygii
        SUPERORDER: Ostariophysi

ORDER: Cypriniformes
    SUBORDER: Characoidei
        (1st) **FAMILY: ANOSTOMIDAE**—headstanders
        [ăn-ŏs-tōm′-ĭ-dē]

The Anostomidae is composed of about 85 species in several genera, including *Leporinus*, *Anostomus*, and *Abramites*, and is widespread throughout most of South America. The common name, headstander, results from the fact that some species orient the long axis of their bodies obliquely about 45° to the bottom. They feed in this fashion with small, nonprotractile mouths that open dorsally. Most species are omnivorous, and some may reach 40 cm. Related South American characoids include the Prochilodontidae, Chilodontidae, and Curi-

matidae. The taxonomy of these groups is confused and needs further work. The aquarium literature complicates matters by using these family names almost interchangeably. See Sterba (1966) and Hoedeman (1974) for life history information and illustrations.

Map references: Eigenmann 1909a, *Eigenmann 1910, Eigenmann 1912, Eigenmann and Allen 1942, Eigenmann and Eigenmann 1892, Sterba 1966*.

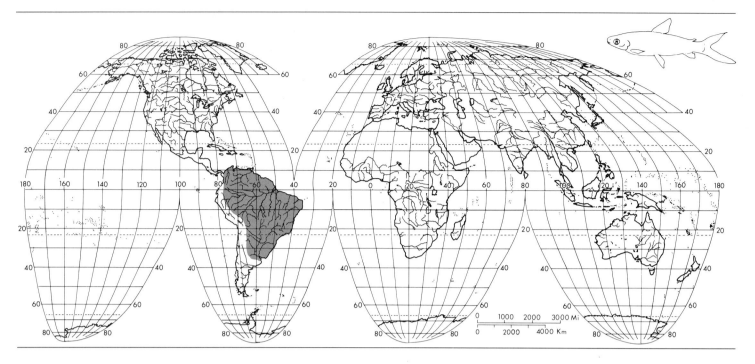

CLASS: Osteichthyes
    SUBCLASS: Actinopterygii
        SUPERORDER: Ostariophysi

ORDER: Cypriniformes
    SUBORDER: Characoidei
        (1st) FAMILY: **HEMIODONTIDAE**—pencil fishes
        [hĕm-ĭ-ō-dŏn′-tĭ-dē]

The pencil fishes are widespread in South America. There are about 27 species in 5−7 genera, such as *Hemiodus*, *Argonectes*, *Bivibranchia*, *Micromischodus*, and *Anodus*. The streamlined, swift-swimming adults may reach 30 cm. *Bivibranchia* and *Argonectes* are the only characoids with truly protrusible upper jaws.

Hemiodontids feed on detritus, plant matter, and insect larvae. *Anodus* is specialized for filter feeding on plankton (Roberts 1972). On all genera except *Micromischodus*, the lower jaw is toothless in adults, hence the family name Hemiodontidae. Many species adopt a tail-standing posture. Max-

imum size may reach about 20 cm. Aquarium books may include *Nannostomus* in this family instead of in the Lebiasinidae. The Parodontidae is a similar family. See Roberts (1974*b*) for a revision of this family with reasons for moving the Anodontidae from the Curimatidae to the Hemiodontidae. Other papers include Regan (1911), Böhlke (1955), Böhlke and Myers (1956) and Roberts (1971*c*).

Map references: Eigenmann 1910, 1912, Roberts 1974*b*, Sterba 1966*.

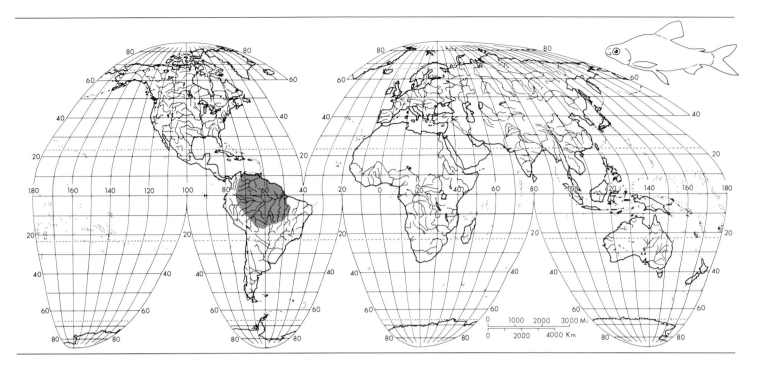

CLASS: Osteichthyes
    SUBCLASS: Actinopterygii
        SUPERORDER: Ostariophysi

ORDER: Cypriniformes
    SUBORDER: Characoidei
        (1st) FAMILY: **Chilodontidae** [kī-lō-dŏn'-tĭ-dē]

This small family consists of *Chilodus punctatus*, *Caenotropus maculosus*, and perhaps 1 or 2 other species. The family is widely distributed in northern South America, the Orinoco, Rio Negro, and upper and middle Amazon basin. These small fishes (up to 15 cm) share the peculiar head-standing behavior with their close relatives the Anostomidae. They have elongate bodies with elevated backs, small mouths, and large scales. They lack jaw teeth, but may have weak teeth on lips and numerous pharyngeal teeth. See Sterba (1966) for illustrations and aquarium care and Roberts (1971c) for taxonomic information.

Map references: Sterba 1966.

55

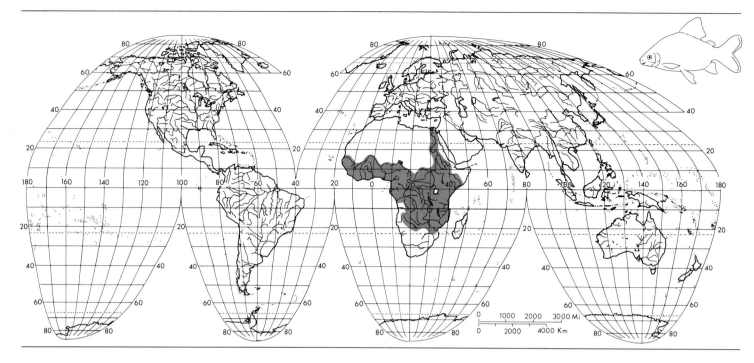

CLASS: Osteichthyes
  SUBCLASS: Actinopterygii
    SUPERORDER: Ostariophysi

ORDER: Cypriniformes
  SUBORDER: Characoidei
    (1st) FAMILY: **DISTICHODONTIDAE**
    [dĭ-stĭ-kō-dŏn′-tĭ-dē]

Distichodontids are found in tropical Africa and the Nile. There are about 50 species in 8 genera, which include *Distichodus*, *Nannocharax*, *Nannaethiops*, and *Neolebias*. Like the Citharinidae, with which they are sometimes grouped, distichodontids possess a straight lateral line. The body form may be robust and compressed to slender and elongate, and size usually ranges from 2.5 to 6.0 cm, but *Distichodus* may reach 35 cm. Ctenoid scales are present, and the adipose fin may be present or absent.

Map references: Jubb 1967, Poll 1973*, Roberts 1975.

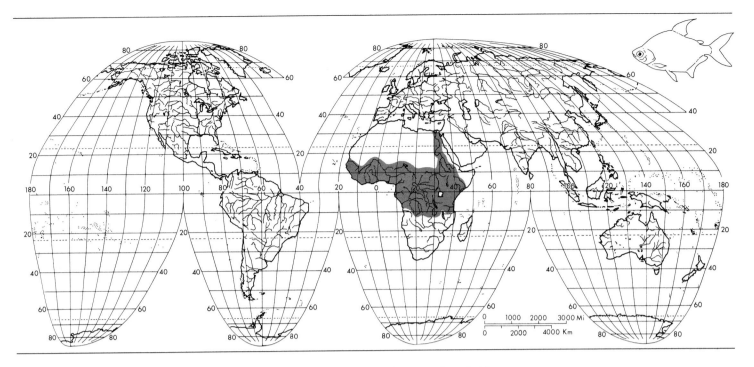

CLASS: Osteichthyes
  SUBCLASS: Actinopterygii
    SUPERORDER: Ostariophysi

ORDER: Cypriniformes
  SUBORDER: Characoidei
    (1st) **FAMILY: CITHARINIDAE** [sĭ-thă-rī′-nĭ-dē]

Citharinids are found in tropical Africa and the Nile River system. There are about 8 species in 2 genera, *Citharidium* and *Citharinus*. These fishes are deep-bodied with a straight lateral line, ctenoid scales, and may reach 18 kg and 84 cm. They are important food fishes in Africa. Most are herbivorous. Some workers include the Distichodontidae in this family.

Map references: Poll 1973*, Roberts 1975, Sterba 1966*.

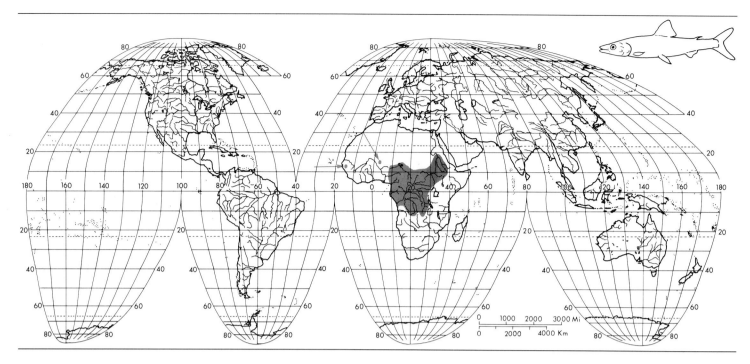

CLASS: Osteichthyes
    SUBCLASS: Actinopterygii
        SUPERORDER: Ostariophysi

ORDER: Cypriniformes
    SUBORDER: Characoidei
        (1st) FAMILY: **ICHTHYBORIDAE** (ĭk'-thĭ-bŏ'-rĭ-dē)
        [ĭk-thȳ-bŏ'-rĭ-dē]

These slender, carnivorous characoids are found in west and central tropical Africa. There are 10 genera and about 20 species, all with ctenoid scales and many with large teeth. Most members of this family have the peculiar habit of feeding on fish fins (Roberts 1972).

Map references: Boulenger 1909, Poll 1973*, Roberts 1975.

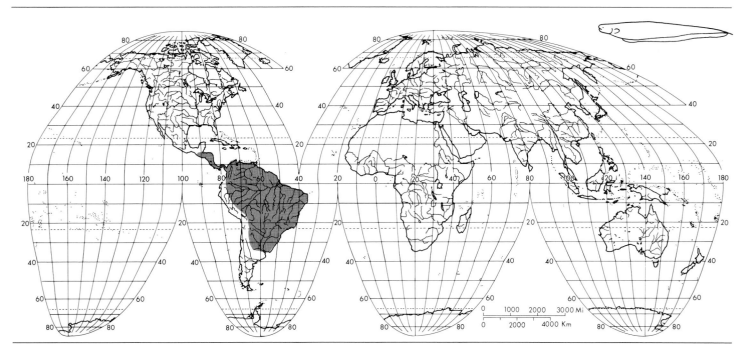

CLASS: Osteichthyes
  SUBCLASS: Actinopterygii
    SUPERORDER: Ostariophysi

ORDER: Cypriniformes
  SUBORDER: Gymnotoidei
    (1st) FAMILY: **GYMNOTIDAE**—gymnotid eels
    (jĭm-nŏt′-ī-dē) [gy̆m-nō′-tī-dē]

The gymnotid eels range from Guatemala to Río de la Plata. Their body form is elongated and compressed. The anal fin is long and flowing, and dorsal and pelvic fins are absent. The body is scaled, and the internal organs are located anteriorly. Damage to the caudal area is not fatal, and regeneration may take place. There are about 3 species in 1 genus; *Gymnotus carapo* is the most common and may reach 60 cm. This family has weak intermittent electrical capabilities which are

used as a sense organ. See Ellis (1913) for a comprehensive study of this suborder, Gery (1973) for a general discussion, Lissmann (1958) and Bennett (1971*a*, *b*) for a discussion of electric organs.

Map references: Eigenmann and Allen 1942, Ellis 1913, Hoedeman 1974*, Miller 1966*, Sterba 1966*.

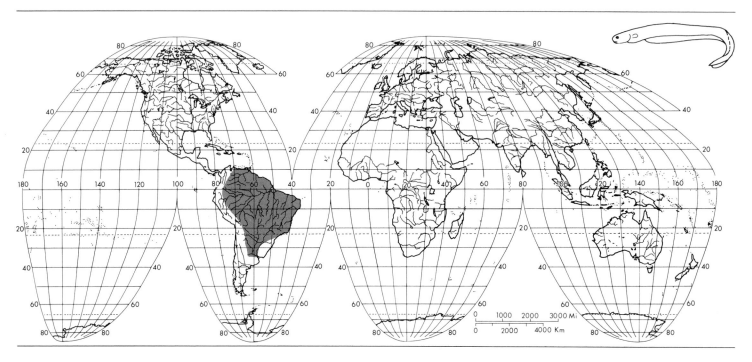

CLASS: Osteichthyes
   SUBCLASS: Actinopterygii
      SUPERORDER: Ostariophysi

ORDER: Cypriniformes
   SUBORDER: Gymnotoidei
      (1st) FAMILY: **ELECTROPHORIDAE**—electric eel
      [ē-lĕc-trō-phō'-rĭ-dē]

The Electrophoridae is a monotypic family composed of *Electrophorus electricus*, which is distributed throughout mid–South America. The electric eel, which can grow to 2.7 m, is cylindrical in cross section and has a very long anal fin of over 500 rays. Scales are absent, as are the dorsal and pelvic fins. The viscera are located anteriorly. This fish can deliver an electrical discharge of from 350 to 650 volts of direct current at up to 2 amps. The current is strong enough to stun fishes in the vicinity, which are then consumed. Larger organisms, including man, may also be injured by the shock, which may be pulsed at 0.002 to 0.005-second intervals. The electric organs are on both sides of the spinal column and make up most of the posterior five-sixths of the animal. The electric eel is linearly polar with a positive head and negative tail. Weak electrical signals are also sent out to locate prey and detect intruders. See Ellis (1913) for life history details. A highly technical explanation of the electric organs can be found in Bennet (1971a, b), and more easily readable accounts are given by Norman and Greenwood (1975) and Grundfest (1960).

Map references: Bartholomew, Clarke, and Grimshaw 1911*, Eigenmann and Allen 1942, Ellis 1913, Grzimek 1973*, Sterba 1966.

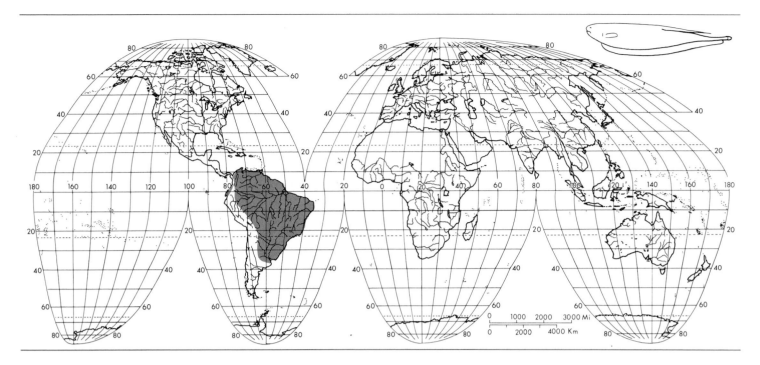

CLASS: Osteichthyes
  SUBCLASS: Actinopterygii
    SUPERORDER: Ostariophysi

ORDER: Cypriniformes
  SUBORDER: Gymnotoidei
    (1st) FAMILY: **APTERONOTIDAE**—knife fishes
    [ăp-tĕ-rō-nō′-tĭ-dē]

The apteronotids (formerly Sternarchidae) range from Panama to Río de la Plata. There are about 20 species in 9 genera. They have the general gymnotid body plan with an elongate anal fin and compressed body, giving rise to the name "knife fish." Some members of the genus *Apteronotus* have a long dorsal filament in place of the dorsal fin. Pelvic fins are missing. Some of the knife fishes, *Sternarchorhynchus* for example, resemble African elephant-nosed mormyrids, but the African family lacks an anal fin and has an undulating dorsal fin. Some apteronotids may reach 80 cm and produce a weak electrical field, which is another similarity shared with the unrelated mormyrids. See Ellis (1913) and Bennett (1971a, b) for life histories and information on electric organs, respectively.

Map references: Eigenmann 1909a*, Eigenmann and Allen 1942, Ellis 1913, Miller 1966, Sterba 1966*.

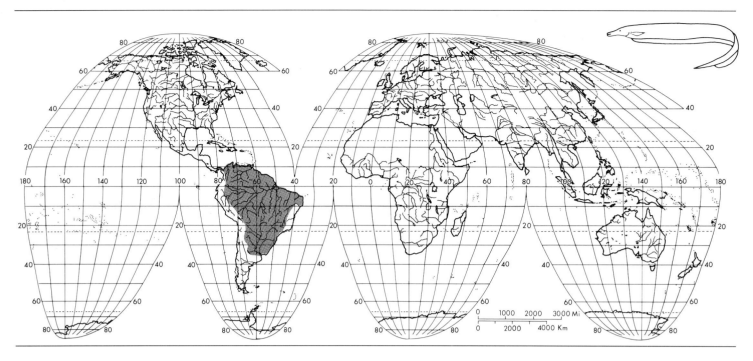

CLASS: Osteichthyes
    SUBCLASS: Actinopterygii
        SUPERORDER: Ostariophysi

ORDER: Cypriniformes
    SUBORDER: Gymnotoidei
        (1st) FAMILY: **RHAMPHICHTHYIDAE**
        [rămf-ĭk-thē′-ĭ-dē]

This family of 7 genera has much the same South American distribution as the other gymnotoids, Panama to Río de la Plata. *Rhamphichthys rostratus* has a scaled body and an elongate snout with which it probes the bottom for food. This species may reach 1.8 m and is valued as a food fish. The anal fin is very long, and the anus is located under the chin region.

Other family members have short snouts and are predators. All have weak electric powers. Refer to Ellis (1913) and Bennett (1971*a*, *b*) for more information.

Map references: Eigenmann 1909*a**, Eigenmann and Allen 1942, Ellis 1913, Sterba 1966*.

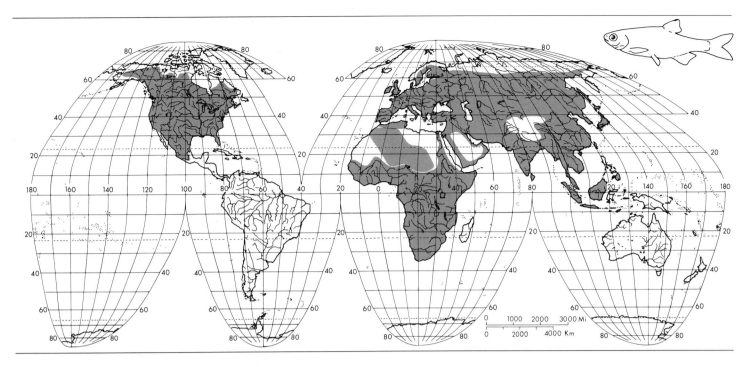

CLASS: Osteichthyes
  SUBCLASS: Actinopterygii
    SUPERORDER: Ostariophysi

ORDER: Cypriniformes
  SUBORDER: Cyprinoidei
    (1st) FAMILY: **CYPRINIDAE**—minnows, carp
    (sī-prĭn′-ĭ-dē) [sī-prĭn′-ĭ-dē]

The minnow family has the widest continuous distribution of any fish family in the world's fresh waters. It is found throughout North America, Eurasia, and Africa. Note its absence from South America, Madagascar, and the Australian realm. The Cyprinidae is the largest fish family in terms of number of species with over 1,500 in about 275 genera (Scott and Crossman 1973). The greatest diversity is in Southeast Asia and China, with fewer species in North America and Africa (Darlington 1957). However, North America does have about 36 genera and 280 species, 118 of which are in the genus *Notropis* (Bailey et al. 1970, Gilbert 1978). Fossil cyprinids date to the Paleocene of Europe, Eocene of Asia, and the Oligocene of North America. The cyprinids are the only primary division family (aside from the osteoglossids) to have dispersed east of Wallace's line without man's help. *Rasbora* and *Puntius* are found on Lombok, and *Rasbora* also reaches Sumbawa (Darlington 1957). Cyprinids reach Borneo but do not cross the Makasar Strait to the Celebes. In the Philippines about 37 native species (including *Rasbora* and *Puntius*) are confined to Mindanao, Palawan, Mindoro, and other southern islands (Herre 1953). In South America the cyprinid's ecological equivalent are the characins, and in Australia and New Guinea the Melanotaeniidae occupy minnow niches. Some species such as the carp, *Cyprinus carpio*, and the goldfish, *Carassius auratus*, have been introduced around the world and exist in wild populations in nonnative areas such as Australia where they are considered pests.

Briggs (1979) thinks that the cyprinoids are more modern than the characoids and siluroids, and they replaced the characoids in Asia and Europe and reached Africa too late to gain access to South America. The greatest diversity and the location of the more advanced taxa, and, therefore, the center of origin is the Oriental region (Matthew 1915, Briggs 1979). However, characoid fossils are yet to be found in Southeast Asia. See Brundin (1975) and Novacek and Marshall (1976) for other views.

Cyprinids, as ostariophysan fishes, have Weberian apparatus as described for the characoids, but unlike most characoids, cyprinids lack an adipose fin. Jaw teeth are also absent, but 1–3 rows of pharyngeal teeth are present. All characoids lack pharyngeal teeth. Fins are soft except in a few genera in which the soft rays are fused. Some species have sensory barbels around the mouth. There is usually a lateral line, and the body is covered with cycloid scales. Males, in breeding condition, may develop tubercles on various regions of the head, body, and fins, the structure and significance of which have been reviewed by Wiley and Collette (1970) and Collette (1977). Color intensification in males may be striking during the breeding season. The family is extremely diverse morphologically and behaviorally. Size ranges from a few centimeters, to 2.5 m in the case of *Catlocarpio siamensis*. There are many peculiar modifications for specialized niches, such as in the bitterling, *Rhodeus sericeus*, which lays its eggs inside a mussel. Most cyprinids are omnivorous, some are herbivorous, and others carnivorous. The western North American genus *Ptychocheilus* subsists primarily on fish. For a general discussion of this family consult Banarescu (1973). Scott and Crossman (1973) and Berg (1949) presented detailed life histories and references for North America and Eurasia respectively. Gosline (1978) discussed subfamilies, and Sterba (1966) and Hoedeman (1974) gave information on cyprinids as aquarium species. See Roberts (1975) for information on the distribution of cyprinids in Saharan oases.

Map references: Bartholomew, Clarke, and Grimshaw 1911*, Berg 1949, Darlington 1957, Grzimek 1973*, Hoedeman 1974*, Innes 1966*, Lagler, Bardach, and Miller 1962*, Miller 1958*, 1966*, Nelson 1976*, Norman and Greenwood 1975*, Roberts 1975, Rostlund 1952*, Scott and Crossman 1973*, Sterba 1966*, Whitaker 1968*.

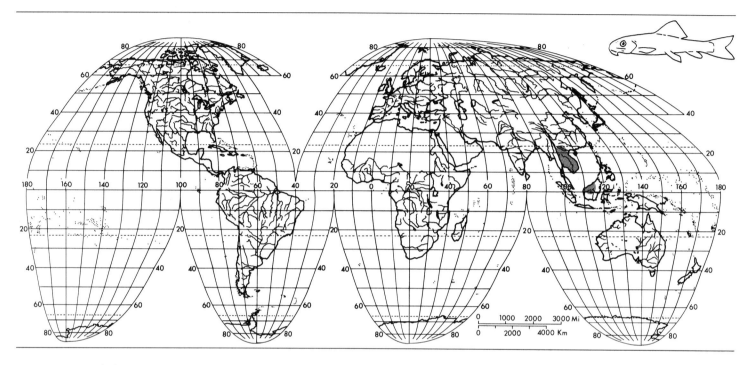

CLASS: Osteichthyes
   SUBCLASS: Actinopterygii
      SUPERORDER: Ostariophysi

ORDER: Cypriniformes
   SUBORDER: Cyprinoidei
      (1st) FAMILY: **GYRINOCHEILIDAE**
      [jī-rī-nō-kī′-lī-dē]

This family contains 1 genus that is only found in Indochina (2 species) and Borneo (1 species). *Gyrinocheilus* lacks pharyngeal teeth and has a suctorial mouth, with which it holds its position in swift-flowing mountain streams by attaching to rocks. While attached, it feeds on algae. A reduced swim bladder is another adaptation to swift current that prevents the fish from rising off the bottom except by swimming effort. This family is most noted for its peculiar means of respiration. It has both inhalent and exhalent gill openings. Water enters an upper opening, passes over the gills via an inhalent route, and then exits through a lower, external gill opening. This unusual modification allows the mouth to be free for adhering to stones and feeding. The respiratory rate is very rapid, 240 times per minute for a 12 cm fish. This compensates for the small inhalent opening. The largest specimen recorded was 27.5 cm. *G. aymonieri* is popular with aquarist because of its ability to clean algae from the walls of aquariums. See Smith (1945) for further life history details and references.

Map references: Grzimek 1973*, Smith 1945*, Sterba 1966*.

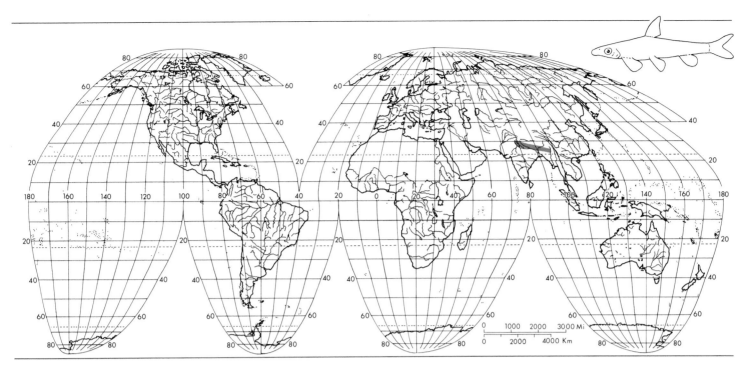

CLASS: Osteichthyes
  SUBCLASS: Actinopterygii
    SUPERORDER: Ostariophysi

ORDER: Cypriniformes
  SUBORDER: Cyprinoidei
    (1st) FAMILY: **PSILORHYNCHIDAE**
    [sī-lō-rǐn'-kǐ-dē]

This family of 3 species in the genus *Psilorhynchus* is found in northeast Bengal, Assam, and north Burma. These small fusiform fishes have thick lips and a deep cleft that extends from the snout to the angle of the subterminal mouth. They live in fast-flowing streams and rivers. For what little is known of their biology, see Hora (1952).

Map references: Day 1878, Grzimek 1973*.

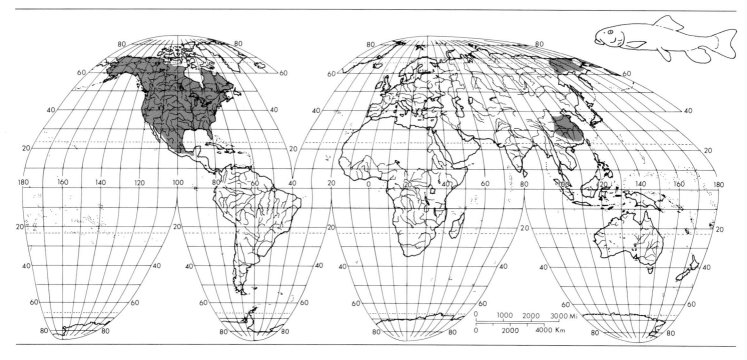

CLASS: Osteichthyes
　　SUBCLASS: Actinopterygii
　　　SUPERORDER: Ostariophysi

ORDER: Cypriniformes
　　SUBORDER: Cyprinoidei
　　　(1st) FAMILY: **CATOSTOMIDAE**—suckers
　　　(kăt'-ō-stŏm'-ĭ-dē)

The suckers are widely distributed across North America south to Guatemala and northwest into Eastern Siberia, where an American species, *Catostomus catostomus*, has dispersed. The family is represented in China by at least 1 species, *Myxocyprinus asiaticus*. Nelson (1976) has found that the Weberian apparatus and body shape of small *Myxocyprinus* resemble *Carpiodes*, whereas the Weberian apparatus and body form of large (adult) *Myxocyprinus* resemble *Cycleptus*. There may be 2 genera or species of suckers in China. The genera *Catostomus* and *Moxostoma* contain the most species. On the bases of area occupied and number of species, North America, with 11 genera and 57 species (Bailey et al. 1970), would appear to be the center of origin of this family. But Darlington (1957) maintained that catostomids originated in Asia and gave rise to cyprinids, which replaced the Asian catostomids, and that the catostomids then spread to North America. Most authorities agree that the suckers are of Asian origin (Gilbert 1976) but feel that cyprinids gave rise to catostomids (Novacek and Marshall 1976), and Miller (1958) cited a number of studies which show a cyprinidlike ancestor. Darlington stated that *Myxocyprinus* is a relict of a larger, earlier oriental catostomid fauna, and that *Catostomus* is definitely of American origin and has reinvaded Asia. Fossil catostomids are from the Eocene of Asia and possibly Eocene of North America (Scott and Crossman 1973).

Suckers are small to large soft-rayed fishes with thick lips and a protrusible mouth devoid of teeth, which accounts for the name "sucker." Pharyngeal teeth are present and occur in 1 row of up to 10 teeth, as opposed to several rows of few teeth in the cyprinids. The dorsal fin of suckers has more than 10 rays, a character that also serves to distinguish catostomids from most cyprinids, which have fewer than 10 rays. No barbels or adipose fins are present, scales are cycloid, and the head is naked. Some species are elongate; others are deep-bodied. Suckers are bottom feeders and may migrate upstream into small tributaries to spawn. The males develop tubercles during the breeding season. See Nelson (1948) and Ramaswami (1957) for information on the comparative morphology of the Weberian apparatus, Miller and Evans (1965) for an anatomical study of catastomid brains and lips, and Eastman (1977) for a study of pharyngeal bones and teeth. Earlier literature is covered by Hubbs (1930). Hubbs, Hubbs, and Johnson (1943) conducted a classic study of hybridization in suckers, and Ferris and Whitt (1978) presented a modern assessment of catostomid phylogeny based on loss of duplicate gene expression. Consult Scott and Crossman (1973) for life histories and references, Eddy and Underhill (1978) and Moore (1968) for keys to species, Nelson (1976) for subfamily and tribe designations, and Fuiman (1979) and Fuiman and Witman (1979) for descriptions of catostomid larvae.

Map references: Berg 1949, Darlington 1957*, Grzimek 1973*, Lagler, Bardach, and Miller 1962*, Miller 1958*, 1966*, Nelson 1976*, Rostlund 1952*, Scott and Crossman 1973*, Whitaker 1968*.

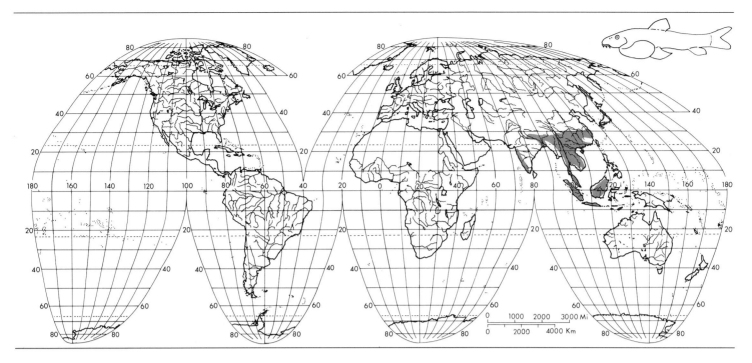

CLASS: Osteichthyes
   SUBCLASS: Actinopterygii
      SUPERORDER: Ostariophysi

ORDER: Cypriniformes
   SUBORDER: Cyprinoidei
      (1st) FAMILY: **HOMALOPTERIDAE**—hillstream loaches [hō-mă-lŏp-tĕ'-rĭ-dē]

These small (up to 10 cm) loachlike fishes are found in torrential streams of western India, Southeast Asia, Malaya, Sumatra, Java, and Borneo. There are fewer than 90 species in about 28 genera, and the group is characterized by the development of a sucking disc composed of elements of the pectoral and, in some species, the pelvic fins. Their hydrodynamic shape allows water to flow over them in such a manner as to press their bodies against the bottom. The swim bladder is reduced, a common adaptation for fishes that live in fast-moving water. Hillstream loaches are algae eaters with a sucking mouth surrounded by at least 3 pairs of barbels. Consult Hora (1932) and Alfred (1969) for a thorough discussion of their classification and habits.

Map references: Grzimek 1973*, Hora 1932, Jayaram 1974*, Smith 1945.

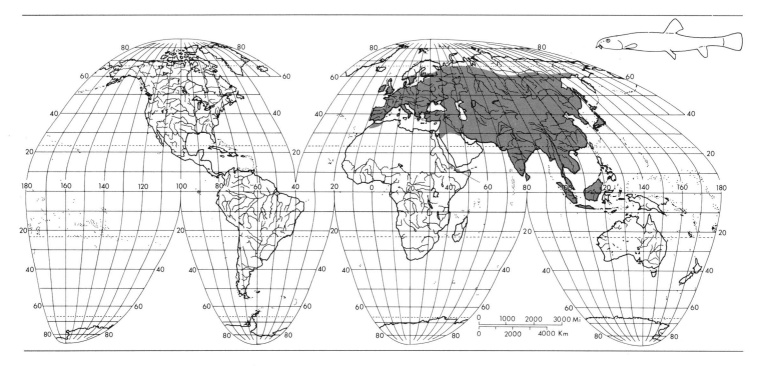

CLASS: Osteichthyes
    SUBCLASS: Actinopterygii
        SUPERORDER: Ostariophysi

ORDER: Cypriniformes
    SUBORDER: Cyprinoidei
        (1st) FAMILY: **COBITIDAE**—loaches (cŏ-bĭt′-ĭ-dē)
        [cŏ-bī′-tĭ-dē]

The loaches have a Eurasian distribution with greatest diversity in Southeast Asia. Two representatives occur in Africa (*Cobitis* in Morocco and *Noemacheilus* in Ethiopia). There are close to 150 species (in 3 subfamilies) which range in size from 3 to 30 cm. Most of these slender, elongate fishes prefer fast-flowing water and feed on invertebrates or algae. Cobitids share the ostariophysan characteristic of Weberian ossicles. They have 3–6 pairs of barbels, and some species may gulp air and extract oxygen via the intestine. Tiny scales may be present or absent. Jaw teeth are absent, but pharyngeal teeth are present. Some have a posteriorly pointed spine beneath the eye. Many loaches are popular aquarium fishes. The oriental weatherfish, *Misgurnus anguillicaudatus* is established in 2 counties in the state of Michigan. See Berg (1949) and Smith (1945) for life histories and references and Nalbant (1973) for a general discussion of this family. Sterba (1966) and Hoedeman (1974) contain useful aquarium information.

Map references: Berg 1949, Darlington 1957, Grzimek 1973*, Hoedeman 1974*, Maitland 1977*, Nelson 1976*, Roberts 1975, Smith 1945, Sterba 1966*, Wheeler 1969*.

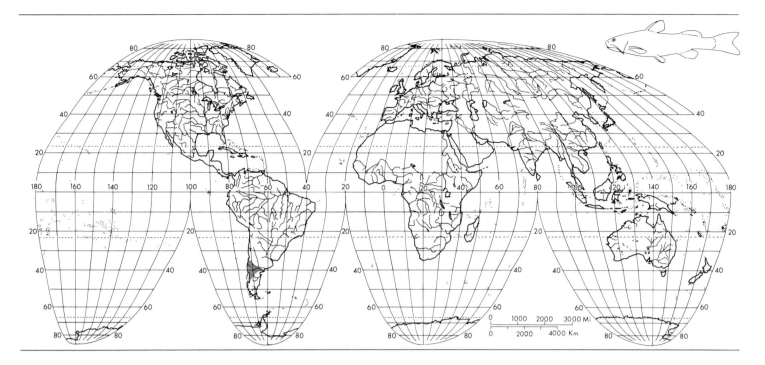

CLASS: Osteichthyes
  SUBCLASS: Actinopterygii
    SUPERORDER: Ostariophysi

ORDER: Siluriformes
  (1st) FAMILY: **DIPLOMYSTIDAE** [dĭp-lō-mĭs'-tĭ-dē]

This relict family of 2 species is found in central Chile and central Argentina. The single genus is characterized by 1 pair of barbels, well developed teeth on the maxilla, a primitive caudal skeleton, and a Weberian apparatus that suggests that *Diplomystes* is the most primitive living catfish. Fossil siluriform fishes date to the Upper Cretaceous of South America (Briggs 1979). See Alexander (1964) and Chardon (1968) for

information on the Weberian apparatus, Lundberg and Baskin (1969) for a discussion of siluriform relationships, Gosline (1975) for a discussion of the palatine-maxillary mechanism, and Novacek and Marshall (1976) and Briggs (1979) for a history of ostariophysan fishes, including catfishes.

Map references: Darlington 1957, Eigenmann 1910, 1927.

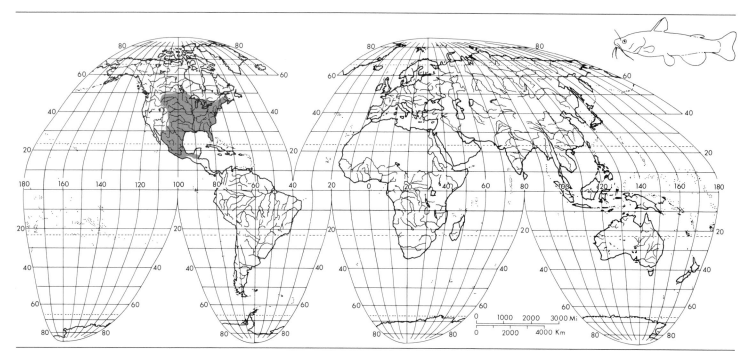

CLASS: Osteichthyes
    SUBCLASS: Actinopterygii
        SUPERORDER: Ostariophysi

ORDER: Siluriformes
    (1st) **FAMILY: ICTALURIDAE**—North American catfishes (īk-tă-lūr'-ī-dē)

The ictalurids are distributed in the fresh waters of North America from the Rocky Mountains eastward and south into drainages of western Mexico and Guatemala. There are 37 species in 5 genera, the largest of which are *Ictalurus* (11 species) and *Noturus* (24 species) (Bailey et al. 1970). These catfishes lack scales, have 4 pairs of barbels, a well-developed Weberian apparatus, possess an adipose fin, and have a spine in the dorsal, anal, and pectoral fins. Madtoms of the genus *Noturus* and some other catfishes possess venom glands, toxic integumentary sheaths, and grooved spines that can inflict a painful sting. All ictalurids have jaw teeth except the blind *Trogloglanis pattersoni*. This species and *Satan eurystomus*, another blind form, also lack swim bladders. Both of these fishes are known from artesian wells near San An-

tonio, Texas. Large members of the genus *Ictalurus* are important sport and food fishes, as is the flathead catfish, *Pylodictis olivaris*, which can reach 50 kg and 1.7 m. Ictalurids have been introduced into other parts of the United States and the world. The channel catfish, *I. punctatus*, is being farmed extensively in ponds in the southeast United States. Fossil ictalurids date from the Paleocene (Gilbert 1976). See Trautman (1957) and Scott and Crossman (1973) for life histories and references, Taylor (1969) for a revision of the genus *Noturus*, and Birkhead (1972) for information on the toxicity of stings.

Map references: Darlington 1957, Miller 1958*, 1966*, Nelson 1976*, Pflieger 1971*, Rostlund 1952*, Scott and Crossman 1973*, Sterba 1966*, Trautman 1957*, Whitaker 1968*.

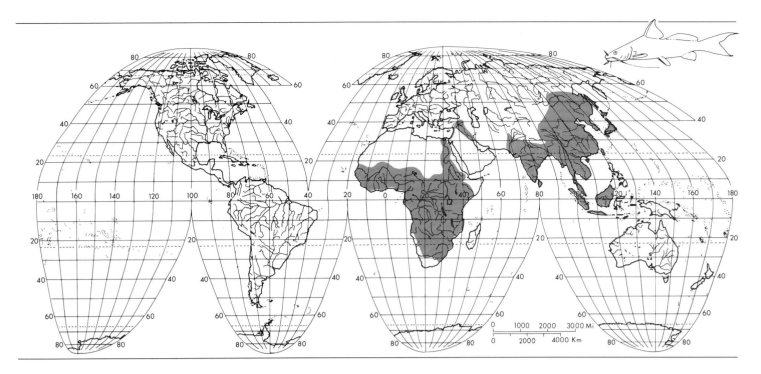

CLASS: Osteichthyes
  SUBCLASS: Actinopterygii
    SUPERORDER: Ostariophysi

ORDER: Siluriformes
  (1st) FAMILY: **BAGRIDAE**—bagrid catfishes
  (bah'-grĭ'-dē)

Bagrids are found in Africa, Asia Minor, Southeast Asia, and throughout the Indo-Australian archipelago. Bagrids are scaleless, with a large adipose fin and 4 pairs of barbels. The barbel in front of the external nares points straight up. A stout dorsal spine (hardened rays) is present, and in one unusual East Indian species, *Bagrichthys hypelopterus*, this spine may reach 30 cm in length, which may be three-fourths the total length of the fish. Bagrids resemble North American ictalurids and South American pimelodids. They are important food fishes and may reach a length of 90 cm. *Mystus* is one of the principal genera of the Bagridae. A general review of major silurid families can be found in Vogt (1973).

Map references: Berg 1949, Boulenger 1911, Darlington 1957, Jayaram 1974*, Lowe-McConnell 1975, Nelson 1976*, Roberts 1975, Smith 1945, Sterba 1966*.

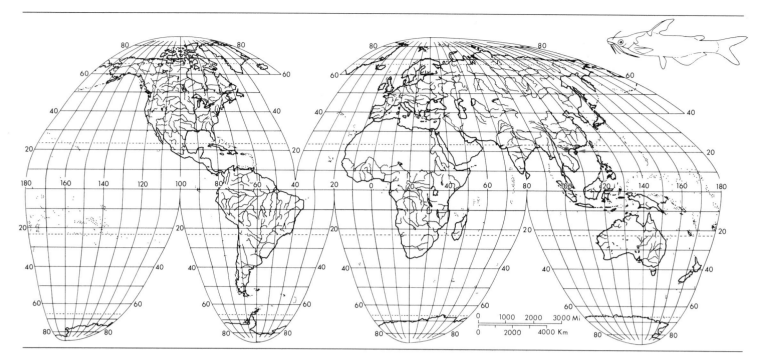

CLASS: Osteichthyes
  SUBCLASS: Actinopterygii
    SUPERORDER: Ostariophysi

ORDER: Siluriformes
  (1st) FAMILY: **CRANOGLANIDIDAE**
  [crā-nō-glă-nĭ′-dĭ-dē]

This catfish family is restricted to Guangxi Zhuang (Kwangsi Chuang) and Hainan Island, China. There are 3 scaleless species, *Cranoglanis sinensis*, *C. bouderius*, and *C. multiradiatus*. They have a rough bony plate on the dorsal surface of the head, short adipose fin, fine jaw teeth, and 4 pairs of bar-

bels. One pair of barbels is situated posterior to the nostrils. Maximum size is probably under 2.5 kg. See Jayaram (1956) for taxonomic details.

Map reference: Nichols 1943.

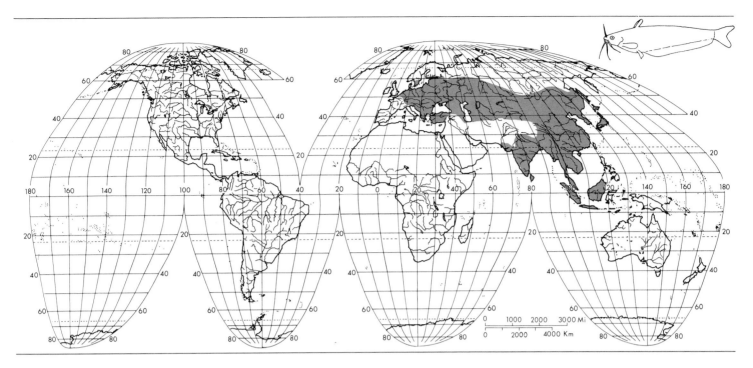

CLASS: Osteichthyes
  SUBCLASS: Actinopterygii
    SUPERORDER: Ostariophysi

ORDER: Siluriformes
  (1st) FAMILY: **SILURIDAE**—silurid catfishes
  (sĭ-lū'-rĭ-dē)

The silurids are found from the Rhine River eastward to the Amur River, south into the Malay Archipelago and west throughout India. They are absent from much of the central Asia plateau. There is a disjunct population of *Silurus* in India (Jayaram 1974), and representatives reach Palawan in the Philippines (Herre 1953). These fishes do not occur in Africa, as some references (Herald 1962, Yerger 1974) state. Silurids lack an adipose fin, and the dorsal fin is reduced to just a few rays with no spine. The anal fin is very long. There are 2 pairs of barbels. The European wels, *Silurus glanis*, ranks as one of the largest freshwater fishes in the world. It may reach 300 kg

and 4 m. It is important as a food fish and has been introduced into England. Other smaller species such as *Kryptopterus* and *Ompok* are popular as aquarium fishes and are collectively called glass catfish. See Berg (1949) and Smith (1945) for life histories, Sterba (1966) for aquarium information, and Haig (1950) for a review of the family.

Map references: Bartholomew, Clarke, and Grimshaw 1911*, Berg 1949, Darlington 1957, Haig 1950, Herre 1953, Hoedeman 1974*, Jayaram 1974*, 1977, Maitland 1977*, Nelson 1976*, Smith 1945, Sterba 1966*, Wheeler 1969*.

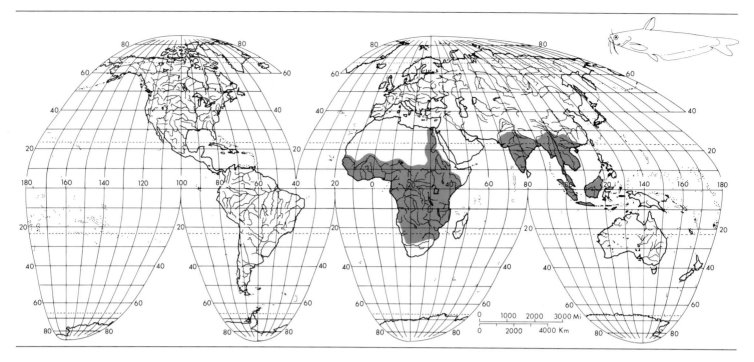

CLASS: Osteichthyes
  SUBCLASS: Actinopterygii
    SUPERORDER: Ostariophysi

ORDER: Siluriformes
  (1st) FAMILY: **SCHILBEIDAE**—schilbeid catfishes
  [shĭl-bē'-ĭ-dē]

These catfishes occur throughout sub-Saharan Africa, India, Southeast Asia, and the East Indies. A similar disjunct distribution is shared by several catfish families.

There are approximately 8 genera in Africa and 8 different genera in Asia. Schilbeids resemble silurids with long anal fins, but an adipose fin may be present, and there is a spine in the dorsal. Two to 4 pairs of barbels are present. Some larger species are used as food, and other smaller, more colorful species serve as aquarium specimens. See Boulenger (1911) for species descriptions.

Map references: Boulenger 1911, Hoedeman 1974*, Jayaram 1974, Jubb 1967, Roberts 1975, Smith 1945, Sterba 1966*.

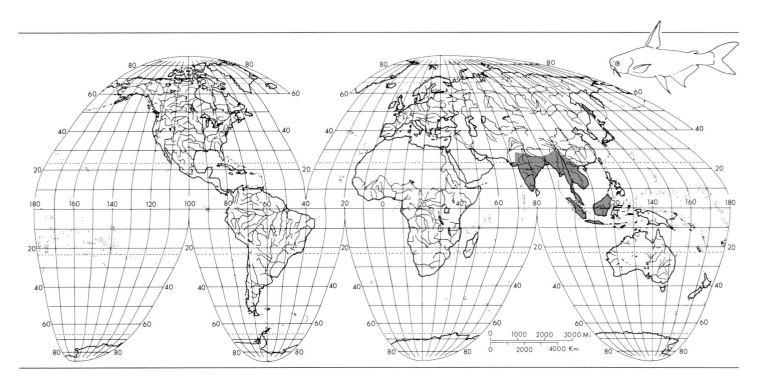

CLASS: Osteichthyes
  SUBCLASS: Actinopterygii
    SUPERORDER: Ostariophysi

ORDER: Siluriformes
  (1st) FAMILY: **PANGASIIDAE** [păn-gā'-sĭ-ĭ-dē]

About 25 species of pangasiids are found in India, Southeast Asia and the East Indies to Java and Borneo. Family members have a rather high dorsal fin with spine, 2–4 pairs of barbels, and an adipose fin. *Pangasius* is the largest genus, with about 15 species. The giant catfish, *Pangasianodon gigas*, is unusual in that adults lack teeth and feed only on plant matter. This species is one of the largest freshwater fish in the world. It may reach 2.5 m and a weight of 112 kg. Smith (1945) in-

cluded photographs of this remarkable animal. *Pangasianodon* makes a spawning migration up the Mekong River to Lake Dali (Ta-li) in China. It is heavily fished during this time. Formerly the Pangassidae were classified with the Schilbeidae. See Smith (1945) for details of life histories and references.

Map references: Day 1878, Smith 1945, Sterba 1966*.

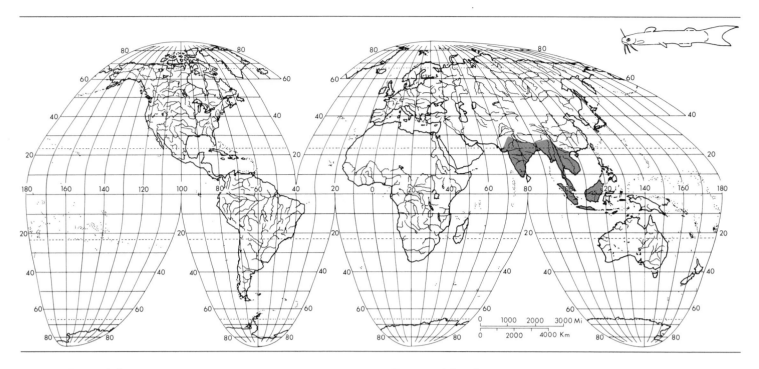

CLASS: Osteichthyes
   SUBCLASS: Actinopterygii
      SUPERORDER: Ostariophysi

ORDER: Siluriformes
   (1st) FAMILY: **AMBLYCIPITIDAE** [ăm-blĭ-sĭ-pĭ′-tĭ-dē]

This family consists of 2 genera, *Liobagrus* and *Amblyceps*, which are distributed from India through Southeast Asia. These small (up to 15 cm) slender catfish with 4 pairs of barbels prefer fast-flowing mountain streams, and have a peculiar respiratory flap in front of the pectoral fins. They also possess a reduced swim bladder. All fins are rather small except the caudal. See Hora (1933) and Smith (1945) for more information.

Map references: Darlington 1957, Day 1878, Hora 1933, Smith 1945.

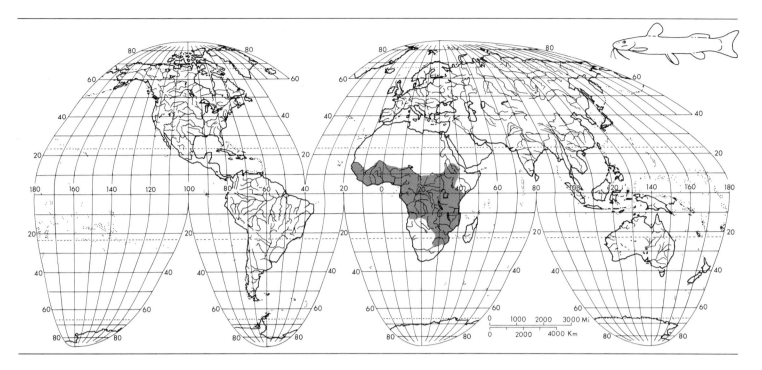

CLASS: Osteichthyes
   SUBCLASS: Actinopterygii
      SUPERORDER: Ostariophysi

ORDER: Siluriformes
   (1st) FAMILY: **AMPHILIIDAE** [ăm-phĭl′-ĭ-ĭ-dē]

This catfish family of about 45 species in 6 genera is found in tropical Africa. The spine is absent in the dorsal and pectoral fins, and 3 pairs of barbels are present. These fishes prefer flowing water, and the pelvic fins are curved to form a weak sucking disc in conjunction with the ventral surface of the body. Eggs are laid under stones, and the newly hatched fishes resemble tadpoles. Amphiliid catfishes feed on insects and other stream invertebrates. Maximum size is about 18 cm. See Harry (1953) for taxonomic information.

Map references: Boulenger 1911, Crass 1964, Jackson 1961, Jubb 1967, Roberts 1975.

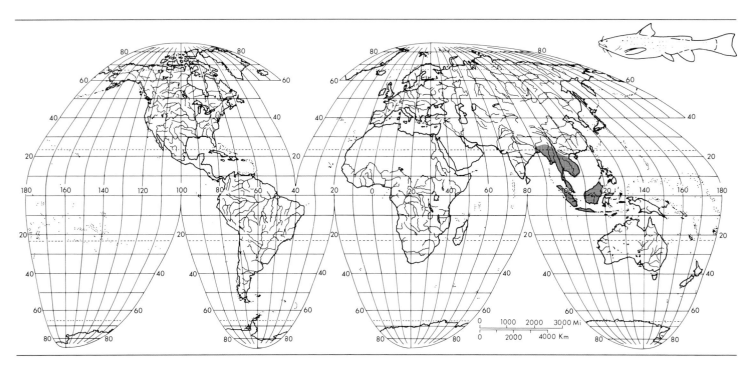

CLASS: Osteichthyes
  SUBCLASS: Actinopterygii
    SUPERORDER: Ostariophysi

ORDER: Siluriformes
  (1st) FAMILY: **AKYSIDAE** [ă-kī'-sĭ-dē]

The akysid catfishes occur from Burma east to Java and Borneo. These small catfishes have skin studded with tubercles, which may be arranged in longitudinal rows. They have a reduced swim bladder and dwell in mountain streams. The dorsal fin is short and has a spine. See Hora (1936) and Smith (1945) for further information.

Map references: Hora 1936, Smith 1945, Weber and De Beaufort 1913.

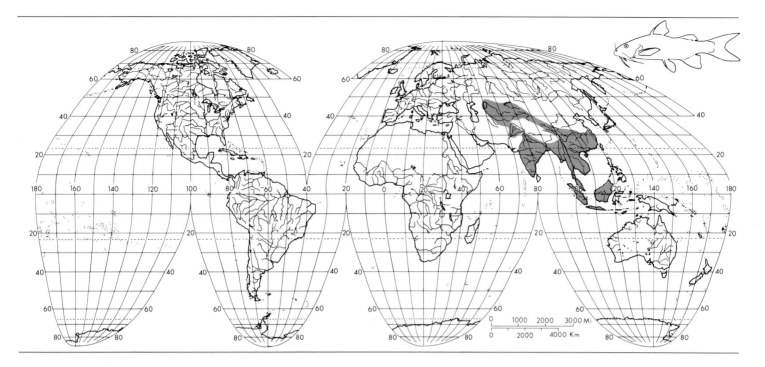

CLASS: Osteichthyes
 SUBCLASS: Actinopterygii
  SUPERORDER: Ostariophysi

ORDER: Siluriformes
 (1st) FAMILY: **SISORIDAE**—sisorid catfishes
 [sī-sō′-rĭ-dē]

This Asian catfish family, which prefers mountain streams, extends from the Aral Sea drainage region through the Himalayas to Southeast Asia and the East Indies. Sisorids have an adipose fin, spine in dorsal and pectoral fins, and 3 pairs of barbels. Some species have a thoracic adhesive disc formed by longitudinal skin folds, whereas others have flattened lips which serve as a sucking organ. One wide-ranging, predatory species, *Bagarius bagarius*, can reach 2 m in length. See Smith (1945) for life histories.

Map references: Berg 1949, Day 1878, Darlington 1957, Jayaram 1974*, Nichols 1943, Smith 1945.

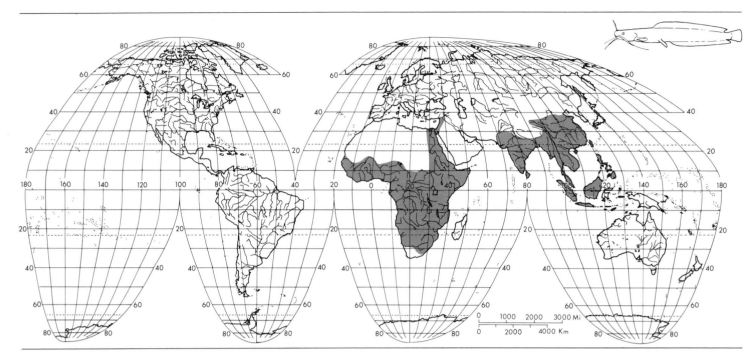

CLASS: Osteichthyes
  SUBCLASS: Actinopterygii
    SUPERORDER: Ostariophysi

ORDER: Siluriformes
  (1st) **FAMILY: CLARIIDAE**—labyrinth catfishes
[clă′-rĭ-ĭ-dē]

The 100 or so labyrinth catfishes are distributed throughout Africa into Syria, and from India eastward to Java, Borneo, and the Philippines. *Clarias* on the Celebes is probably an introduction (Darlington 1957). These catfishes are unique because of the presence of an accessory respiratory organ, which occupies the upper part of each branchial cavity. These suprabranchial arborescent organs enable the fish to utilize atmospheric oxygen by providing an increased surface area for absorption. Some species such as *Clarias batrachus*, the walking catfish, can leave the water and crawl about on land. This improves dispersal chances and also facilitates transport by man over extended distances and time. *C. batrachus* has been accidentally established as an aquarium escapee in Florida and may develop into a severe pest (Idyll 1969*b*, Lachner,

Robins, and Courtenay 1970). Other family traits include long dorsal and anal fins without spines and 4 pairs of barbels. Spines are present in pectoral fins, and an adipose fin is usually absent. *Clarias* is an important food fish in some places, and some species may reach 1.3 m. Others are utilized as aquarium species, such as the burrowing, wormlike *Gymnallabes* and *Channallabes*. See Smith (1945) for life history details of some species, and Boulenger (1911) for descriptions of African species. The latter should be used with caution because of confused taxonomy.

Map references: Boulenger 1911, Darlington 1957, Day 1878, Herre 1953, Hoedeman 1974*, Jubb 1967, Nelson 1976*, Roberts 1975, Smith 1945, Sterba 1966*.

80

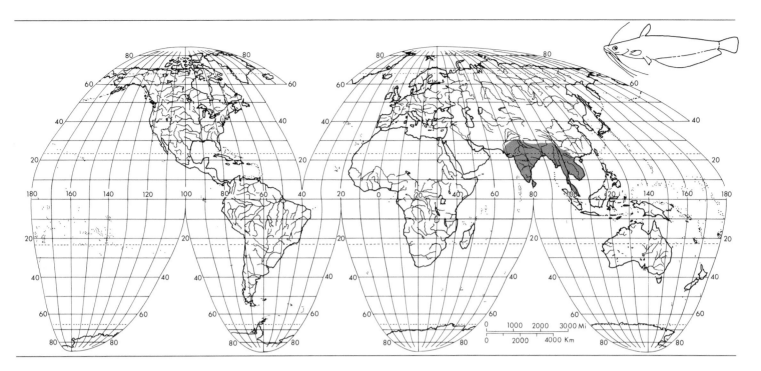

CLASS: Osteichthyes
  SUBCLASS: Actinopterygii
    SUPERORDER: Ostariophysi

ORDER: Siluriformes
  (1st) FAMILY: **HETEROPNEUSTIDAE**—stinging
  catfishes [hĕ-tĕ-rŏp-nū′-stĭ-dē]

This family is found in India, Ceylon, Burma, and Southeast Asia. The 2 species, *Heteropneustes fossilis* and *H. microps*, are closely related to the clariid catfishes. They have a pair of hollow air sacs extending from the gill chamber to the caudal peduncle which enables the fish to breathe air. Like the Clariidae, *Heteropneustes* has 4 pairs of barbels and a long anal fin. The spineless dorsal fin is short, and the pectoral fins con-

tain a sharp spine that can inflict a nasty wound and has earned the name "stinging catfish" for this species. Maximum size is 30 cm. Hora (1936) and Smith (1945) have further details.

Map references: Day 1878, Smith 1945.

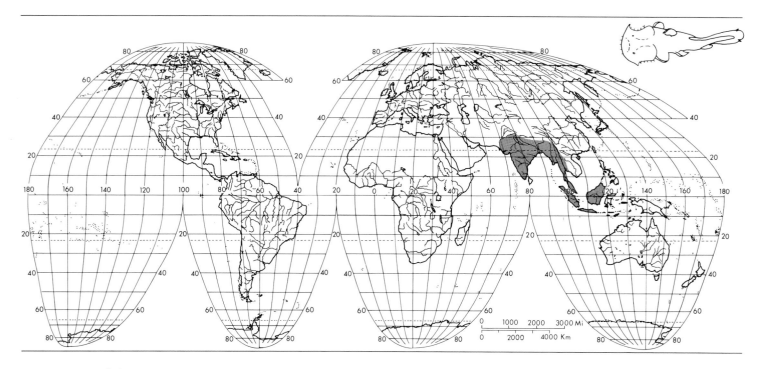

CLASS: Osteichthyes
   SUBCLASS: Actinopterygii
     SUPERORDER: Ostariophysi

ORDER: Siluriformes
   (1st) FAMILY: **CHACIDAE** [kă'-sī-dē]

The distribution of the Chacidae extends from India to the Malay Archipelago. *Chaca chaca*, the only species, has an enlarged, depressed head with a very wide mouth. An arborescent fringe dangles from the ventral surface of the head. The adipose fin is confluent with the caudal fin, which extends foward along the dorsal and ventral surfaces. A spine is present in the dorsal and pectoral fins. The eyes are minute and dorsally oriented. This omnivorous, nocturnal fish is sluggish and lies in wait for its prey. See Jayaram and Majumbar (1964) for futher details.

Map references: Day 1878, Sterba 1966*.

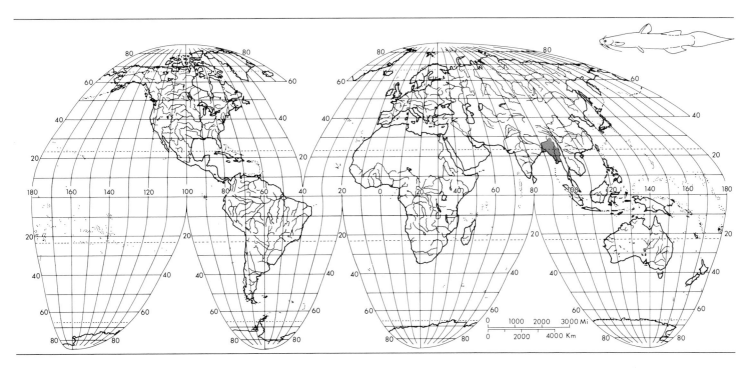

CLASS: Osteichthyes
  SUBCLASS: Actinopterygii
    SUPERORDER: Ostariophysi

ORDER: Siluriformes
(1st) FAMILY: **OLYRIDAE** [ō-lȳ′-rĭ-dē]

The only genus, *Olyra*, which has several species, is endemic to the eastern Himalayas and Burma. These small fishes have an elongate body, a long, low adipose fin, 4 pairs of barbels, and a pectoral spine. Some species have a lanceolate caudal fin. See Hora (1936) for more details.

Map references: Day 1878, Jayaram 1974.

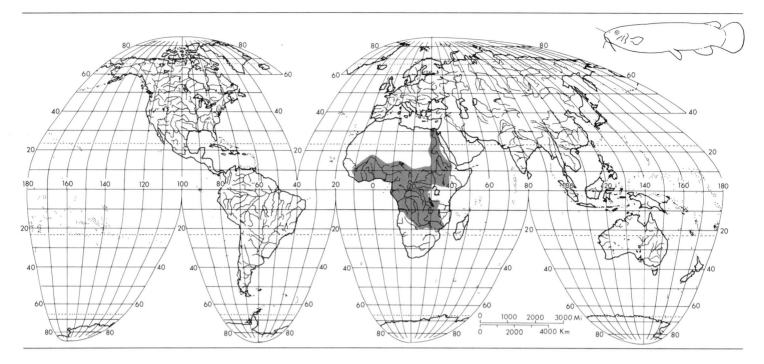

CLASS: Osteichthyes
SUBCLASS: Actinopterygii
SUPERORDER: Ostariophysi

ORDER: Siluriformes
(1st) FAMILY: **MALAPTERURIDAE**—electric catfishes
(măl-ăp'-tē-rōō'-rĭ-dē)

The Malapteruridae occurs through tropical Africa and the Nile Valley, except Lake Victoria and east coast rivers north of the Zambezi River. *Malapterurus electricus* and the recently described *M. microstoma* are the only catfishes known to have the ability to generate an electrical current. These species lack a rayed dorsal fin but have an adipose fin. *M. electricus* can reach 1.2 m, weigh 23 kg, and is capable of delivering over a 100 volt jolt. The polarity of *Malapterurus*, negative at the anterior end and positive at the posterior end, is the re-verse of the electric eel. The electric organs extend through the dorsal length of the body and are derived from modified muscle tissue. The discharge is used to capture prey, and the electric field may be used as a detection system as is done by gymnotids and mormyrids. See Bennett (1971a, b) and Grund-fest (1960) for a discussion of electrical properties, and Poll and Gosse (1969) for a revision of the genus.

Map references: Boulenger 1911, Roberts 1975, Sterba 1966*.

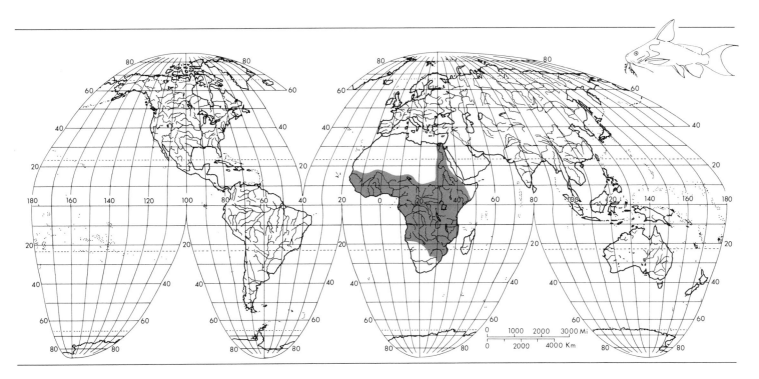

CLASS: Osteichthyes
   SUBCLASS: Actinopterygii
      SUPERORDER: Ostariophysi

ORDER: Siluriformes
   (1st) FAMILY: **MOCHOKIDAE**—upside-down catfishes [mō-kō'-kĭd-dē]

This family of 9 genera and 155 species is endemic to tropical Africa and the Nile Valley. Mochokids have a bony head and nape shield and 3 pairs of barbels, some of which may be extensively feathered. The adipose fin may be large, and lockable spines are present in the dorsal and pectoral fins. As the common name implies, some species, such as *Synodontis nigriventris*, actually swim with their ventral surfaces up. The species which swim in this unusual position may exhibit rever-

sal of countershading, with the dorsal surface light and the ventral surface dark, as the specific name *nigriventris* denotes. Larger species (up to 60 cm) are used as food fishes, and the smaller, more colorful species are popular with aquarists.

Map references: Hoedeman 1974*, Jubb 1967, Poll 1973*, Roberts 1975, Sterba 1966*.

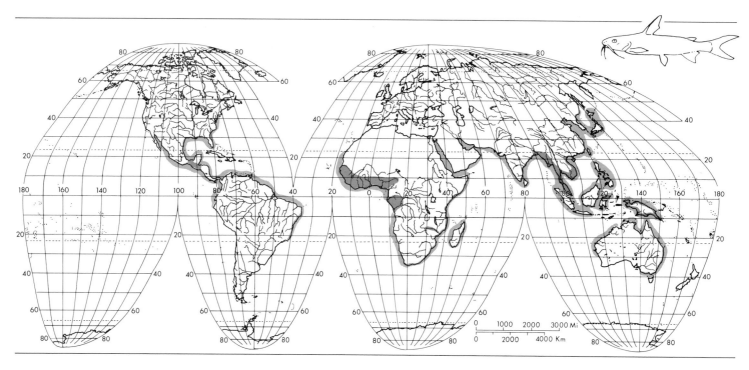

CLASS: Osteichthyes
    SUBCLASS: Actinopterygii
        SUPERORDER: Ostariophysi

ORDER: Siluriformes
    (Per) FAMILY: **ARIIDAE** (ă-rī′-ĭ-dē) [ă-rī′-ĭ-dē]

This marine family is worldwide in tropical and subtropical seas. Some species enter estuaries and coastal rivers. Stout spines arm the dorsal and pectoral fins. An adipose fin is present, and the anterior and posterior nasal openings are very close together, with flaps covering the posterior openings. A head shield may be present. Males incubate the large eggs in their mouths. Large species can reach 1 m and are used as food. The main genera are *Arius*, *Bagre*, *Hexanematichthys*, and *Tachysurus*. An American species, the sea catfish *Arius felis*, enters fresh water from Cade Cod to Panama. *Potamarius izabelensis* is endemic to Lake Izabal in Guatemala.

Map references: Boulenger 1911, Breder 1929, Darlington 1957, Day 1878, Eigenmann 1922, Herre 1953, Kiener and Richard-Vindard 1972, Lake 1971, Miller 1966, Smith 1965, Smith 1945.

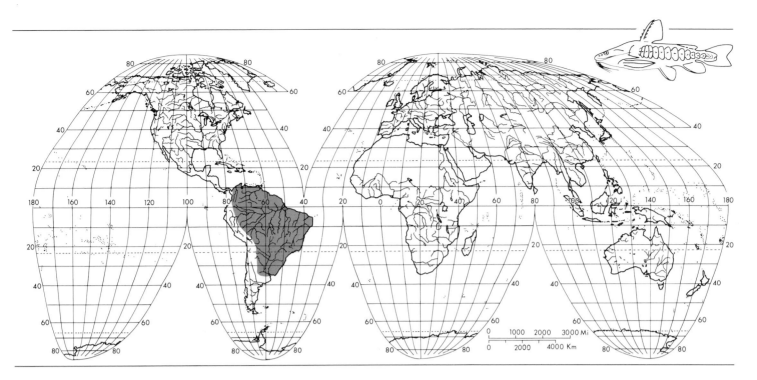

CLASS: Osteichthyes
  SUBCLASS: Actinopterygii
    SUPERORDER: Ostariophysi

ORDER: Siluriformes
  (1st) FAMILY: **DORADIDAE**—thorny catfishes
  (dō-răd'-ĭ-dē)

This South American family extends from Colombia to Río de la Plata and has about 75 species in 30 genera. Most are small, but some reach 1 m. The doradids are heavily armored fishes with studded bony plates along the sides. The pectoral and dorsal fin spines are stout and serrated. The skull extends as a bony plate to the base of the dorsal fin. Three pairs of barbels and an adipose fin are present. These fishes possess the ability to extract oxygen from gulped air via the intestinal tract and can emit growling sounds by moving the fin rays. The smaller species are used as aquarium specimens.

Map references: Eigenmann 1910, 1912*, Eigenmann and Allen 1942, Eigenmann and Eigenmann 1892, Gery 1969, Hoedeman 1974*, Sterba 1966*.

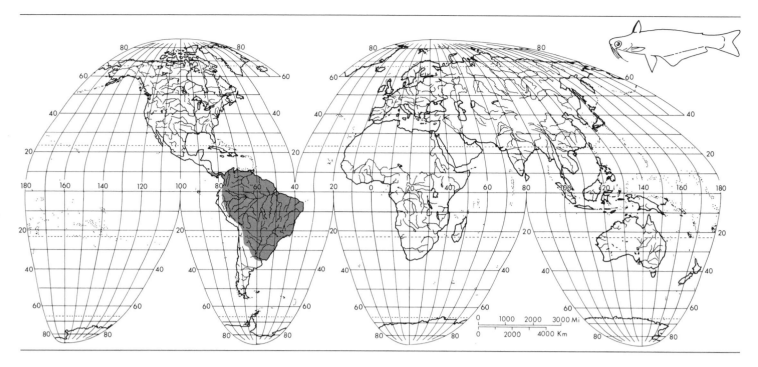

CLASS: Osteichthyes
   SUBCLASS: Actinopterygii
      SUPERORDER: Ostariophysi

ORDER: Siluriformes
(1st) FAMILY: **AUCHENIPTERIDAE**
[ŏw-kĕn-ĭp-tĕr'-ĭ-dē]

The auchenipterids range from Panama to Río de la Plata. There are about 16 genera and 50 species, which had previously been classified with the Doradidae. The naked-flanked auchenipterids, however, lack the armor of the dor-adids, and the dorsal and adipose fins are small.

Map references: Eigenmann 1912*, Gery 1969, Hoedeman 1974*, Miller 1966*, Sterba 1966*.

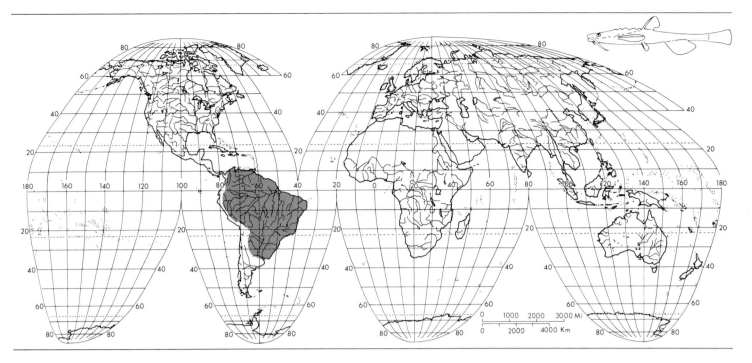

CLASS: Osteichthyes
   SUBCLASS: Actinopterygii
      SUPERORDER: Ostariophysi

ORDER: Siluriformes
   (1st) FAMILY: **ASPREDINIDAE**—banjo catfishes
   (ăs'-prē-dĭn'-ĭ-dē)

These catfishes, formerly the Bunocephalidae, are found from Colombia through the Amazon to Río de la Plata. There are about 8 genera and 25 species. The name banjo catfish, or frying pan catfish, as they are called by European aquarists, refers to the depressed, almost circular, head followed by a long slender tail with very narrow caudal peduncle. The adipose fin is absent. Pectoral spines may be strongly serrated, and the skin is naked but covered with tubercles. Max-imum size is 50 cm. Most inhabit fresh water (Bunocephalinae), but some species are euryhaline (Aspredininae). See Myers (1960) for further information.

Map references: Eigenmann 1910, Eigenmann 1912, Eigenmann and Allen 1942, Gery 1969, Hoedeman 1974*, Myers 1960, Schultz 1944, Sterba 1966*.

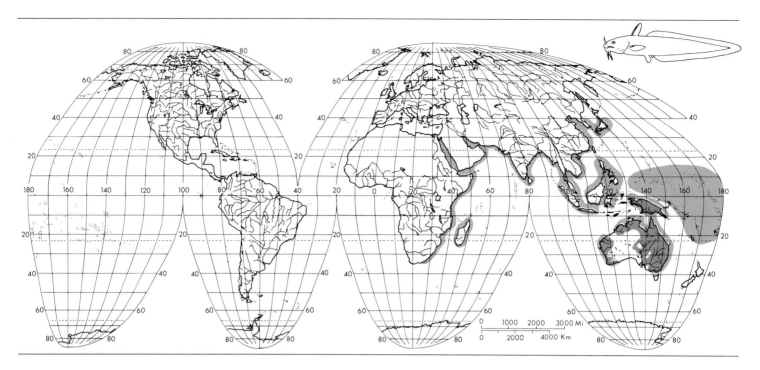

CLASS: Osteichthyes
   SUBCLASS: Actinopterygii
      SUPERORDER: Ostariophysi

ORDER: Siluriformes
   (Per) FAMILY: **PLOTOSIDAE**—plotosids
   [plō-tō'-sĭ-dē]

Plotosid catfishes are a marine family restricted to the Indo-Pacific region, but some species enter rivers, and others can live their entire life in fresh water far above the zone of tidal influence. This is especially true in Australia and New Guinea (Berra, Moore, and Reynolds 1975). There are about 30 species in 7 genera. Plotosids are referred to as eel-tailed catfish because the caudal and anal fins are confluent and extend dorsally. There is no adipose fin. Dorsal and pectoral spines are present, and a few species, the colorful *Plotosus anguillaris* for example, can inflict a venomous sting that is extremely painful. Other species have a peculiar preanal dendritic organ of unknown function. The body is naked. Max-

imum size is about 90 cm, and, like most catfish, plotosids are omnivorous. Some species such as the Australian *Tandanus tandanus* have an elaborate courtship ritual and build gravel nests. The larger species provide food and sport in some areas, and the smaller *Neosilurus* appears to be an ecological equivalent of the North American madtoms, *Noturus*. See Lake (1971) for life history notes and Halstead (1970) for information on venomous species.

Map references: Darlington 1957, Fowler 1932, 1959, Hoedeman 1974*, Lake 1971, Nelson 1976*, Smith 1965, Sterba 1966*.

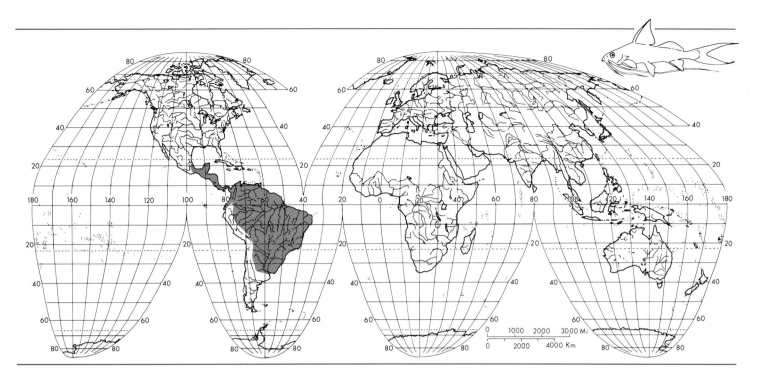

CLASS: Osteichthyes
    SUBCLASS: Actinopterygii
        SUPERORDER: Ostariophysi

ORDER: Siluriformes
    (1st) FAMILY: **PIMELODONTIDAE**—long-whiskered catfishes (pĭm'-ē-lō-dŏn'-tĭ-dē)

Pimelodontid catfish are found from southeastern Mexico and Central America throughout South America to Río de la Plata. It is the second largest family of South American catfish (after the Loricariidae), with about 55 genera and over 280 species. The genus *Rhamdia* extends throughout the range of the family. Other important genera are *Pimelodella*, *Pimelodus*, and *Pseudoplatystoma*. Pimelodontids resemble the Old World Bagridae. Three pairs of exceptionally long barbels are present in some species; the body is naked; adipose fin, dorsal and pectoral spines, and jaw teeth are present.

Many species are small, such as the 7 cm *Microglanis*; however, some species reach 1.3 m and a weight of 65 kg. Pimelodontids are used as aquarium and food species. This family is usually called the Pimelodidae; however, George S. Myers informed me that the family name should be based upon the stem *odont-* rather than *odous*.

Map references: Darlington 1957, Eigenmann 1909a*, Eigenmann 1912*, Eigenmann and Allen 1942, Gery 1969, Hoedeman 1974*, Miller 1966*, Nelson 1976*, Sterba 1966*.

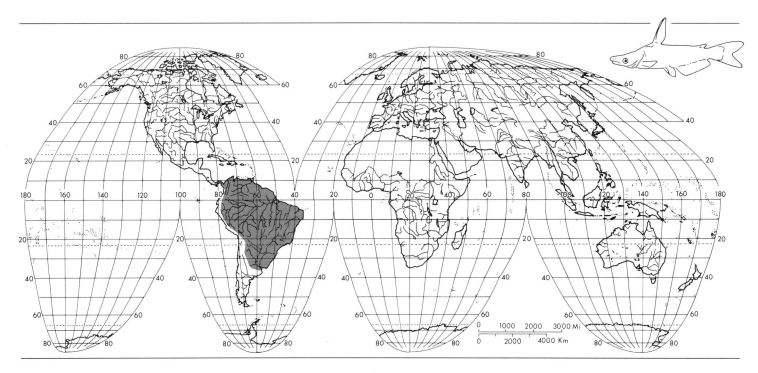

CLASS: Osteichthyes
  SUBCLASS: Actinopterygii
    SUPERORDER: Ostariophysi

ORDER: Siluriformes
  (1st) FAMILY: **AGENEIOSIDAE**—barbel-less catfishes
  [ă-gĕn-ē-ō′-sĭ-dē]

The Ageneiosidae occurs from Panama to Río de la Plata. There are 2 genera, of which *Ageneiosus* contains most of the 30-odd species in the family. There is only 1 pair of barbels, which may be rudimentary. The dorsal and pectoral spines are pungent, and the anal fin is long. An adipose fin is present but very small, and the swim bladder is reduced.

Map references: Eigenmann 1909*a*, 1910, 1912, Eigenmann and Allen 1942, Eigenmann and Eigenmann 1892, Gery 1969, Miller 1966*.

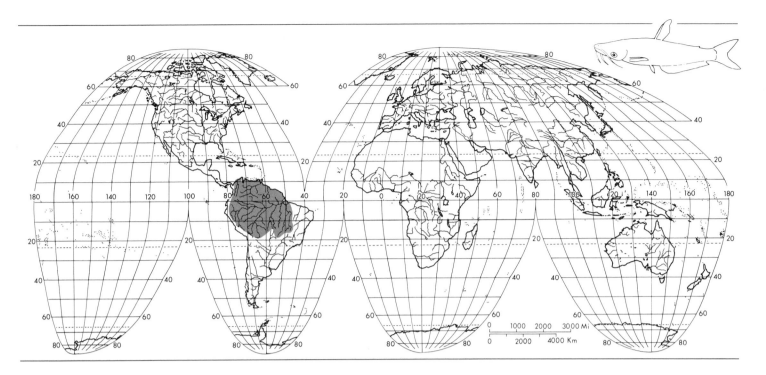

CLASS: Osteichthyes
  SUBCLASS: Actinopterygii
    SUPERORDER: Ostariophysi

ORDER: Siluriformes
  (1st) FAMILY: **HYPOPHTHALMIDAE**—low-eyed catfish [hȳ-pŏf-thăl′-mĭ-dē]

This monotypic family consists of *Hypophthalmus edentatus*, which is found from Colombia through the Brazilian Amazon. The specific epithet refers to this species' toothless condition. The body is compressed, and the head is depressed. The adipose fin is reduced, as is the swim bladder, and the anal fin is long. The eyes of this fish are set far down on the side of the head.

Map references: Eigenmann 1910, 1912, Eigenmann and Allen 1942.

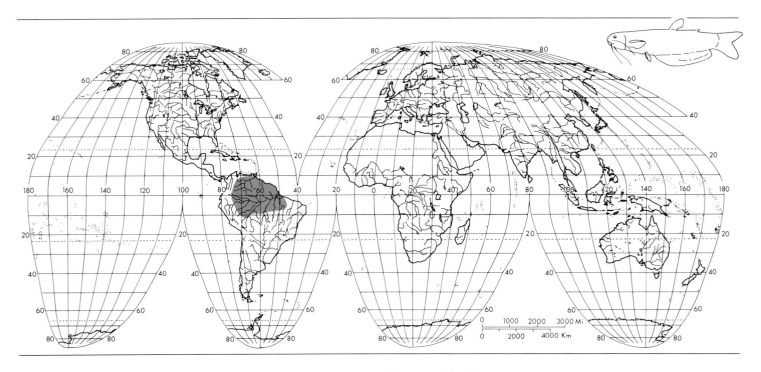

CLASS: Osteichthyes
   SUBCLASS: Actinopterygii
      SUPERORDER: Ostariophysi

ORDER: Siluriformes
   (1st) FAMILY: **HELOGENEIDAE** [hē-lō-jĕ-nē'-ĭ-dē]

This small family occurs in northern South America. *Helogenes marmoratus* has a spineless dorsal, very small adipose fin, a long anal fin, and 3 pairs of barbels. This omnivorous fish can grow to 10 cm in length. In captivity it may give the impression of being dead by lying on its back or side for long periods of time (Hoedeman 1974). Until recently it was the only recognized species in the family, but now about 5 species and a second genus (*Leyvaichthys*) may be recognized.

Map references: Eigenmann 1910, 1912, Gery 1969.

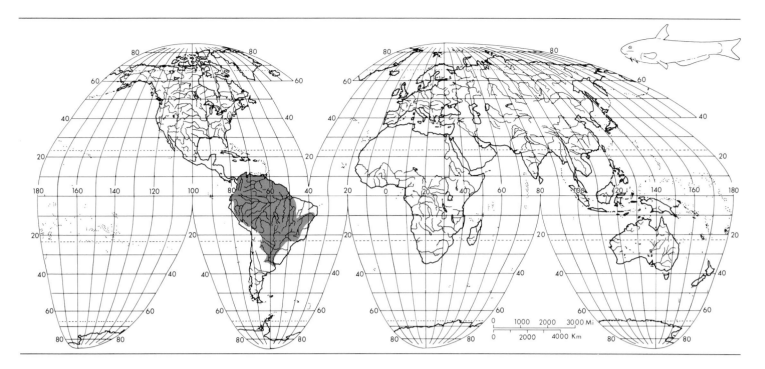

CLASS: Osteichthyes
  SUBCLASS: Actinopterygii
    SUPERORDER: Ostariophysi

ORDER: Siluriformes
  (1st) FAMILY: **CETOPSIDAE** [sē-tŏp′-sĭ-dē]

This family of 4 genera and about 14 species is present in northern South America in the Orinoco and Amazon drainages and the Paraná and São Francisco rivers. These small, streamlined, naked fishes have a long anal fin and lack an adipose fin. Their swim bladder is reduced and covered with a bony sheath. Their eyes are almost concealed in skin, and jaw teeth are present. The largest cetopsids are under 20 cm.

Cetopsids lack the opercular spines typical of their parasitic relatives, the Trichomycteridae. Three pairs of barbels are present. Consult Schultz (1944) for an explanation of taxonomic problems in this family.

Map references: Eigenmann 1910, 1912, Gery 1969, Schultz 1944.

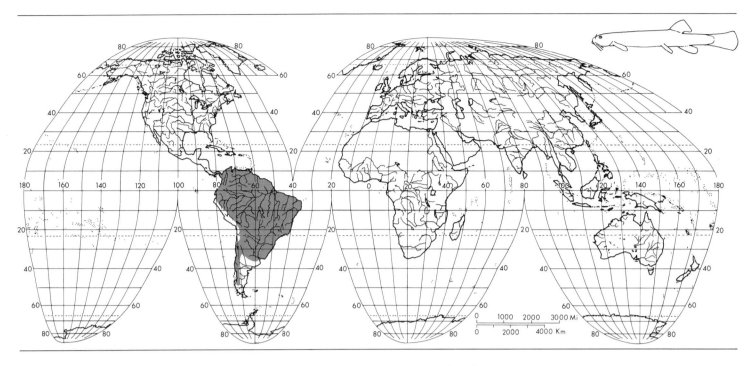

CLASS: Osteichthyes
    SUBCLASS: Actinopterygii
        SUPERORDER: Ostariophysi

ORDER: Siluriformes
    (1st) **FAMILY:** **TRICHOMYCTERIDAE**—parasitic
    catfishes [trĭ-kō-mĭk-tĕ′-rĭ-dē]

This family, formerly known as the Pygidiidae, ranges from Panama (*Pygidium*) throughout most of South America to as far south as lat. 47°30′ (*Hatcheria*). This is farther south than any other primary freshwater fish (Darlington 1957). The family contains about 27 genera and probably 150 species. The size of these fishes is very small, from 2 to 10 cm. Body form is wormlike, with a short dorsal and anal fin, no adipose fin, naked skin, and posteriorly pointed spines on the operculum. Many species are free-living in torrential Andean streams, but some species have evolved a curious parasitic way of life. *Stegophilus* and its relatives feed on the blood from the gills of larger catfishes such as the Pimelodontidae. The small parasitic species enter the branchial chamber and nip the blood-rich gills with their tiny teeth. An even more extraordinary, but probably accidental, mode of living is attributed to the infamous candiru, a collective name applied to several species, such as *Vandellia cirrhosa*. This slender, 6 cm fish has been reported to enter the urethra of men and women who urinate while bathing in rivers. Once a candiru has entered the urethra, excruciating pain is generated, and the fish must be removed surgically before it reaches the bladder. The poste-

riorly directed opercular spines which dig into the flesh prevent the removal of the candiru by urination or external pressure. Amazon natives have developed several types of penis sheaths and G-strings to prevent the candiru's admission. Since the water is turbid and the fish has very small eyes, it probably locates an appropriate entrance by orienting to the current (rheotaxis), whether it be a stream of urine or the exhaled water from a larger fish's gill cavity. Gudger (1930) has written a fascinating book on this group. Further information on life history and taxonomy can be found in Eigenmann (1918), Eigenmann and Allen (1942), Myers (1944), Kelley and Atz (1964), Masters (1968), Roberts (1972), Ricciuti (1973) and Gordon (1977). Vinton and Stickler (1941) describe several eyewitness accounts and report that the unripe fruit of a native tree, *Gunipa americana*, is used to purge the fish.

Map references: Darlington 1957, Eigenmann 1909a*, 1912, 1918*, 1927, Eigenmann and Allen 1942, Eigenmann and Eigenmann 1892, Gery 1969, Miller 1966*, Sterba 1966*.

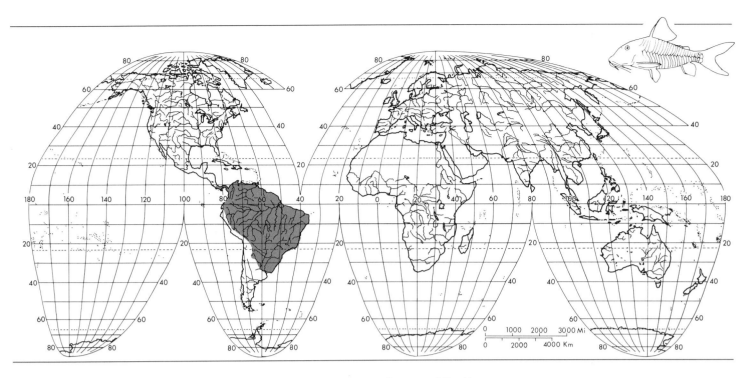

CLASS: Osteichthyes
    SUBCLASS: Actinopterygii
        SUPERORDER: Ostariophysi

ORDER: Siluriformes
    (1st) FAMILY: CALLICHTHYIDAE [kăl-lĭk-thī'-ĭ-dē]

Callichthyids range from Panama to Río de la Plata. There are about 8 genera and over 100 species, with *Corydoras* containing most of the species. These fishes have overlapping bony plates arranged in 2 longitudinal rows along the flanks. Spines are present in the dorsal and pectoral fins, and even the adipose fin is armored with a spine. Callichthyids are capable of gulping air at the surface and extracting oxygen via the gut. Most species are small from 3.5 to 25 cm, and are probably the most popular aquarium catfishes. Their spawning behavior involves the female holding her eggs in a cup formed by her pectoral fins while the male releases his sperm. See Vogt (1973) and Sterba (1966) for more details and aquarium information.

Map references: Eigenmann 1912*, Eigenmann and Allen 1942, Gery 1969, Hoedeman 1974*, Miller 1966*, Sterba 1966*.

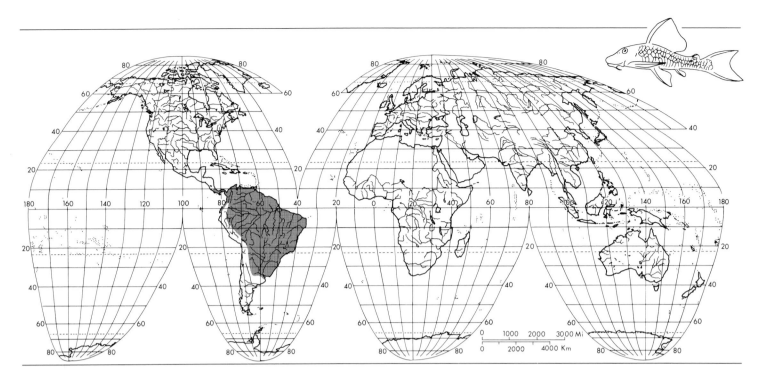

CLASS: Osteichthyes
  SUBCLASS: Actinopterygii
    SUPERORDER: Ostariophysi

ORDER: Siluriformes
  (1st) FAMILY: **LORICARIIDAE**—armored catfishes
  (lŏr'-ĭ-kă-rī'-ĭ-dē) [lō-rĭ-că-rī'-ĭ-dē]

The loricariids range from Costa Rica to Río de la Plata and are the largest family of South American catfishes, with about 50 genera and over 400 species. The body of these fishes is covered with smooth overlapping bony plates in 3–4 rows. These bottom-feeding vegetarians have a high dorsal fin and a suctorial mouth, which may help maintain a position in rapid-flowing water. Stout spines are present in all fins except the caudal. Body form is diverse. Some species are rather heavy-bodied (*Plecostomus*), while others such as *Farlowella* are elongate and very slender. *Loricaria* may have a filament extending from either lobe of the caudal fin. Many species are small (4–20 cm) and make interesting aquarium animals, while some *Plecostomous* exceed 1 m. See Vogt (1973), Sterba (1966), and Hoedman (1974) for life history details, aquarium data, and illustrations. See Freihofer and Neil (1967) for an interesting account of a commensal relationship between midge larvae and some catfish.

Map references: Bartholomew, Clarke, and Grimshaw 1911*, Darlington 1957*, Eigenmann 1909a*, 1912*, Eigenmann and Allen 1942, Gery 1969, Hoedeman 1974*, Miller 1976*, Sterba 1966*.

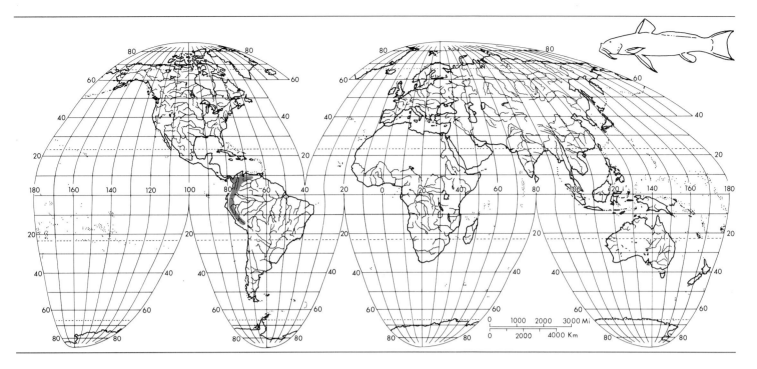

CLASS: Osteichthyes
  SUBCLASS: Actinopterygii
    SUPERORDER: Ostariophysi

ORDER: Siluriformes
  (1st) FAMILY: **ASTROBLEPIDAE** [ăs-trō-blē′-pĭ-dē]

The astroblepids are found in the northern Andes from Panama to Bolivia. There is only 1 genus, *Astroblepus*, with about 37 species, all of which are scaleless. A suctorial mouth and modified pelvic fins help these fishes maintain their position in rapid-water habitats. Some species have a stout spine associated with the adipose fin.

Map references: Darlington 1957, Eigenmann 1909a*, Eigenmann and Allen 1942, Eigenmann and Eigenmann 1892, Gery 1969, Miller 1966, Schultz 1944.

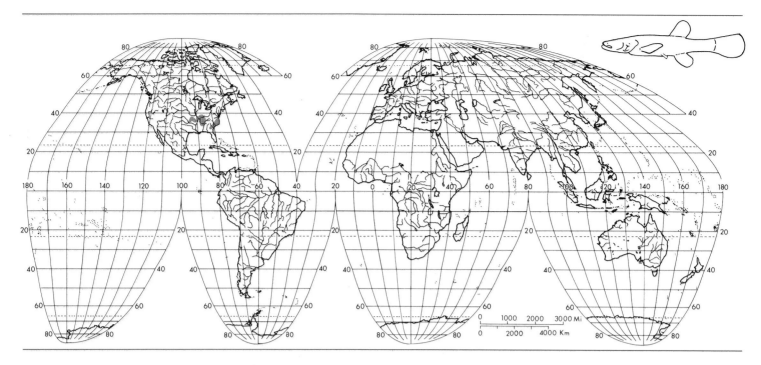

CLASS: Osteichthyes
    SUBCLASS: Actinopterygii
        SUPERORDER: Paracanthopterygii

ORDER: Percopsiformes
    SUBORDER: Amblyopsoidei
        (2d) FAMILY: **AMBLYOPSIDAE** (ăm'-blĭ-ŏp'-sĭ-dē)

This interesting family of cave, spring, and swamp-dwelling fishes occurs in central and southeastern United States. There are 6 described species in 4 genera, all of which are small in size, the maximum length being about 9 cm. All species except the swampfish (*Chologaster cornuta*), which lives in surface waters of the Atlantic coastal plain from Virginia to Georgia, are associated with limestone formations. The Ozark cavefish, *Amblyopsis rosae*, occurs in caves in southwest Missouri and northwest Arkansas. *A. spelaea*, the northern cavefish, inhabits caves of south central Indiana and the Mammoth Cave region of west central Kentucky. The southern cavefish, *Typhlichthys subterraneus*, is disjunctly distributed in Kentucky, central Tennessee, northern Alabama, and the Ozark region of Missouri and northeastern Oklahoma. *C. agassizi*, the springfish, occurs in southwest Illinois, central Tennessee, and Kentucky. *Speoplatyrhinus poulsoni* is

only known from a cave in northwestern Alabama. All except the 2 species of *Chologaster* lack eyes or have rudimentary eyes at best. Pelvic fins are either absent or very reduced. In this family the anus is jugular, cycloid scales are minute and imbedded, and there is a profusion of sensory papillae on the heads and bodies. The eggs are retained by the female in her gill chamber. See Woods and Inger (1957) for a thorough study of this family. Rosen (1962) reviewed the family relationship, and Nelson (1974) gave an overview of this superorder, whose morphological characters are transitional between those of the soft-rayed fishes and spiny-rayed fishes.

Map references: Cooper and Kuehne 1974, Darlington 1957, Eddy 1969, Moore 1968, Nelson 1976*, Pflieger 1971*, Whitaker 1968*, Woods and Inger 1957*.

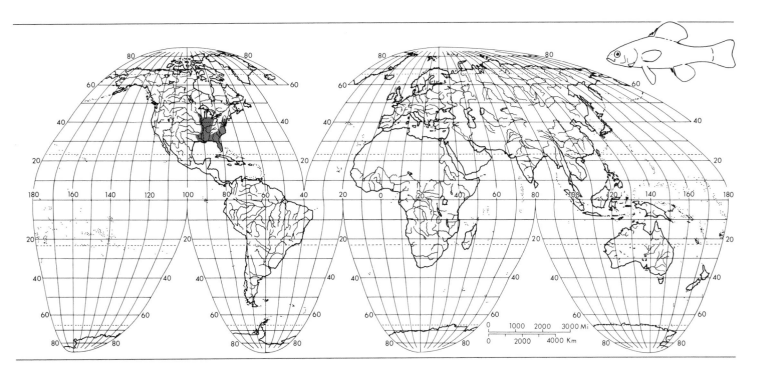

CLASS: Osteichthyes
  SUBCLASS: Actinopterygii
    SUPERORDER: Paracanthopterygii

ORDER: Percopsiformes
  SUBORDER: Aphredoderoidei
    (1st) FAMILY: **APHREDODERIDAE**—pirate perch
    [ă-frē-dō-dĕ'-rĭ-dē]

This family of 1 species, *Aphredoderus sayanus*, is found in the Mississippi River valley and along the coastal plain from eastern Texas to New York. Pirate perch have ctenoid scales, a large mouth, deep body anteriorly, 3 dorsal spines, 2 anal spines, and 1 pelvic spine. Their most peculiar characteristic is the migration of the anal opening from the normal position in juveniles to the throat region in adults. Maximum size is about 14 cm. The preferred habitat of *Aphredoderus* is sluggish water, ponds, oxbows, marshes, and other places which have bottoms of decomposing organic matter and are heavily vegetated. Fossils date from the Oligocene of Montana. See Trautman (1957) for life history information and Mansueti (1963) for ontogeny.

Map references: Darlington 1957, Eddy 1969, Miller 1958*, Moore 1968, Nelson 1976*, Pflieger 1971*, Sterba 1966*, Trautman 1957*, Whitaker 1968*.

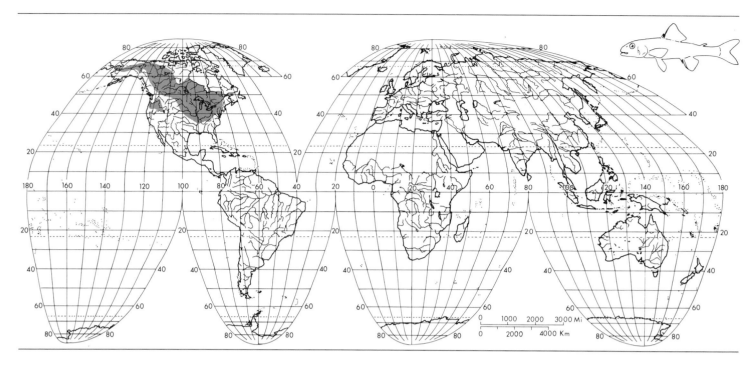

CLASS: Osteichthyes
　SUBCLASS: Actinopterygii
　　SUPERORDER: Paracanthopterygii

ORDER: Percopsiformes
　SUBORDER: Percopsoidei
　　(1st) FAMILY: **PERCOPSIDAE**—troutperch
　　[pĕr-kŏp′-sĭ-dē]

This family is composed of 2 species of *Percopsis*, which are disjunctly distributed in northern North America. The trout perch, *Percopsis omiscomaycus*, is the more widely distributed species. It is found from the Yukon to the Atlantic coast and south in the Mississippi Valley to Missouri. The sand roller, *P. transmontana*, is found in Oregon and Washington in the Columbia River basin and in the Snake River of western Idaho. Troutlike characteristics include an adipose fin in conjunction with perchlike spines in the dorsal, anal, and pelvic fins. Scales are ctenoid. Diet consists of insects and crustacea, and the maximum size is about 20 cm. Habitat includes lakes and streams, where *P. omiscomaycus* is an important forage species for pike, trout, burbot, perch, and walleye. Fossils date from the middle Eocene of North America. Consult Scott and Crossman (1973) for life history details and references.

Map references: Carl, Clemmens, and Lindsey 1959*, Darlington 1957, McPhail and Lindsey 1970*, Miller 1958*, Moore 1968, Nelson 1976*, Pflieger 1971*, Rostlund 1952*, Scott and Crossman 1973*, Trautman 1957*, Whitaker 1968*.

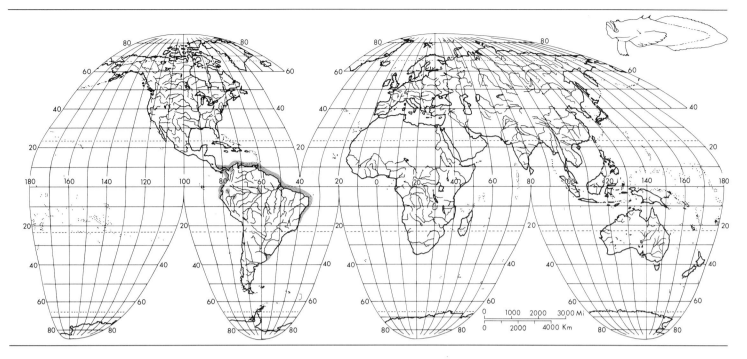

CLASS: Osteichthyes
    SUBCLASS: Actinopterygii
        SUPERORDER: Acanthopterygii

ORDER: Batrachoidiformes
    (Per) **FAMILY: BATRACHOIDIDAE**—toadfishes
    (băt'-ră-koi'-dĭ-dē)

Members of this family of bottom-dwelling fishes have a large head with large dorsally located eyes, jugular pelvic fins, and 3 pairs of gills. Some species can produce sound with their swim bladders. The toadfishes are divided into 3 subfamilies. The Batrachoidinae (14 genera and about 30 species) is found off the coasts of North and South America, Africa, Europe, southern Asia, and Australia. The Porichthyinae (2 genera and 12 species) occurs from southeastern Alaska to Chile and Virginia to Argentina. Only the Thalassophryninae has freshwater representatives, and it is this group that is shown on the map.

The Thalassophrynine is distinguished from the other 2 subfamilies by the presence of 2 hollow dorsal spines and a hollow opercular spine. These spines are connected to venom glands. This is the only group of venomous fishes to have hollow spines for the delivery of venom. Other groups have less sophisticated grooved spines. The Batrachoidinae and the Porichthyinae have 3 and 2 solid dorsal spines, respectively, and are nonvenomous.

The venomous toadfishes are placed in 2 genera, *Daector* (5 species) and *Thalassophryne* (6 species). Five *Thalassophryne* are found along the east coast of South America, and *T. amazonica* occurs in the fresh water of the Amazon and its tributaries. Four *Daector* occur along the east coast of South America, with *D. quadrizonatus* being found in freshwater tributaries of the Atrato River in Colombia. The venomous toadfishes are scaleless and have a single lateral line. They lack photophores and canine teeth, which some members of the other subfamilies possess. They may lie buried in the sand, and a very painful wound results when stepped on. See Collette (1968, 1973) for a review of the Thalassophryninae and description of a new freshwater species. Fossils date to the Upper Miocene of Algeria.

Map reference: Collette 1968*, 1973.

103

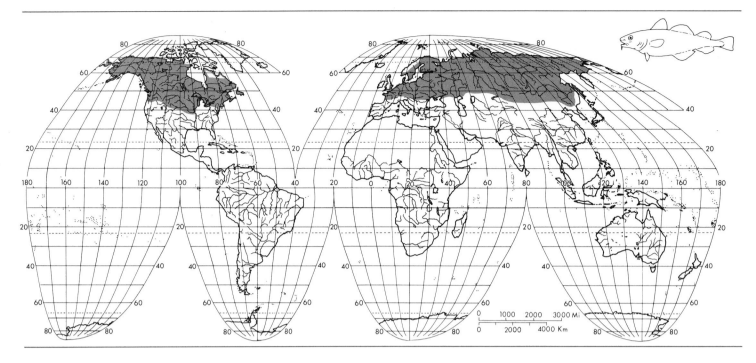

CLASS: Osteichthyes
  SUBCLASS: Actinopterygii
    SUPERORDER: Paracanthopterygii

ORDER: Gadiformes
  SUBORDER: Gadoidei
    (Per) FAMILY: **GADIDAE**—cods
    (găd′-ĭ-dē) [gā′-dĭ-dē]

The Gadidae is a marine family of about 60 species with only 1 representative, the burbot (*Lota lota*), living entirely in fresh water of North America and Eurasia, where it has a holarctic distribution. Some of the marine species may enter rivers in coastal areas in both the Northern and Southern hemispheres. In tropical regions gadids are deep-water fishes. Cods have an elongate body, a thin barbel at the tip of the chin, a large head, and small cycloid scales. Three dorsal and 2 anal fins may be present, and the fins may be confluent and long. Cods, especially *Gadus morhua*, are of enormous commercial importance second only to the clupeids. Size varies up to 2 m. Burbots may reach 1.2 m and weigh 34 kg, are found in waters as deep as 200 m, and are winter spawners. Burbots are highly predacious on other fish species. Fossils of this suborder date from the Lower Eocene of England. See Svetovidov (1962) for a technical review of the order and Messtorff (1973) for general information about the family. Scott and Crossman (1973) provide references and life history details of *Lota*.

Map references: Berg 1949, Darlington 1957, Grzimek 1973*, McPhail and Lindsey 1970*, Maitland 1977*, Meek 1916*, Nelson 1976*, Pflieger 1971*, Rostlund 1952*, Trautman 1957*, Scott and Crossman 1973*, Svetovidov 1961*, Wheeler 1969*, Whitaker 1968*, Whitley 1968.

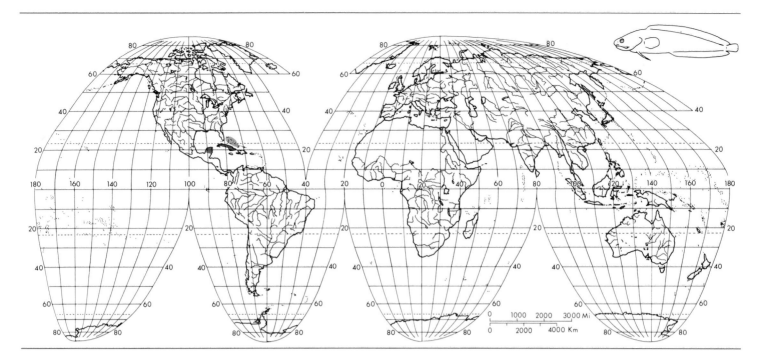

CLASS: Osteichthyes
  SUBCLASS: Actinopterygii
    SUPERORDER: Paracanthopterygii

ORDER: Gadiformes
  SUBORDER: Ophidioidei
    (Per) FAMILY: **OPHIDIIDAE**—cusk eels and
    brotulas (ŏf-ĭ-dī'-ĭ-dē) [ŏ-fĭ-dī'-ĭ-dē]

Ophidiids are a marine family with a worldwide deep-sea distribution. However, there are several blind freshwater forms from sinkholes and caves in the Bahamas, Cuba, and Yucatan. Only the freshwater distribution is shown on the map. Cusk eels and brotulas are elongated fishes with slender pelvic fins located very far forward near the head. The dorsal and anal fins are ribbonlike. There are approximately 230 species in 48 genera. Most are less than 30 cm in length, but one South American form can reach 1.5 m. The freshwater ophidiids are *Lucifuga subterranea* and *L.* (= *Stygicola*) *dentatus* from Cuba, *L. spelaeotes* from the Bahamas, and

Ogilbia (= *Typhlias*) *pearsei* from Yucatan. The eyeless troglodytes from Cuba were studied by Eigenmann (1909*b*). Ophidiids are viviparous, and males have a clasperlike copulatory organ. The anterior region of the head is compressed, and the caudal fin is lanceolate and separated from the dorsal and anal fin. Fossils of this suborder date to the Lower Eocene of England. See Hubbs (1938), Cohen and Robins (1970), and Cohen and Nielson (1978) for more information.

Map references: Cohen and Nielson 1978, Hubbs 1938.

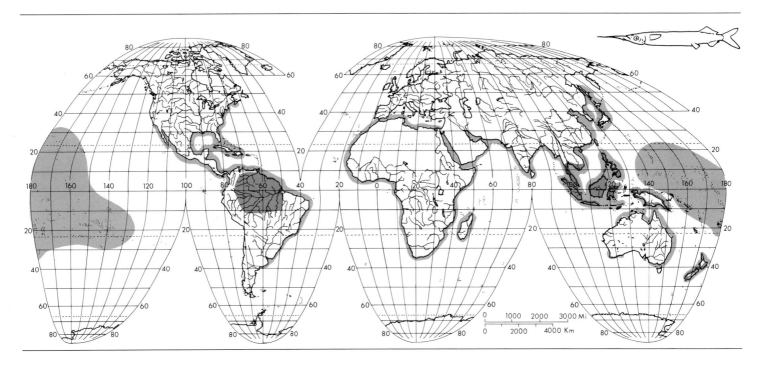

CLASS: Osteichthyes
  SUBCLASS: Actinopterygii
    SUPERORDER: Atherinomorpha

ORDER: Atheriniformes
  SUBORDER: Exocoetoidei
    (Per) FAMILY: **HEMIRAMPHIDAE**—halfbeaks
    (hĕm'-ĭ-răm'-fĭ-dē)

This surface-dwelling marine family is cosmopolitan. A few halfbeaks (sometimes classified with flying fishes as Exocoetidae) live in rivers, especially in the Indo-Australian region. Halfbeaks are slender, elongate fishes with the lower jaw extending far beyond the upper jaw in most species. The dorsal, anal, and pelvic fins are set extremely far posteriad. The lower lobe of the caudal may be enlarged, reflecting a relationship to the flying fishes, which use the expanded caudal fin for generation of sufficient propulsive force to leap over the water surface. A skulling motion of the tail allows halfbeaks to make short leaps, but they do not have the expanded pectoral fins necessary for gliding. *Oxypohamphus micropterus* is a flying fish with relatively small pectoral fins that effectively bridge the morphological gap between halfbeaks and flying fishes. Some halfbeaks have internal fertilization and give birth to live young. The males of such species have an anal fin probably modified as a copulatory organ. There are at least 65 species of halfbeaks in approximately

10 genera, such as *Hemirampus* and *Zenarchopterus*. *Hyporhamphus brederi* accounts for the inland South American distribution. Maximum size is about 45 cm, but most halfbeaks are less than half that size. Two species of the genus *Nomorhampus* are found in the Celebes and have jaws of equal length. Smith (1945) presented an interesting account of *Dermogenys* being cultivated as a fighting fish by the Thai people. Fossil halfbeaks date to the middle Eocene of Italy. Patterson (1974) presented an overview of the order. See Herre (1944) for a review of halfbeaks, and Rosen (1964) and Rosen and Patterson (1969) for a discussion of their relation to other atheriniform fishes.

Map references: Berg 1949, Breder 1929, Collette 1965*, 1976*, Fitch and Levenberg 1971, Fowler 1959, Herre 1953, Kiener and Richard-Vindard 1972, Lake 1971, Miller 1966, Smith 1945, Tinker 1978, Wheeler 1969, Whitley 1968.

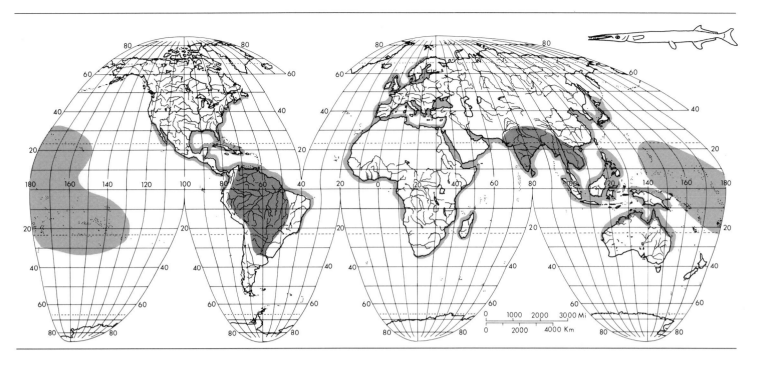

CLASS: Osteichthyes
    SUBCLASS: Actinopterygii
        SUPERORDER: Atherinomorpha

ORDER: Atheriniformes
    SUBORDER: Exocoetoidei
        (Per) FAMILY: BELONIDAE—needlefishes
        (bĕ-lŏn′-ĭ-dē) [bĕ-lō′-nĭ-dē]

Needlefishes are a worldwide marine family of about 28 species with a few freshwater genera such as the South American *Potamorrhaphis*, *Pseudotylosurus*, and *Belonion* and the Indian *Xenentoden* and freshwater representatives of the cosmopolitan genus *Strongylura*. The largest species is probably *Tylosurus crocodilus* found in coastal waters around the world, which may reach 1.5 m, but most species are half that size. The belonids are thin, elongate fishes with teeth-studded jaws of equal length extended to form a beak. They are very fast and voracious predators. The dorsal and anal fins are fairly long, and the paired fins are reduced. The skeleton and sometimes the flesh have a greenish color, but this peculiarity does not affect edibility. Munro (1967) reported that death has been caused by needlefish leaping at great speed and piercing the bodies of naked natives. Fossils date to the Oligocene. See the 1974 papers of Collette for more details and information on the inverse freshwater distributional relationship between the Hemiramphidae and the Belonidae.

Map references: Collette 1966, 1974a*, b*, c*, d*, Collette and Parin 1970*, Cressy and Collette 1971*, Day 1878, Eigenmann and Allen 1942, Fitch and Lavenberg 1971, Fowler 1959, Gery 1969, Herre 1953, Lake 1971, Miller 1966, Smith 1945, Smith 1965, Sterba 1966, Tinker 1978, Wheeler 1969*, Whitaker 1968*.

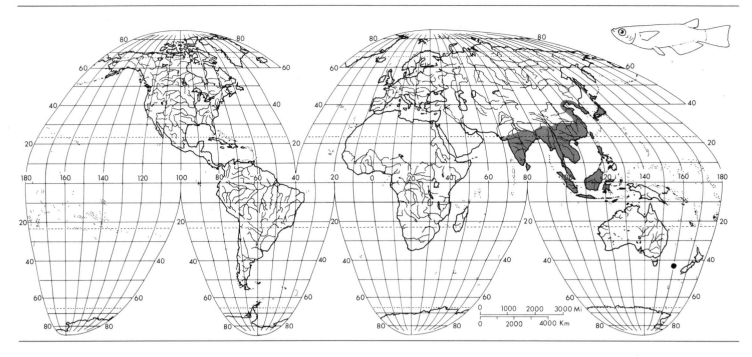

CLASS: Osteichthyes
  SUBCLASS: Actinopterygii
    SUPERORDER: Atherinomorpha

ORDER: Atheriniformes
  SUBORDER: Cyprinodontoidei
    (2d) FAMILY: **ORYZIATIDAE**—rice fishes, medakas
    [ō-rī-zǐ-ǎ'-tǐ-dē]

This family of 7 species is the most primitive of the cyprinodontoids and is found in fresh and brackish waters from India through Southeast Asia across Wallace's line to Timor, Celebes, Luzon, and Japan. The only genus is *Oryzias*. These small fishes (under 10 cm) are compressed with a short dorsal and larger anal fin, both posteriorly placed. They commonly dwell in rice paddies, hence their vernacular name. The

Oryziatidae are egg layers with nonprotrusible jaws and a terminal or superior mouth which makes surface feeding the usual behavior. See Rosen (1964) for family description and Sterba (1966) for aquarium care information.

Map references: Day 1878, Herre 1953, Hoedeman 1974*, Nichols 1943, Rosen 1973, Smith 1945, Sterba 1966.

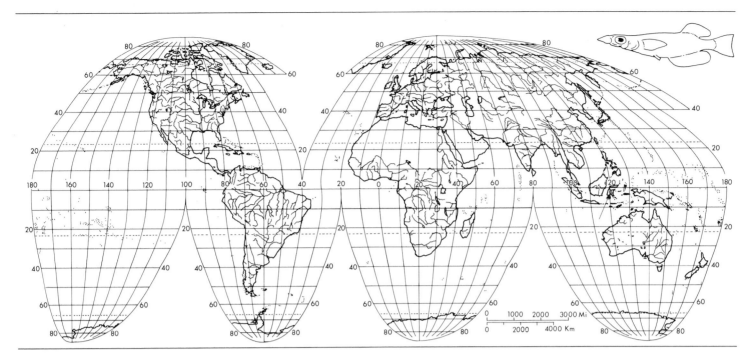

CLASS: Osteichthyes
  SUBCLASS: Actinopterygii
    SUPERORDER: Atherinomorpha

ORDER: Atheriniformes
  SUBORDER: Cyprinodontoidei
    (2d) **FAMILY: ADRIANICHTHYIDAE—**
    adrianichthyids [ā-drĭ-ăn-ĭk'-thĭ-ĭ-dē]

The 2 genera and 3 species which make up this family are found in Lakes Poso and Lindu on the Celebes. Their mouth is shovellike, and their size ranges from 7 to 20 cm. *Xenopoecilus poptae* in Lake Poso is the object of a November to January hook-and-line fishery, which coincides with their spawning period. These fishes have internal fertilization, and the eggs hatch immediately upon deposition. Broken egg membranes reportedly cover extensive regions of the lake surface during the spawning season. Celebes fossils date to the late Tertiary. For further details see Weber and De Beaufort (1922) and Rosen (1964).

Map references: Darlington 1957, Weber and De Beaufort 1922.

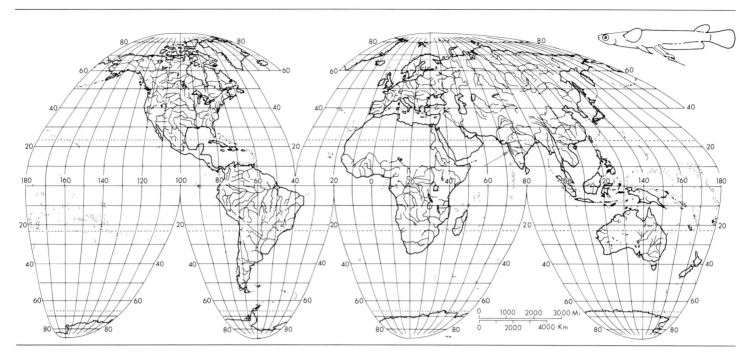

CLASS: Osteichthyes
    SUBCLASS: Actinopterygii
        SUPERORDER: Atherinomorpha

ORDER: Atheriniformes
    SUBORDER: Cyprinodontoidei
        (2d) FAMILY: **HORAICHTHYIDAE**
        [hō-ră-īk′-thī-ĭ-dē]

This endemic Indian family consists of a single species, *Horaichthys setnai*, which is found in brackish backwaters about 160 km north and south of Bombay. This tiny fish (2 cm) wasn't described until 1940 by Kulkarni. It is transparent, and the male has an anal fin modified for transmission of packets of sperm (spermatophores) to the female. Both pelvic fins are present in the male, but in females the genital opening is deflected to the left, the right pelvic fin is absent, and the left pelvic fin is medial. *Horaichthys* has a remarkable range of salt tolerance, related to monsoon flooding and summer evaporation. It feeds at the surface on copepods, diatoms, and crustacean larvae. Breeding occurs all year round, but reaches a peak in July and August. Eggs are laid in weedy areas. See Kulkarni (1940) for a thorough study of morphology and life history, and Hubbs (1941) for further comments.

Map references: Kulkarni 1940.

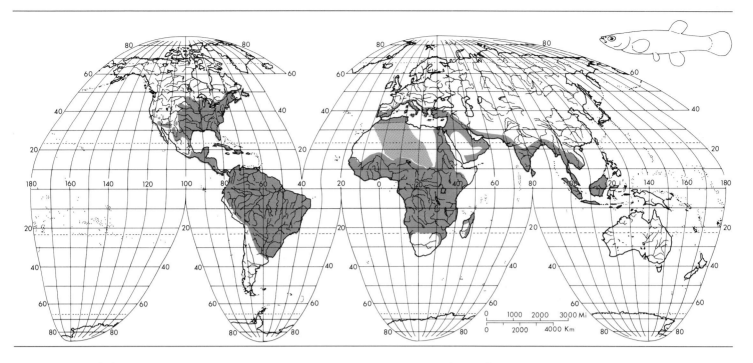

CLASS: Osteichthyes
  SUBCLASS: Actinopterygii
    SUPERORDER: Atherinomorpha

ORDER: Atheriniformes
  SUBORDER: Cyprinodontoidei
    (2d) FAMILY: **CYPRINODONTIDAE**—killifishes, topminnows (sĭ-prĭn′-ō-dŏn′-tĭ-dē)

Cyprinodontids are found in North, Central, and South America, Africa, Mediterranean Europe, the Near East, India, Southeast Asia, and the Malay Archipelago. They are secondary division freshwater fishes, which means they have some salt tolerance and may be able to cross saltwater barriers. This is borne out by their presence in the West Indies, Madagascar, Ceylon, and the East Indies. There are isolated natural populations in the southwestern United States (notably in the genus *Cyprinodon*) that have undergone considerable differentiation, including the loss of pelvic fins in some species. The greatest species diversity is in the southeastern United States, and the least diversity is in the Orient. It is interesting to note that the major South American genera are more closely related to African forms rather than to North American genera (Myers 1938). Cyprinodonts do not occur east of Weber's line into the Australian realm. There are about 300 species in 45 genera, which range in occurrence from fresh and brackish to salt waters.

Many killifish species are diminutive fishes; the largest, *Fundulus grandissimus*, may reach 18 cm. They are surface feeders, and the head is adapted with a terminal, protractile mouth. The fins are soft-rayed, (*Jordanella floridae* has the first dorsal ray modified as a stout grooved spine), the caudal is not forked, females have cycloid scales, and males have ctenoid scales. The lateral line is incomplete or partially developed. Egg laying (oviparity) and external fertilization are the rule. Family members have evolved a variety of interesting ecological adaptations that match the diversity of their ex-

tensive range of habitats. The various desert-dwelling pupfish, *Cyprinodon*, of the southwest United States can tolerate temperatures as high as 44° C. The Mediterranean *Aphanius* can live in water almost twice as salty as the ocean and is also found in isolated Saharan oases (Roberts 1975). Other species such as the African *Nothobranchus* survive hostile conditions by laying eggs that are resistant to desiccation. Their habitat may dry up and adult fish perish, but when the rains come, the eggs deposited in the bottom mud hatch. Such annual fishes usually live less than 1 year but can survive several years if given the chance. *Rivulus marmoratus* is hermaphroditic and fertilizes its own eggs. Cyprinodonts are an important link in the food web of larger aquatic animals and can benefit man by controlling mosquito larvae. Various species of *Fundulus* have served as laboratory animals, and the family is probably the most important aquarium group. Fossils date back to the Oligocene. See Harrington (1961) and Breder and Rosen (1966) for details of reproductive adaptations, Sterba (1966) for aquarium information, and Soltz and Naiman (1978) for the natural history of Death Valley fishes.

Map references: Bartholomew, Clarke, and Grimshaw 1911*, Bertin and Arambourg 1958*, Darlington 1957, Hoedeman 1974*, Innes 1966*, Kiener and Richard-Vindard 1972*, Lagler, Bardach, and Miller 1962*, Maitland 1977*, Meek 1916*, Miller 1958*, 1961*, 1966, Nelson 1976*, Roberts 1975, Scott and Crossman 1973*, Sterba 1966*.

111

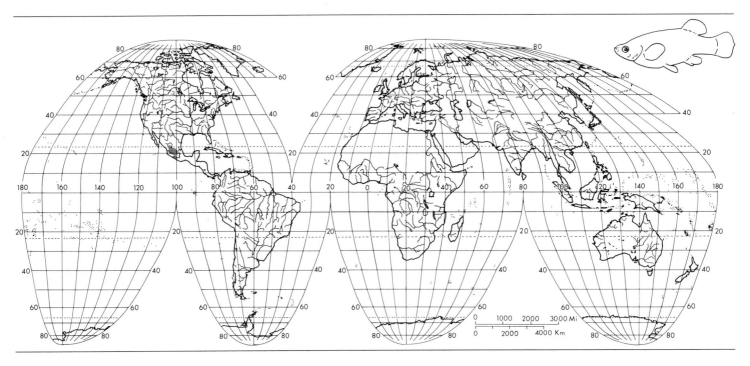

CLASS: Osteichthyes
   SUBCLASS: Actinopterygii
      SUPERORDER: Atherinomorpha

ORDER: Atheriniformes
   SUBORDER: Cyprinodontoidei
      (2d) FAMILY: **GOODEIDAE** [gŏŏd-ĭ'-ĭ-dē]

The goodeids are confined to the highlands of the Mesa Central of Mexico, with a center of concentration in the Rio Lerma system. There are about 10 genera and 35 species, with a maximum size of 20 cm. Most species are less than half that size, however. The goodeids give birth to live young (viviparity) that receive nutrition from the female through structures analogous to the mammalian placenta, but the males lack the elaborate gonopodium of the poeciliids. Instead, the first 6–7 rays of the male anal fin are separated from the rest of the fin by a distinct notch. Body form ranges from streamlined to deep-bodied, and various species are carnivores, herbivores or omnivores. See Hubbs and Turner (1939), Turner (1946), Miller and Fitzsimons (1971), and Fitzsimons (1972, 1976) for a review of the literature. Miocene fossils are found on the Mesa Central.

Map references: Darlington 1957, Fitzsimons 1972, Grzimek 1973*, Hoedeman 1974*, Sterba 1966*, Turner 1946.

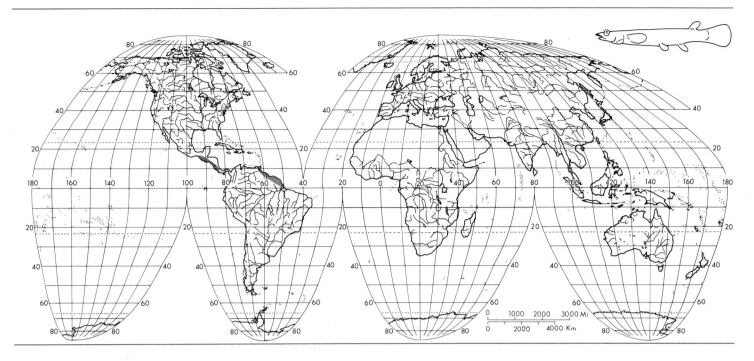

CLASS: Osteichthyes
   SUBCLASS: Actinopterygii
      SUPERORDER: Atherinomorpha

ORDER: Atheriniformes
   SUBORDER: Cyprinodontoidei
      (2d) FAMILY: **ANABLEPIDAE**—four-eyed fishes
      (ăn′-ă-blĕp′-ĭ-dē)

The four-eyed fishes are found in fresh and coastal waters of the Pacific slope of middle America and northern South America. There is 1 genus, *Anableps*, and 3 species: *anableps*, *dowi*, and *microlepis*. *A. dowi* is found on the Pacific slope of middle America, and the other 2 species are found in northern South America. Adult size is 15–30 cm. The body is elongate with a posteriorly positioned dorsal fin and a broad head. The eyes of these surface-dwelling fishes are adapted for seeing in air and under water. The cornea is divided into an upper and lower half by a band of tissue. The iris is partially divided, resulting in two pupils, and a divided retina forms images of above water and below water objects simultaneously. Even the lens is differentially thickened to adjust for the different indices of refraction between air and water. If this peculiar visual system is not enough to ingratiate this family to ichthyologists, then the reproductive modifications should do it. These fishes are viviparous and have internal fertilization. The male intromittent organ has either a left or a right mobility. The females have a scale that occludes the genital opening on either the left or right side. Consequently, a "left-handed" male must copulate with a "right-handed" female and vice versa. The left-right ratios are not equal in the populations, which may function to limit population size. See Herald (1962) for references to reproductive habits, Schwassmann and Kruger (1965) and Graham (1972) for information on this unique visual system, and Zahl, McLaughlin, and Gomprecht (1977), Zahl (1978), and Miller (1979) for natural history and illustrations.

Map references: Hildebrand 1925, Mago Leccia 1970, Miller 1966, 1979, Rosen 1973.

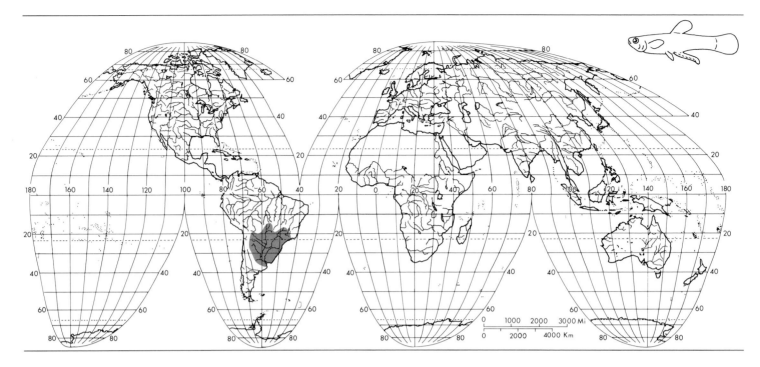

CLASS: Osteichthyes
   SUBCLASS: Actinopterygii
      SUPERORDER: Atherinomorpha

ORDER: Atheriniformes
   SUBORDER: Cyprinodontoidei
      (2d) FAMILY: **JENYNSIIDAE** [jĕ-nĭ'-sĭ-ĭ-dē]

This small family of viviparous fishes, with about 3 species in a single genus, is found in southern Brazil and northern Argentina. *Jenynsia lineata* females may reach 10 cm, while males are only about 2.5 cm long. The male's tubular gonopodium and the female's genital aperture are either dextral or sinistral as in the Anablepidae. See Breder and Rosen (1966) for references to reproductive behavior and structure.

Map references: Gery 1969, Sterba 1966.

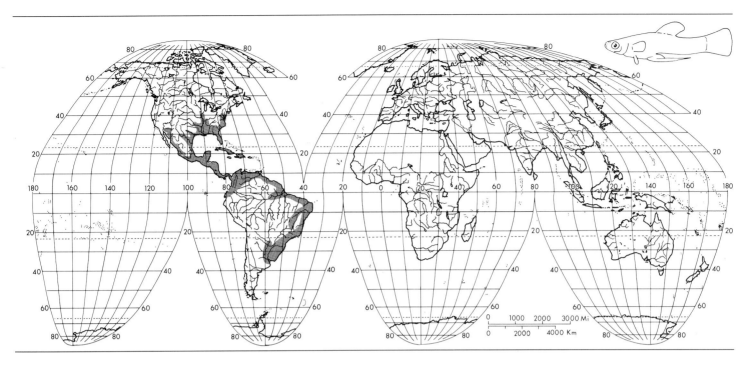

CLASS: Osteichthyes
SUBCLASS: Actinopterygii
SUPERORDER: Atherinomorpha

ORDER: Atheriniformes
SUBORDER: Cyprinodontoidei
(2d) FAMILY: **POECILIIDAE**—livebearers
(pē'-sĭ-lĭ'-ĭ-dē) [pē-sĭ-lĭ'-ĭ-dē]

The viviparous topminnows are known from southeastern United States, Mexico, Central America, and South America to Río de la Plata. A considerable degree of salt tolerance has allowed the spread of these secondary-division fishes to some West Indian islands. The livebearers range in size from 1.5 to 15 cm, and, in fact, the least killifish, *Heterandria formosa*, of the southeastern United States may be the smallest live-bearing vertebrate in the world. There are 21 genera and about 160 species, with the greatest diversity in Central and tropical America. Diversity declines as one proceeds north to the United States or south to Argentina. The mosquitofish, *Gambusia affinis*, from the southeast United States, has been introduced around the world as a mosquito control agent and can be collected in streams in Australia and even New Guinea (Glucksman, West, and Berra 1976), as can the guppy, *Poecilia reticulata*, which is an aquarium escapee.

Internal fertilization and sperm storage are the rule in this family. Males transmit spermatophores (the only other fish family to have sperm encased in a spermatophore is the Horaichthyidae) via their gonopodium, which is formed from modified anal fin rays. Females are able to store sperm over 10 months, and several successive broods may be fertilized from 1 mating. Some forms exist as all-female "species" (*Poecilia formosa*) and utilize males of closely related spe-

cies, the sperm of which stimulates egg cleavage but does not contribute to inheritance. Sex reversals have been reported in this family. Breder and Rosen (1966) have details and references to the variety of poeciliid reproductive habits. Males are usually more colorful than females (for example, guppies); have larger, more ornate fins (for example, *P. latipinna*); or have additional secondary sexual characteristics (for example, swordtails, genus *Xiphophorus*). These characteristics have attracted the attention of aquarists and have made the Poeciliidae one of the most important families in the aquarium industry. *Xiphophorus* has been an important laboratory animal in genetic research. See Sterba (1966) and Hoedemann (1974) for aquarium information and Breder and Rosen (1966), Moore, Miller, and Schultz (1970), and Schultz (1973) for references to reproduction. Rosen and Bailey (1963) have presented a thorough monograph on the osteology, zoogeography, and systematics of the Poeciliidae, and Rosen (1975, 1978) has used the distribution patterns of this family as an example of vicariance.

Map references: Eigenmann and Allen 1942, Gery 1969, Hoedeman 1974*, Innes 1966*, Miller 1966, Myers 1938, Nelson 1976*, Pflieger 1971*, Rosen 1975*, 1978*, 1979*, Rosen and Bailey 1963*, Whitaker 1968*.

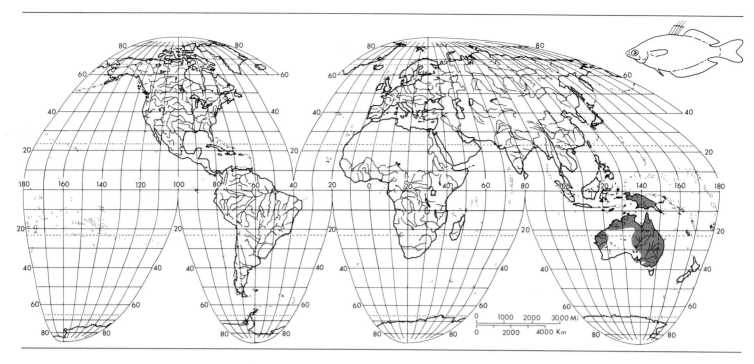

Class: Osteichthyes
   Subclass: Actinopterygii
      Superorder: Atherinomorpha

Order: Atheriniformes
   Suborder: Atherinoidei
      (2d) **Family:** **MELANOTAENIIDAE**—rainbow fishes [mĕ-lă-nō-tē′-nĭ-ĭ-dē]

Melanotaeniids are small (5–18 cm), colorful fishes of Australia and New Guinea. They do not occur west of Weber's line, nor do they reach the Bismarck Archipelago or the Solomon Islands to the east. There are approximately 6 genera and 40 species, with *Melanotaenia* and *Nematocentris* having the most species. They are compressed fishes with large scales and no lateral line. There are 2 dorsal fins; the first is much shorter than the second and may have filamentous rays in older individuals. The anal fin is long. Dorsal and anal fins have a spine. The mouth is small, usually terminal, and studded with fine conical teeth. Melanotaeniids are useful in mosquito control, and are being utilized by tropical fish hobbyists. See Munro (1967), Lake (1971), and McDowall (1980) for more details and a list of species. Allen (1980) has revised the family.

Map references: Lake 1971, Munro 1967.

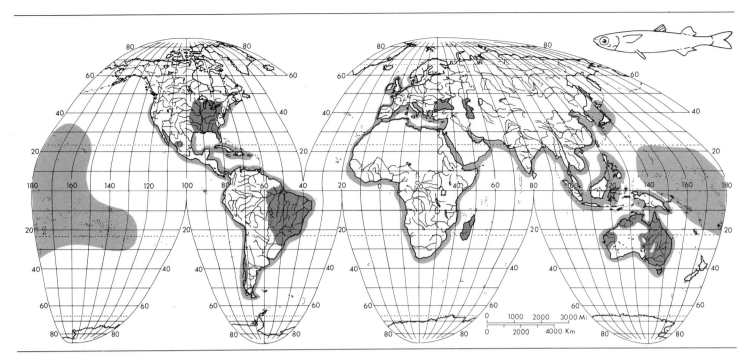

CLASS: Osteichthyes
  SUBCLASS: Actinopterygii
    SUPERORDER: Atherinomorpha

ORDER: Atheriniformes
  SUBORDER: Atherinoidei
    (Per) FAMILY: **ATHERINIDAE**—silversides
    (ăth'-ĕr-ĭn'-ĭ-dē) [ă-thĕ-rī'-nĭ-dē]

The silversides are a worldwide peripheral division family, about half of whose species enter coastal rivers or can be found far inland, especially in eastern North America and Australia. Atherinids are small, silvery, elongate, compressed fishes with a terminal mouth, large eyes, and no lateral line. Two dorsal fins are present, the first of which is very small and has spines. The pelvic fins are abdominal, and the pectorals are high on the body. Silversides are egg layers. Size range is from 5 to 70 cm, but most are less than 15 cm. There are roughly 30 genera and 160 species. *Labidesthes sicculus*, the brook silverside, is common in larger streams and lakes in eastern North America, and 2 species of *Menidia* may also be taken in United States brackish or fresh waters. There are 18 species of *Chirostoma* in the fresh waters of the Mexican plateau. Australia has 6 species in inland waters, most of which are in the genera *Pseudomugil* or *Craterocephalus*. *Odontesthes* is found in fresh water from Brazil to Argentina,

and *Basilichthys* occurs in Andean streams from Peru to Chile. *Bedotia* occupies streams of Madagascar, and *Telmatherina* is found in fresh water on the Celebes.

Atherinids are schooling fishes and are important as forage species. The California grunion, *Leuresthes tenuis*, is well known for its nighttime beach spawning during spring high tides. See Idyll (1969a) for photographs of this striking event. Fossils date from the middle Eocene. See Jordan and Hubbs (1919), Schultz (1948), and Barbour (1973) for taxonomic reviews and McDowall (1980) for information on Australian species.

Map references: Barbour 1973*, Berg 1949, Darlington 1957, Eigenmann 1927, Fowler 1959, Jordan and Hubbs 1919, Kiener and Richard-Vindard 1972, Lake 1971, Maitland 1977*, Miller 1966, Pflieger 1971*, Scott and Crossman 1973*, Schultz 1948, Tinker 1978, Trautman 1957*, Whitaker 1968*, Whitley 1968.

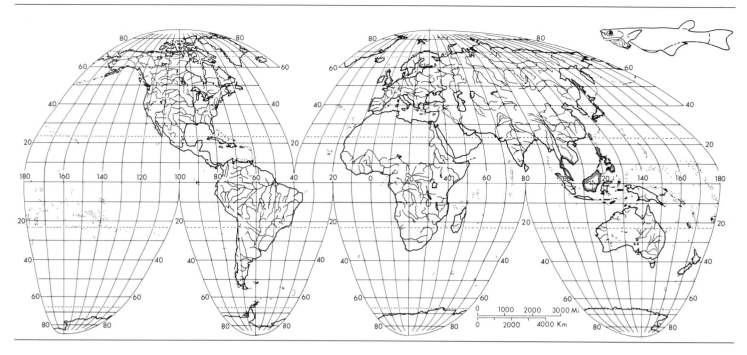

CLASS: Osteichthyes
   SUBCLASS: Actinopterygii
      SUPERORDER: Atherinomorpha

ORDER: Atheriniformes
   SUBORDER: Atherinoidei
      (Per) FAMILY: **NEOSTETHIDAE** [nē-ō-stĕth′-ĭ-dē]

This family is found in coastal waters of Thailand, Malaya, Sumatra, and Borneo and throughout the Philippines. These tiny fishes (2 cm) are closely related to the Phallostethidae. Males possess a copulatory organ called the priapium which is supported by skeletal elements of the first pair of ribs and parts of the pelvic and pectoral girdles. Roberts (1971a) lists 8 genera for this family. See the Phallostethidae for references.

Map references: Herre 1953, Roberts 1971a, b.

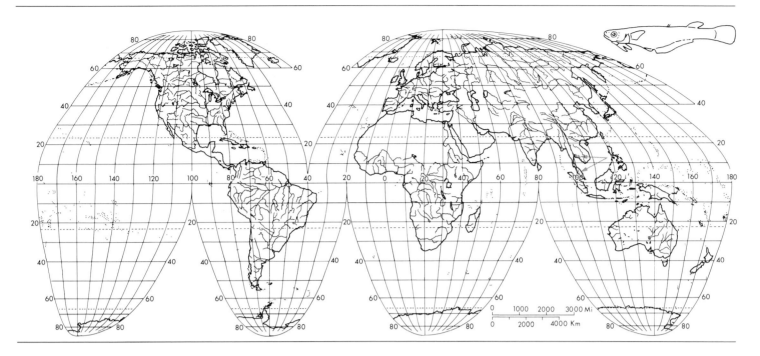

CLASS: Osteichthyes
   SUBCLASS: Actinopterygii
      SUPERORDER: Atherinomorpha

ORDER: Atheriniformes
   SUBORDER: Atherinoidei
      (Per) FAMILY: **PHALLOSTETHIDAE**
      [făl-ō-stĕth'-ī-dē]

These peculiar little fishes (15 cm) are found in fresh and brackish waters of the Malay Peninsula and adjacent southeast Asia. The first dorsal fin is easily overlooked and consists of 1 or 2 short spines. The anal fin is long, and pelvics are absent. A thin keel is present on the abdomen. The most unusual feature is the presence in males of a fleshy appendage called the priapium. It is jugular in position and supported by the head and shoulder girdle. The priapium bears the anus and urogenital openings and also functions as a clasper. In females the vent is located between the pectoral fins. Phallo-stethidae are separated from the closely related Neostethidae by the presence of the toxactinium, part of the bony skeleton of the priapium. Roberts (1971a), lists 2 genera, *Phallostethus* and *Phenacostethus*, and 3 species. Consult Bailey (1936), Herre (1939, 1942), Myers (1935, 1937), Smith (1945) and Roberts (1971a, b) for more details, references, and illustrations.

Map references: Berg 1940, Darlington 1957, Herre 1942, Herre 1953, Roberts 1971a*, Sterba 1966*.

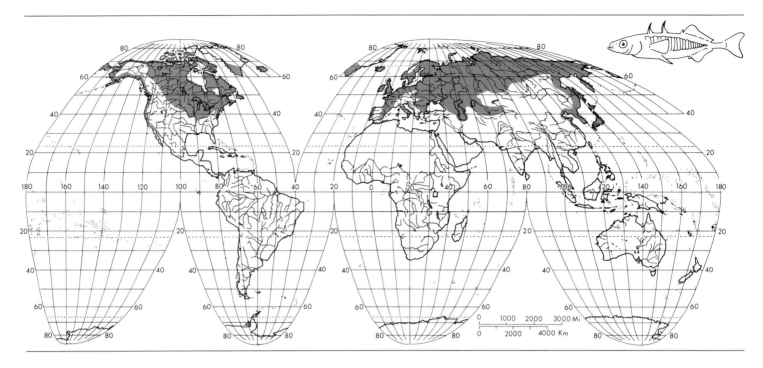

CLASS: Osteichthyes
    SUBCLASS: Actinopterygii
        SUPERORDER: Acanthopterygii

ORDER: Gasterosteiformes
    SUBORDER: Gasterosteoidei
        (Per) FAMILY: **GASTEROSTEIDAE**—sticklebacks
        (găs'-tĕr-ō-stē'-ĭ-dē)

The 5 genera and 8 species of sticklebacks are found in shallow, cool, fresh, and marine waters of the north temperate zone. The common name is derived from the 3–16 individual dorsal spines, each of which has its own membrane. These spines provide a defense mechanism against hungry predators. Pelvic fins also have a stout spine and up to 3 soft rays. A spine precedes the anal fin as well. Most marine species may be heavily armored with bony plates, while freshwater species usually lack plates and scales. The jaws are small and studded with teeth. The caudal peduncle is very narrow. Maximum size is about 15 cm. The elaborate courtship behavior has been well studied. In the threespine stickleback, *Gasterosteus aculeatus*, the ventral surface of the male becomes bright red in breeding season. The male constructs a tubular nest of plant material cemented together with a sticky kidney secretion. The female is lured to the nest and spawns. The male enters, fertilizes the eggs, and tends the eggs and young. He may entice several different females to spawn in the same nest. The fossil record of this family dates to the

middle Miocene of Siberia. See Tinbergen (1952) for a classical study of this instinctive behavior. Other genera include the holarctic *Pungitius* and *Gasterosteus*. The latter even occurs in North Africa. *Spinachia spinachia* is a European marine species, and the brook stickleback, *Culaea inconstans*, is only found in North American fresh waters. *Apeltes quadracus* is found only along the north Atlantic coast of North America. See Scott and Crossman (1973) and Berg (1949) for life histories and references, and Krueger (1961), McPhail (1963), Hagen and McPhail (1970), Nelson (1971), and Bell (1976) for statements of taxonomic problems. For an entire volume on the biology of sticklebacks, consult Wootton (1976).

Map references: Bartholomew, Clarke, and Grimshaw 1911*, Berg 1949, Grzimek 1974*, McPhail and Lindsey 1970*, Maitland 1977*, Meek 1916*, Nelson 1976*, Scott and Crossman 1973*, Trautman 1957*, Whitaker 1968*, Wootton 1976*.

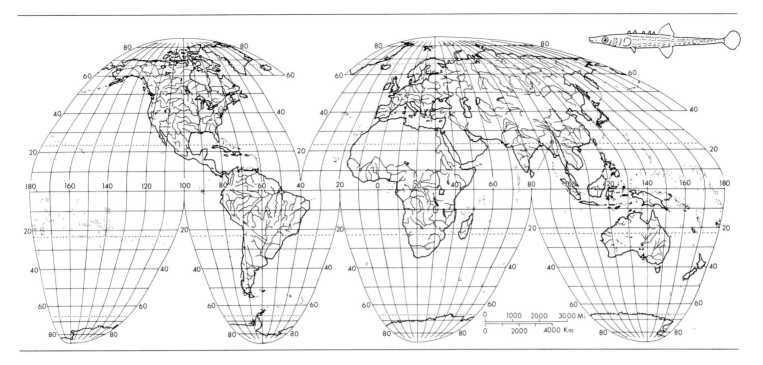

CLASS: Osteichthyes
    SUBCLASS: Actinopterygii
        SUPERORDER: Acanthopterygii

ORDER: Gasterosteiformes
    SUBORDER: Gasterosteoidei
        (Per) FAMILY: **INDOSTOMIDAE** [ĭn-dŏs-tō′-mĭ-dē]

This family is monotypic and consists of *Indostomus para-doxus*, which is found in Lake Indawygi, Burma. This elongate fish has 5 predorsal spines, which resemble those of a stickleback, and a tubelike snout and external bony skeleton, which resembles a pipefish. Little is known about the species. See Prashad and Mukerji (1929) for the original description and Banister (1970) for a recent discussion of anatomy and taxonomy, in which he removed it from the superorder Acanthopterygii and placed it in its own order (Indostomiformes) within the superorder Paracanthopterygii.

Map references: Grzimek 1974*, Prashad and Mukerji 1929.

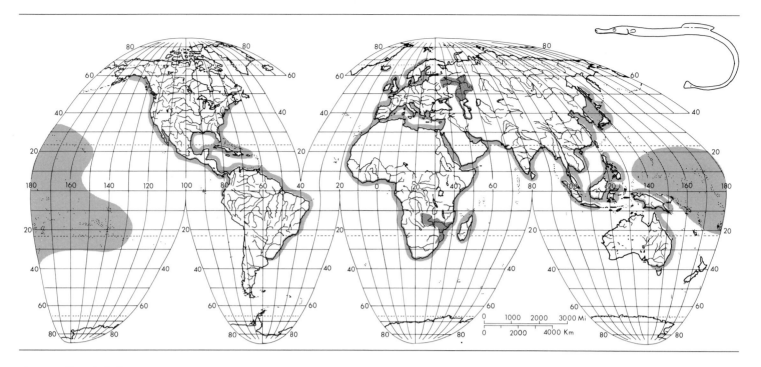

CLASS: Osteichthyes
    SUBCLASS: Actinopterygii
        SUPERORDER: Acanthopterygii

ORDER: Gasterosteiformes
    SUBORDER: Syngnathoidei
        (Per) **FAMILY: SYNGNATHIDAE**—pipefishes and sea horses (sĭng-năth′-ĭ-dē) [sўng-nā′-thĭ-dē]

This family is composed of the sea horses and pipefishes. Some species (all of them pipefishes) enter coastal rivers around the world. For example, the Gulf pipefish, *Syngnathus scovelli*, may occur some distance upstream from Florida to Mexico. There are about 150 species of pipefish, all of which have ringlike plates around their elongated bodies, tiny tubular snouts, and no pelvic fins. Sea horses, of which there are about 24 species, usually do not enter fresh water, although Myers (1979) reported the possible presence of a sea horse from the Mekong River. They resemble pipefishes whose heads have been bent 90° downward. Their tail is prehensile and has no caudal fin. The pipehorse, *Amphelikturus dendriticus* of Bermuda and the Bahamas, has characteristics of both groups. It has a prehensile tail and a caudal fin, and its head is held at a slight angle to the body. In both pipefishes and sea horses, the male incubates the eggs in a brood pouch on the abdomen. Size range of pipefishes is 2.5–45 cm. This suborder dates to the middle Eocene of Italy. See Whitley and Allan (1958), Kahsbauer (1974), and Herald (1962) for popular accounts of members of this family and Dawson (1972, 1978 and papers cited therein) for taxonomic information. Read Herald (1959) for a discussion of the relationship between sea horses and pipefishes.

Map references: Berg 1949, Boulenger 1915, Breder 1929, Clemens and Wilby 1961, Day 1878, Fowler 1934, 1959, Herre 1953, Lake 1971, Maitland 1977*, Miller 1966, Roberts 1975, Smith 1945, Smith 1965, Sterba 1966, Tinker 1978, Wheeler 1969*, Whitaker 1968*, Whitley 1968.

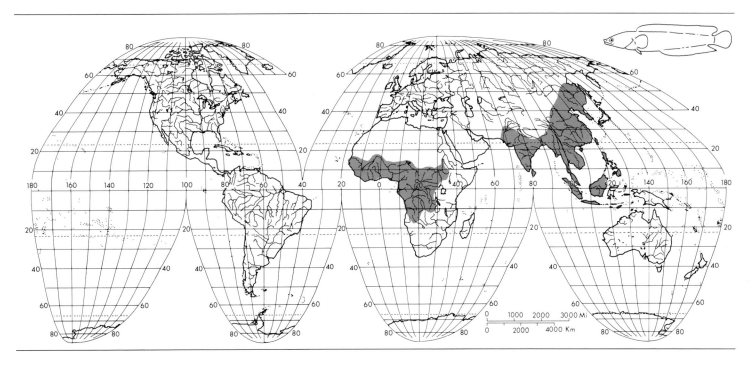

CLASS: Osteichthyes
  SUBCLASS: Actinopterygii
    SUPERORDER: Acanthopterygii

ORDER: Channiformes
  (1st) FAMILY: **CHANNIDAE**—snakeheads [kăn'-nī-dē]

The snakeheads are found in west central Africa, India through southeast Asia to the Philippines, and north to the Amur River. The Channidae is the only family in the order. They are cylindrical with long dorsal and anal fins. The head and mouth are very large, and the anterior nostril is distinctly tubular. The ventral fins are reduced (absent in *Channa*). Snakeheads lack a labyrinth organ; however, these fishes are capable of breathing air via a suprabranchial cavity that communicates with the pharynx. They may remain alive out of water for many hours. This trait makes them suitable for transportation, and live fish may be purchased at markets. The air-breathing ability allows accidental or deliberate introduction of this highly predacious group, which may account for its

eastward encroachment upon Wallace's line. In fact, *Ophicephalus striatus* occurs on the Celebes and as far east as Halmahera, but this presence is probably due to introduction by man (Darlington 1957) and is not shown on the map. The major genus is *Ophicephalus*, and size ranges from 15 cm to 1.2 m. Fossils date to the Pliocene of India and Java. See Smith (1945) for life histories and Nelson (1976) for literature concerning the taxonomic placement of this order.

Map references: Bartholomew, Clarke, and Grimshaw 1911*, Berg 1949, Boulenger 1916, Darlington 1957, Grzimek 1974*, Meek 1916*, Nelson 1976*, Roberts 1975, Sterba 1966*.

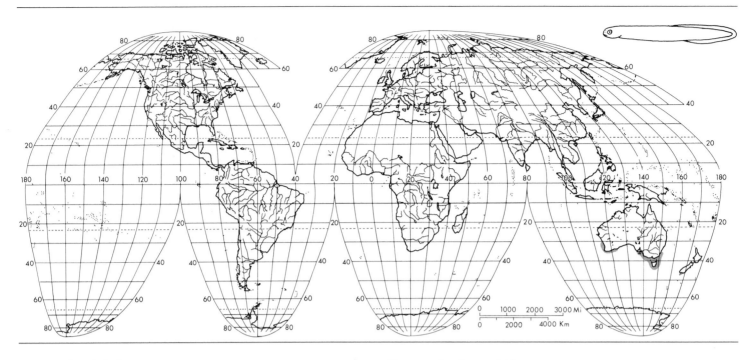

CLASS: Osteichthyes
  SUBCLASS: Actinopterygii
    SUPERORDER: Acanthopterygii

ORDER: Synbranchiformes
  SUBORDER: Alabetoidei
    (Per) FAMILY: **ALABETIDAE**—shore eels
    [ăl-ă-bĕt'-ĭ-dē]

This small family of 4 species is confined to coastal southeast Australia, Tasmania, and Western Australia, although Mc-Culloch (1929) incorrectly lists India and northwest Australia as well. These fishes are small (5–10 cm) and eellike. There is only a single gill opening on the ventral surface, and the body is scaleless. The dorsal, caudal, and anal fins are joined, and paired fins are absent. *Alabes* (formerly *Cheilobranchus*) is the only genus. Rosen and Greenwood (1976) think that *Alabes* is more closely related to blennylike fishes than to syn-branchids. On the other hand, Springer and Fraser (1976) presented cogent osteological reasons for placing the family, Cheilobranchidae (= Alebetidae) in synonymy with the Gobiesocidae. Alabetids are found in shallow rock pools. See Munro (1938) and Springer and Fraser (1976) for species descriptions.

Map references: McCulloch 1929, Meek 1916*, Munro 1938, Scott, Glover, and Southcott 1974, Springer and Fraser 1976.

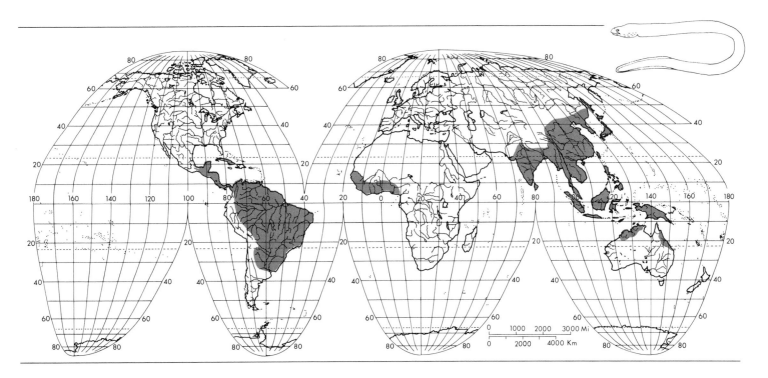

CLASS: Osteichthyes
  SUBCLASS: Actinopterygii
    SUPERORDER: Acanthopterygii

ORDER: Synbranchiformes
  SUBORDER: Synbranchoidei
    (Per) FAMILY: **SYNBRANCHIDAE**—swamp eels
    [sўn-brăn'-kĭ-dē]

The synbranchids are found in fresh and brackish waters in Central and South America, tropical west Africa, and from India east to Australia. Although synbranchids are eellike, they are not related to eels. They lack both pectoral and pelvic fins, and the dorsal and anal fins exist only as a ridge. The left and right gill openings are fused into one opening at throat to mid-body level. Gills may be reduced, but bucco-pharyngeal or intestinal air breathing allows these fish to inhabit stagnant waters. The eyes are very small. Some species may aestivate during drought. There are 4 genera, including *Ophisternon* (6 species) and *Monopterus* (6 species). The genus *Synbranchus*

(2 species) has representatives throughout the family range. The New World *S. marmoratus* reaches 1.5 m. See Rosen and Greenwood (1976) for a phylogenetic review in which they include the Amphipnoidae, consisting of *Amphipnous* (= *Monopterus*) *cuchia*, within the Synbranchidae.

Map references: Bartholomew, Clarke, and Grimshaw 1911*, Boulenger 1915, Darlington 1957, Eigenmann 1909a*, Eigenmann and Allen 1942, Gery 1969, Grzimek 1974*, Lake 1971, Meek 1916*, Miller 1966, Nelson 1976*, Roberts 1975, Rosen 1975*, Rosen and Greenwood 1976, Sterba 1966*.

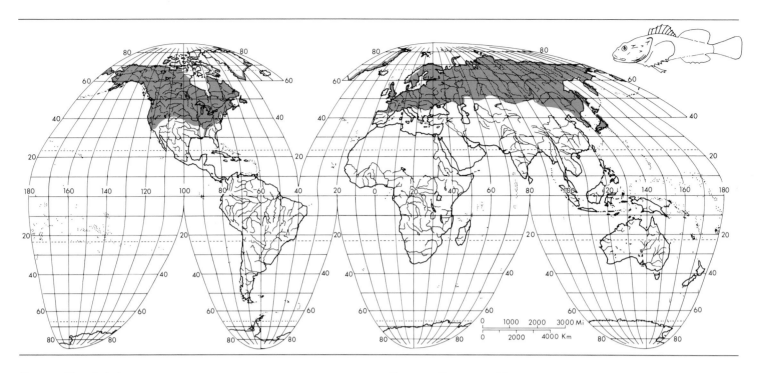

Class: Osteichthyes
   Subclass: Actinopterygii
      Superorder: Acanthopterygii

Order: Scorpaeniformes
   Suborder: Cottoidei
      (Per) **Family**: **COTTIDAE**—sculpins (kŏt′-ĭ-dē)

This family of over 300 species is largely marine; however, the genus *Cottus* is found in the fresh waters of northern North America and northern Eurasia. DeWitt (1969) lists 2 species in the genus *Antipodocottus* from deep water off New Zealand, and Nelson (1976) mentions an Argentinian species. These Southern Hemisphere marine cottids are not represented on the map. The greatest diversity is in the Pacific Northwest, with numbers of species decreasing westward through Eurasia. Cottids are bottom-dwelling fishes with large heads. The preopercular bone bears spines. The first dorsal fin is spiny, and the pectoral fins are fanlike. The body of cottids is usually covered with tubercles with just a few ctenoid scales at the lateral line. A swim bladder is absent. The freshwater species rarely exceed 17 cm, but marine forms may reach 60 cm. Cottids are oviparous. Fossils date back to the Oligocene of Belgium. See Scott and Crossman (1973) and Berg (1949) for life histories, species description, and references.

Map references: Berg 1949, Carl, Clemens, and Lindsey 1959*, Darlington 1957, McPhail and Lindsey 1970*, Maitland 1977*, Meek 1916*, Pflieger 1971*, Scott and Crossman 1973*, Trautman 1957*, Wheeler 1969*, Whitaker 1968*, Williams and Robins 1970*.

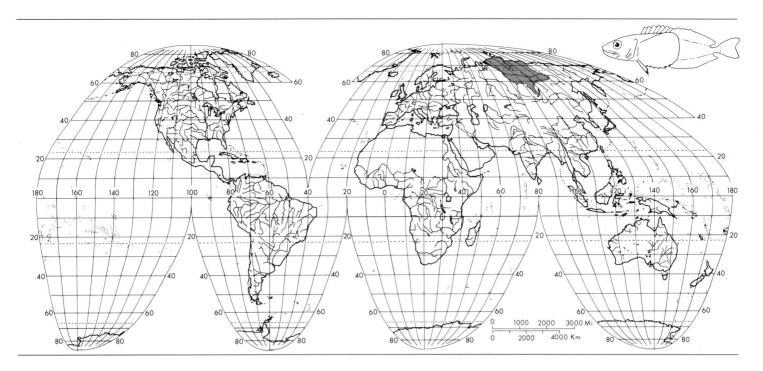

CLASS: Osteichthyes
  SUBCLASS: Actinopterygii
    SUPERORDER: Acanthopterygii

ORDER: Scorpaeniformes
  SUBORDER: Cottoidei
    (Per) FAMILY: **COTTOCOMEPHORIDAE**
      [cŏt-tō-cō-mē-fōr′-ĭ-dē]

This family of about two dozen species in 8 genera is primarily found in Lake Baikal, but several species are also in the Lena and Yenisei rivers. They are similar to cottids except that the postclavicular bone is absent or rudimentary. The genus *Cottocomephorus* feeds in open waters, whereas the other genera are sculpinlike bottom feeders. Lake Baikal is famous for its high degree of endemism (Kozhov 1963), and the cot-tocomephorids represent a good example of an endemic freshwater fauna derived from marine ancestors via adaptive radiation. See Berg (1949) for species descriptions and life histories, and Brooks (1950) for more on speciation in lakes.

Map references: Berg 1949, Darlington 1957.

127

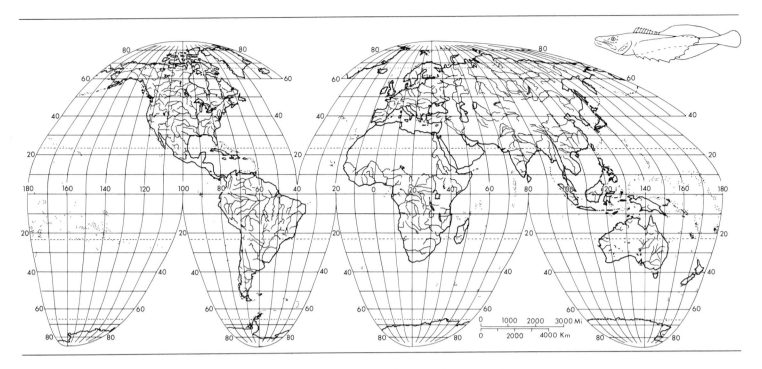

CLASS: Osteichthyes
  SUBCLASS: Actinopterygii
    SUPERORDER: Acanthopterygii

ORDER: Scorpaeniformes
  SUBORDER: Cottoidei
    (Per) FAMILY: **COMEPHORIDAE** [cō-mē-fōr'-ī-dē]

The 2 known species of comephorids are endemic to Lake Baikal. These fishes are scaleless and less than 20 cm long. The pelvic fins are absent, although portions of the pelvic girdle remain. The pectoral fins are extremely large, and the head has well developed sensory pores. *Comephorus baicalensis* and *C. dybowskii* prefer deep water, 750 and 1000 m, respectively. *C. baicalensis* undertakes a diurnal vertical mi-

gration ascending to within 10 m of the surface at night. These fishes give birth to live young, and there is a strange imbalance in the ratio of males to females (1:24), according to Wheeler (1974). See Kozhov (1963) and Berg (1949) for details and references.

Map references: Berg 1949.

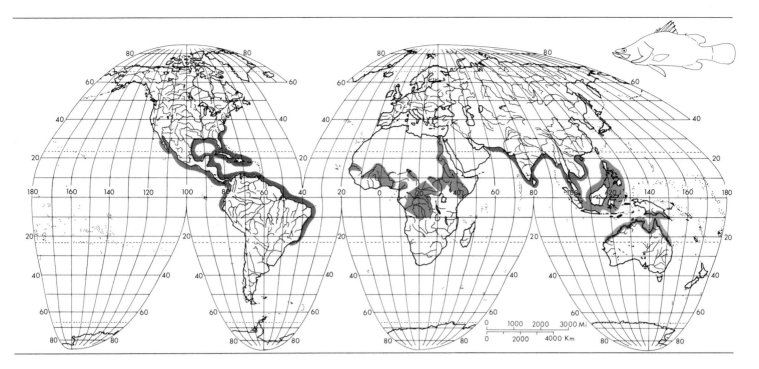

Class: Osteichthyes
  Subclass: Actinopterygii
    Superorder: Acanthopterygii

Order: Perciformes
  Suborder: Percoidei
    (Per) **Family: CENTROPOMIDAE**—snooks, giant perches (sĕn-trō-pŏm'-ĭ-dē)

This family, related to the Serranidae, has recently been defined by Greenwood (1976). It includes 9 species of *Centropomus* from the coastal waters of the New World. *C. undecimalis* is a familiar American species that ascends rivers from Florida to Brazil and can grow to 22.5 kg. A second subfamily, Latinae, includes 8 species of *Lates* and *Psammoperca waigiensis*. The latter, plus *L. calcarifer*, are widely distributed in coastal waters of the Indo-Pacific, whereas the other 7 species of *Lates* are African. The African distribution of *Lates* includes the Nile, Congo, Niger, Volta, and Senegal rivers, as well as lakes Tanganyika, Albert, Chad, and Rudolf (Midgley 1968). The African species breed in fresh water and have been introduced into other lakes, whereas the Australian species requires a spawning migration into salt walter (Lake

1971). Some species, such as *L. niloticus*, can reach 180 cm and 140 kg. *L. calcarifer* is called barramundi in Australia and New Guinea and is widely sought as a food fish. All members of this family except one have the lateral line extending to the posterior margin of the caudal fin, and the neural spine of the second vertebra is expanded. Fossil centropomids date to the Eocene. Consult Greenwood (1976), Midgley (1968), and Lake (1971) for further information and references. Freihofer and Lin (1974) gave an overview of the order, Perciformes.

Map references: Boulenger 1915, Day 1878, Greenwood 1976*, Grzimek 1974*, Herre 1953, Lake 1971, La Monte 1952, Midgley 1968, Miller 1966, Munro 1967, Smith 1945.

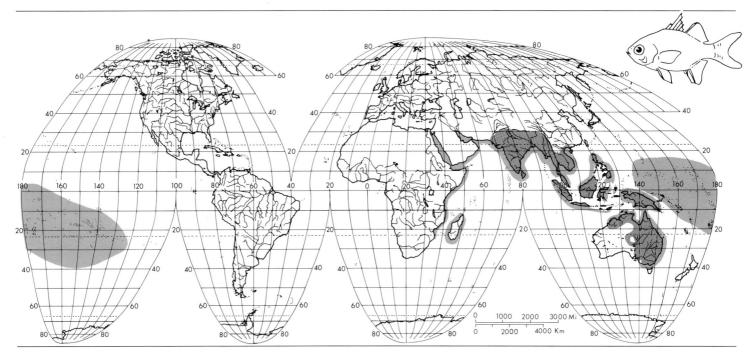

CLASS: Osteichthyes
   SUBCLASS: Actinopterygii
      SUPERORDER: Acanthopterygii

ORDER: Perciformes
   SUBORDER: Percoidei
      (Per) FAMILY: **AMBASSIDAE**—glass perches
      (ăm-băs'-ĭ-dē)

This family of small, perchlike fishes has, until recently, been lumped in a heterogenous assemblage with the large snooks and giant perches. Greenwood (1976) removed the Ambassidae from the Centropomidae because the lateral line of *Chanda* (= *Ambassis*) does not extend far onto the caudal fin and the neural spine of the second vertebra is not expanded. There has been much confusion over the use of *Chanda* versus *Ambassis*, and this is detailed by Smith (1945). Members of this family continue to be listed under Centropomidae, Ambassidae, or Chandidae.

This mostly marine family of about 24 species, called glass perches because of their translucency, is distributed from the east coast of Africa through India, and from Southeast Asia to New Guinea and Australia. They are small schooling fishes of estuaries and fresh water. Some have found their way into the aquarium trade. Most are under 15 cm, but *Parambassis gulliveri* of Australia and New Guinea may reach 30 cm.

Map references: Day 1878, Fowler 1959, Herre 1953, Kiener and Richard-Vindard 1972, Lake 1971, Munro 1967, Smith 1945, Smith 1965, Sterba 1966.

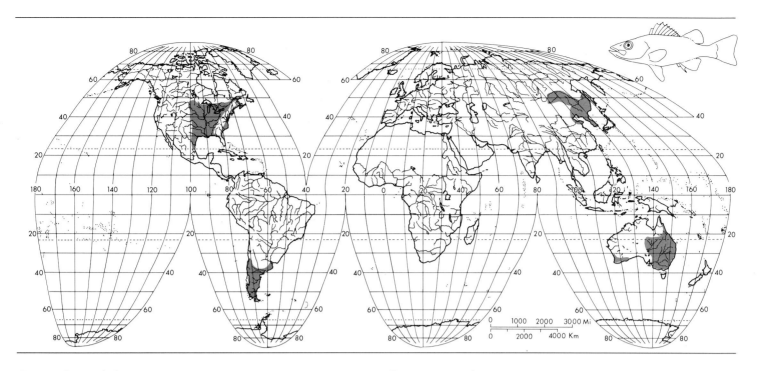

CLASS: Osteichthyes
    SUBCLASS: Actinopterygii
        SUPERORDER: Acanthopterygii

ORDER: Perciformes
    SUBORDER: Percoidei
        FAMILY: **PERCICHTHYIDAE**—percichthyids
        [pĕrs-ĭk-thē′-ĭ-dē]

This family of about 5 genera inhabits fresh waters of North America, Argentina, Chile, Asia, and eastern Australia. Gosline (1966) made the case for separating these freshwater basal percoids from the specialized marine serranids, but their taxonomy remains to be clarified. Percichthyids are typical perciform fishes with spiny fins. They have an anteriorly bilobed swim bladder, while serranid gas bladders are rounded at both ends. The dorsal fins are usually distinct or deeply notched, and the spiny portion has a longer base than the soft portion. The anal fin typically bears 3 spines. There are 1 or 2 opercular spines, whereas many serranids have 3. The mouth is large and has well developed teeth. The pelvic fins are composed of 1 spine and 5 soft rays positioned far forward on the body. Some dorsal and anal rays have pterygiophores divided into 3 bony parts, while in many serranids there are only 2 parts. The lateral line is well developed. There are about three dozen freshwater species. Some examples in-

clude the 4 species of *Morone* of eastern North America, *Percichthys* from South America, *Siniperca* from the Amur River, and 7 species in 3 genera from Australia (*Bostockia, Macquaria,* and *Maccullochella*). The latter genus reaches 68 kg and may even go as high as 114 kg (Berra and Weatherley 1972). MacDonald (1978) revised the Australian genera and reexamined Gosline's (1966) familial characters. This family contains many important food and sport fishes. See Scott and Crossman (1973), Eigenmann (1927), Berg (1949), Lake (1971) and McDowall (1980) for more details and references.

Map references: Bartholomew, Clarke, and Grimshaw 1911*, Berg 1949, Berra and Weatherley 1972*, Eigenmann 1927, Grzimek 1974*, Kiener and Richard-Vindard 1972, Lake 1971, Nichols 1943, Pflieger 1971*, Scott and Crossman 1973*, Wheeler 1969*, Whitaker 1968*, Whitley 1968.

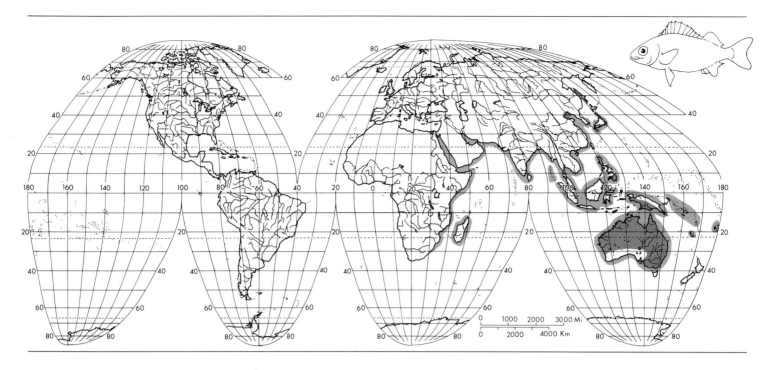

CLASS: Osteichthyes
   SUBCLASS: Actinopterygii
      SUPERORDER: Acanthopterygii

ORDER: Perciformes
   SUBORDER: Percoidei
      (Per) FAMILY: **TERAPONIDAE**—terapon perches
      [tĕ-ră-pŏn'-ĭ-dē]

This Indo-west Pacific marine family of 15 genera and 37 species extends from the east African coast, and the Red Sea through coastal India, China, Japan, the Malay Archipelago into New Guinea and Australia. In the absence of primary division fishes in Australia, the teraponids have invaded fresh water, and many species can be found in Australia and New Guinea. There are also freshwater species in Japan, the Philippines, and the Celebes.

These compressed, oblong perchlike fishes are of small to moderate size (65–800 mm) and have 2 spines on the operculum. The dorsal fin is fairly deeply notched, and a scaled sheath is present at the base of the spinous dorsal and anal fin. Ctenoid scales are present. Some species emit a grunting noise produced by extrinsic swimbladder muscles which vibrate the resonant transversely divided swim bladder. The Australian *Bidyanus bidyanus* is one of the few freshwater fishes that lay planktonic eggs. Several teraponids are important game fishes in Australia. Many references spell the family name "Theraponidae." Vari (1978) in his comprehensive review of the family explained that, although *Terapon* is an incorrect transliteration, it is the original spelling and must apply to both generic and familiar names. See Lake (1971), Munro (1967), and McDowall (1980) for life histories and species descriptions, and Vari (1978) for a taxonomic revision and zoogeographic information.

Map references: Day 1878, Fowler (1959), Herre 1953, Kiener and Richard-Vindard 1972, Lake 1971, Munro 1967, Smith 1965, Vari 1978*.

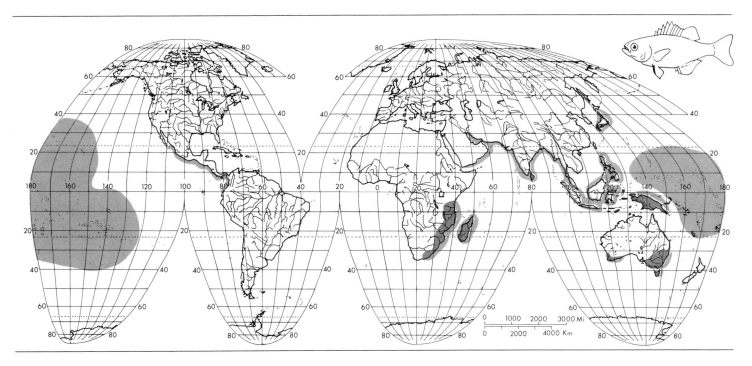

CLASS: Osteichthyes
  SUBCLASS: Actinopterygii
    SUPERORDER: Acanthopterygii

ORDER: Perciformes
  SUBORDER: Percoidei
    (Per) FAMILY: KUHLIIDAE—flagtails [kōō'-lǐ-ǐ-dē]

The flagtails are a marine, Indo-Pacific family found from South Africa and the Red Sea along the Asian coast to New Guinea, Australia, and the Solomon Islands. *Kuhlia taeniura* is the only kuhliid in the eastern Pacific. Most of the dozen or so species are marine, but some inhabit fresh water. *Kuhlia* is the principal genus. These fishes resemble the North American centrarchids in body form. The dorsal fin is single and notched. Both the dorsal and anal fins fold into a scale covered sheath. Scales are large and ctenoid, and the operculum has two spines. Maximum size is about 45 cm. *Nannatherina*

balstoni and *Edelia vittata* occur in southwestern Australia, and *Nanoperca australis* is found in the Murray-Darling system of eastern Australia. Llewellyn (1974) has reported on the natural history of *Nannoperca*, and McDowall (1980) mentions the species from southeastern Australia.

Map references: Boulenger 1915, Day 1878, Fowler 1959, Herre 1953, Kiener and Richard-Vindard 1972, Lake 1971, Llewellyn 1974*, Meek 1916*, Mendis 1954, Munro 1967, Smith 1965, Thomson, Findley, and Kerstitch 1979, Tinker 1978.

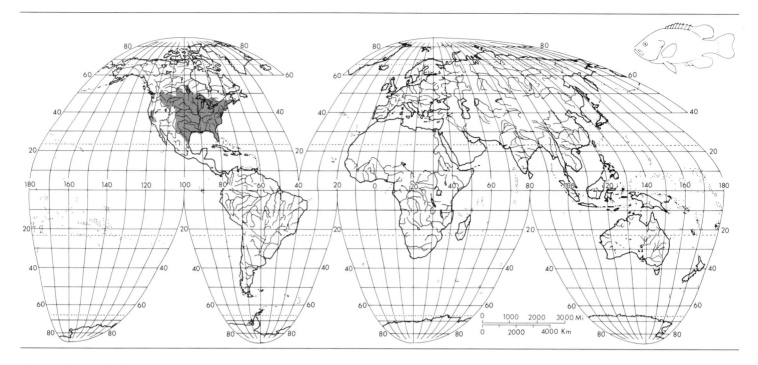

CLASS: Osteichthyes
  SUBCLASS: Actinopterygii
    SUPERORDER: Acanthopterygii

ORDER: Perciformes
  SUBORDER: Percoidei
    (1st) FAMILY: **CENTRARCHIDAE**—sunfishes,
basses (sĕn-trăr'-kĭ-dē)

The centrarchids are autochthonous to North America east of the Rocky Mountains with a disjunct, endemic population of *Archoplites interruptus* in the Sacramento and San Joaquin river systems of California. There are 32 species and 9 genera, with the sunfishes, *Lepomis* species, being most numerous (11 species), followed by 6 species of basses, *Micropterus*. The centrarchids are important sport fishes and have been introduced to many parts of the world (Europe and Africa for example), and are stocked throughout the United States in farm ponds. These colorful, compressed fishes have the spiny and soft dorsal fin joined but separated by a notch, and the anal spines can number 3–9. Size varies from a few grams and 4 cm for the pygmy sunfishes, *Elassoma*, to over 10 kg and 83 cm for the largemouth bass, *M. salmoides*. Centrarchids, especially within the genus *Lepomis*, readily hybridize with one another and make juvenile identification difficult.

All but the primitive *Archoplites* have elaborate courtship, nest building, and territorial behavior, and occupy a definite home range. Centrarchids feed on insects, crustaceans, and fishes. Fossils date to the Eocene. See Branson and Moore (1962) for a detailed taxonomic study and Scott and Crossman (1973) for a variety of references to this group. Berra and Gunning (1972) summarize home range information, Bennett (1971) and Lagler (1956) provide management details, and Carlander (1977) provides a thorough bibliography of life history references.

Map references: Darlington 1957, Grzimek 1974*, Lagler, Bardach, and Miller 1962*, Meek 1916*, Miller 1958*, 1961*, Moyle 1976, Nelson 1976*, Pflieger 1971*, Rostlund 1952*, Scott and Crossman 1973*, Sterba 1966*, Trautman 1957*, Whitaker 1968*.

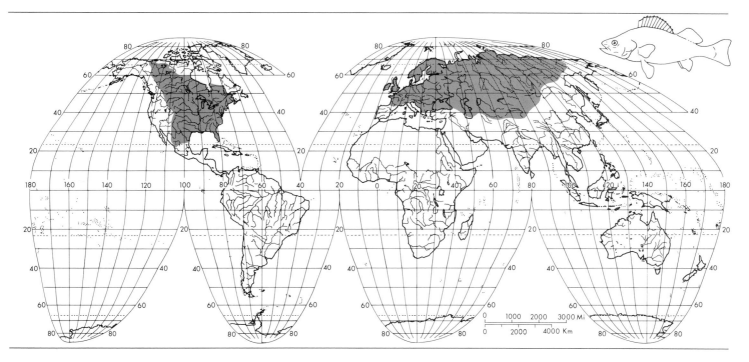

CLASS: Osteichthyes
  SUBCLASS: Actinopterygii
    SUPERORDER: Acanthopterygii

ORDER: Perciformes
  SUBORDER: Percoidei
    (1st) FAMILY: **PERCIDAE**—perch, darters
    (pŭr′-sĭ-dē)

This large family of about 160 species and 9 genera has a holarctic distribution from eastern North America through Europe and northern Asia. Percids are absent from eastern Asia and western North America. The body is elongate and covered with ctenoid scales. The spiny and soft parts of the dorsal fin are not joined, and 1 or 2 anal spines are present. Collette and Banarescu (1977) and Collette et al. (1977) have recently summarized the systematics and biology of this family. There are 2 distinct subfamilies: the Percinae, which has large anal spines, and the Luciopercinae, which has poorly developed anal spines. The Percinae is divided into 2 tribes. The first is the Percini, with 3 genera and 8 species, including *Perca flavescens* in North America and the almost identical *P. fluviatilis* across Eurasia. *P. fluviatilis* has been introduced into Australia, where it has become a pest in stunted, overpopulated situations. The second tribe of the Percinae is the Etheostomatini, with 3 genera of North American darters: *Percina*, 30 valid described species and about 8 undescribed forms; *Ammocrypta*, 7 species; and *Etheostoma*, 84 species with about 17 undescribed forms known (Collette and Banarescu 1977, Jenkins 1976). The Luciopercinae likewise has 2 tribes, Luciopercini with 5 species of *Stizostedion* (walleye, sauger, pikeperch), and the darterlike European Romanichthyini with 2

genera and 4 species. The largest members of this family may grow to 90 cm and 11 kg, while the diminutive darters range in size from about 2.5 to 15 cm. Male darters can be extremely colorful during the breeding season. Two darters, *E. australe* and *E. pottsi*, are recorded from the Chihuahua River (Moore 1968) and the Rio Mezquital (*E. pottsi*, Darlington 1957), which are westward flowing Mexican streams that cross the Tropic of Cancer. This represents the southernmost range for the family. Fossils date to the Eocene, but the family apparently reached North America only relatively recently, possibly not before the Pliocene (Gilbert 1976). See Scott and Crossman (1973) for a bibliography of this family and life histories of some species. Consult Collette (1963, 1967), Collette and Knapp (1966), Williams (1975), Collette and Banarescu (1977), and Collette et al. (1977) for taxonomic information.

Map references: Bartholomew, Clarke, and Grimshaw 1911*, Berg 1949, Collette and Banarescu 1977*, Darlington 1957*, Grzimek 1974*, McPhail and Lindsey 1970*, Maitland 1977*, Meek 1916*, Norman and Greenwood 1975*, Pflieger 1971*, Nelson 1976*, Scott and Crossman 1973*, Rostlund 1952*, Sterba 1966*, Trautman 1957*, Whitaker 1968*.

135

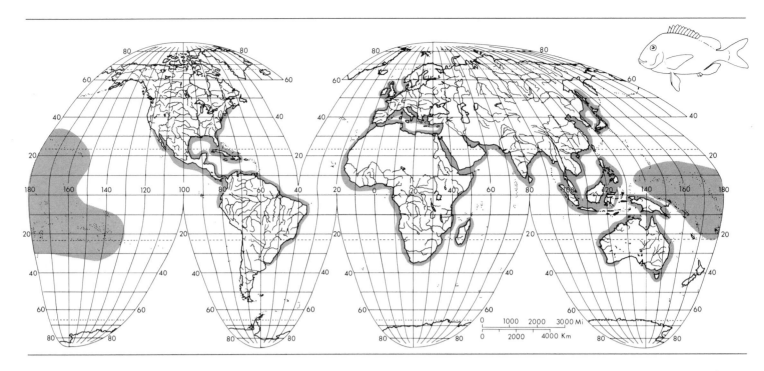

CLASS: Osteichthyes
    SUBCLASS: Actinopterygii
        SUPERORDER: Acanthopterygii

ORDER: Perciformes
    SUBORDER: Percoidei
        (Per) FAMILY: **SPARIDAE**—porgies (spăr′-ĭ-dē)

Sparids are a worldwide marine family with the greatest diversity and endemism in South African coastal waters. A few of the 100-plus species occasionally enter rivers. The size of the deep-bodied, compressed sparids ranges from 30 to 120 cm. They have small mouths with well developed incisors, as well as molariform dentition with which they crush shellfish. The sheepshead, *Archosargus probatocephalus*, ranges from Nova Scotia to Texas and may be taken in fresh water from Florida to Texas. Four species occur in Australian fresh waters near the zone of tidal influence. Porgies are important food and sport fishes and date to the Eocene.

Map reference: Berg 1949, Boulenger 1915, Breder 1929, Fitch and Lavenberg 1971, Fowler 1959, Grzimek 1974*, Herre 1953, Kiener and Richard-Vindard 1972, Lake 1971, Thomson, Findley, and Kerstitch 1979, Tinker 1978, Whitley 1968.

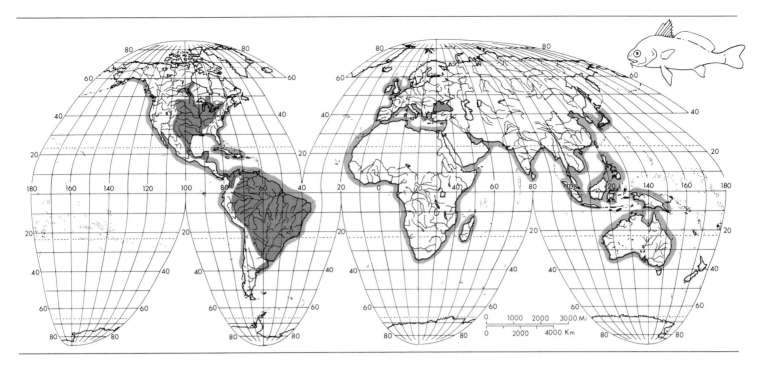

CLASS: Osteichthyes
  SUBCLASS: Actinopterygii
    SUPERORDER: Acanthopterygii

ORDER: Perciformes
  SUBORDER: Percoidei
    (Per) FAMILY: **SCIAENIDAE**—drums and croakers
    (sī-ĕn'-ĭ-dē) [sī-ē'-nĭ-dē]

Sciaenids are a marine family found on the continental shelves of tropical seas and extend into temperate areas. Only a few of the 245 species in 56 genera enter fresh water. The freshwater drum, *Aplodinotus grunniens,* is a wide-ranging species that is entirely confined to the fresh waters of central North America, and *Plagioscion* is a freshwater South American genus. Drums are unusual for perciform fishes in having only 2 anal spines and a lateral line that extends onto the caudal fin as it does in centropomids. The 2 dorsal fins are separate, and 1 or more barbels may be present on the lower jaw. The common name is derived from the fish's ability to make resonating sounds with the swim bladder and its muscles. The resulting underwater noise was a source of confusion to navy sonar operators until its nature was understood. Size range is from 28 to 213 cm, and weights may reach 80 kg. Many of the world's important food fishes are sciaenids. Fossils date to the Upper Cretaceous. Consult Druzhinin (1974) and Trewavas (1977) for a review and discussion of family characters.

Map references: Bartholomew, Clarke, and Grimshaw 1911*, Darlington 1957, Druzhinin 1974*, Eigenmann 1912, Eigenmann and Allen 1942, Grzimek 1974*, Lake 1971, Miller 1966, Pflieger 1971*, Scott and Crossman 1973*, Trautman 1957*, Whitaker 1968*.

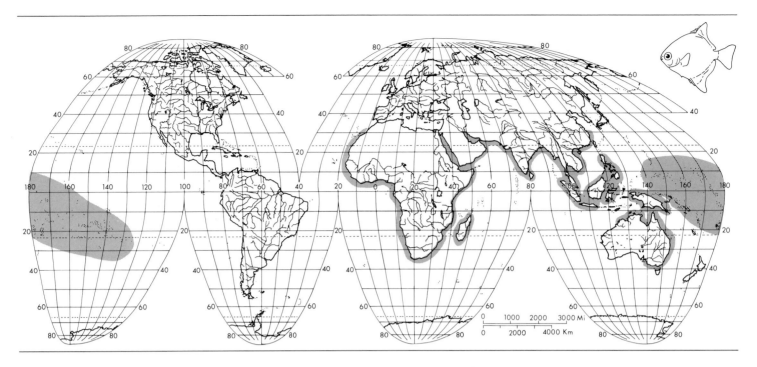

CLASS: Osteichthyes
  SUBCLASS: Actinopterygii
    SUPERORDER: Acanthopterygii

ORDER: Perciformes
  SUBORDER: Percoidei
    (Per) FAMILY: **MONODACTYLIDAE**—batfishes
    (mŏn'-ō-dăk'-tĭl'-ĭ-dē)

These marine fishes are found in coastal waters from tropical west Africa to Australia. There are only about 5 species, and some of these enter fresh water, such as *Monodactylus falciformis* from South Africa and *M. argenteus* in Australia. Monodactylids are small, 23 cm at most, with an almost disc-shaped body. The dorsal and anal fins are undivided and long. The pelvics are rudimentary. The mouth is small and protractile. The tiny ctenoid scales of the highly compressed body extend into the fins, and the lateral line is arched.

Map references: Day 1878, Fowler 1959, Herre 1953, Lake 1971, Smith 1965, Sterba 1966*.

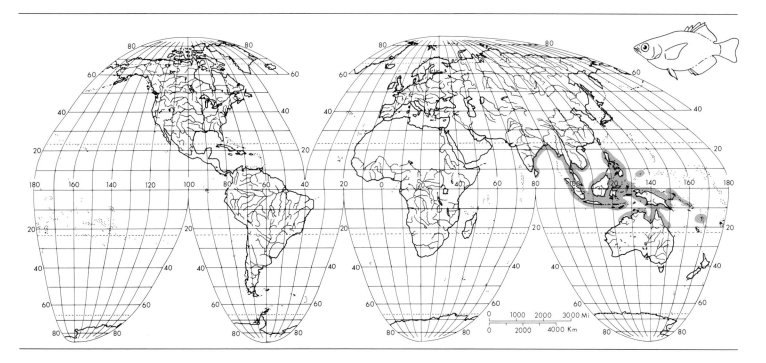

CLASS: Osteichthyes
    SUBCLASS: Actinopterygii
        SUPERORDER: Acanthopterygii

ORDER: Perciformes
    SUBORDER: Percoidei
        (Per) FAMILY: **TOXOTIDAE**—archer fishes
        (tŏks-ŏt'-ĭ-dē)

This small family of 1 genus and 6 species is found in coastal and fresh waters from India to Australia. Some species of *Toxotes* can be found many kilometers upstream (Berra, Moore, and Reynolds 1975) and probably breed in fresh water. Their compressed body shape is rather rhomboidal, with a straight slope from snout to dorsal fin. The spiny and soft dorsal and the anal fin are undivided and posteriorly set. The mouth is large and slanted upward, with the lower jaw protruding. These fishes are known for their remarkable ability to "shoot down" insects from vegetation overhanging the water surface. This ability was first explained by Smith (1936). *T. jaculator*, the most widespread species, has a palatine groove that, together with the tongue, forms a tube through which water drops are forcefully ejected by strong compression of the opercula. *Toxotes* can accurately hit an insect 1.6 m above the water's surface. When the prey is knocked into the water, it is quickly devoured. Archer fishes reach 25 cm in length and feed on crustaceans, insect larvae, and other food in addition to what they can shoot into the water. See Smith (1936, 1945) for more absorbing details of this unique mode of existence. Herald (1962) includes action photographs, and Lake (1971) reported that his cigarette was extinguished from 90 cm by an aquarium based *Toxotes*. Allen (1978) reviewed the family and provided keys and photographs. Fossils of this family date back to the Lower Tertiary.

Map references: Allen 1978*, Darlington 1957, Grzimek 1974*, Herre 1953, Hoedeman 1974*, Lake 1971, Meek 1916*, Munro 1967, Nelson 1976*, Smith 1945, Sterba 1966*.

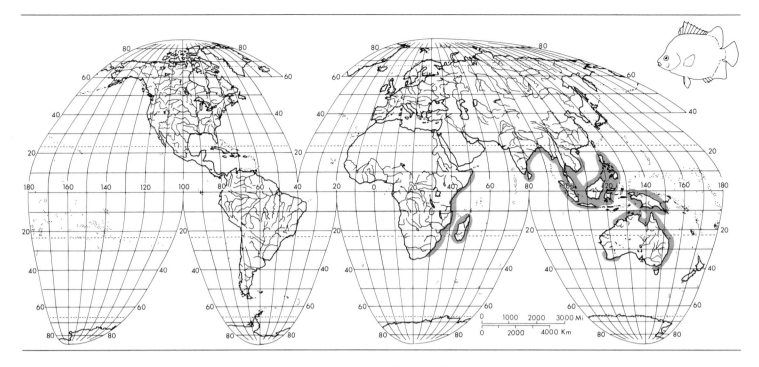

CLASS: Osteichthyes
    SUBCLASS: Actinopterygii
        SUPERORDER: Acanthopterygii

ORDER: Perciformes
    SUBORDER: Percoidei
        (Per) FAMILY: **SCATOPHAGIDAE**—scats
        [scă-tō-fāj'-ĭ-dē]

This marine family of about 6 species in 2 genera is found along the east African coast and from the Indian coast eastward to Australia and New Guinea. Scats are coastal fishes that freely enter fresh water. The generic name, *Scatophagus*, means "feces feeder"; however, these scavengers eat a variety of decaying organic matter and, in turn, constitute an item in human diets. Scats have a quadrangular, deep, compressed body with tiny ctenoid scales that cover the dorsal and anal fins. The dorsal fin is deeply notched, and the anal fin has 4 spines. The larval stage has a bony head covering, which is lacking in adults. Maximum size is around 40 cm. Fossils date to the Eocene.

Map references: Grzimek 1974*, Herre 1953, Kiener and Richard-Vindard 1972, Lake 1971, Munro 1967, Nelson 1976, Smith 1965, Sterba 1966*.

140

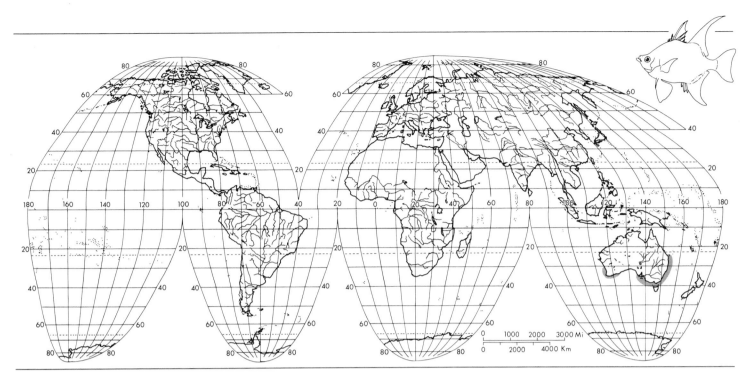

CLASS: Osteichthyes
   SUBCLASS: Actinopterygii
      SUPERORDER: Acanthopterygii

ORDER: Perciformes
   SUBORDER: Percoidei
      (Per) FAMILY: **ENOPLOSIDAE**—old wife
      [ē-nō-plō′-sĭ-dē]

This marine family is monotypic and consists of *Enoplosus armatus*, which is found in schools near rocky foreshores and jetties along Australia's south and east coast. It occasionally enters fresh water. These fishes reach 25 cm and are edible. The deep body is compressed, and the snout is pointed and bears a small mouth. The pelvic fins are large and located anteriorly. Both dorsal fins and the anal fin are elevated, with the 2 separate dorsal fins borne on 2 camellike humps. See Coleman (1974) for a color illustration. Fossils date to the Eocene.

Map references: Lake 1971, Scott, Glover, and Southcott 1974.

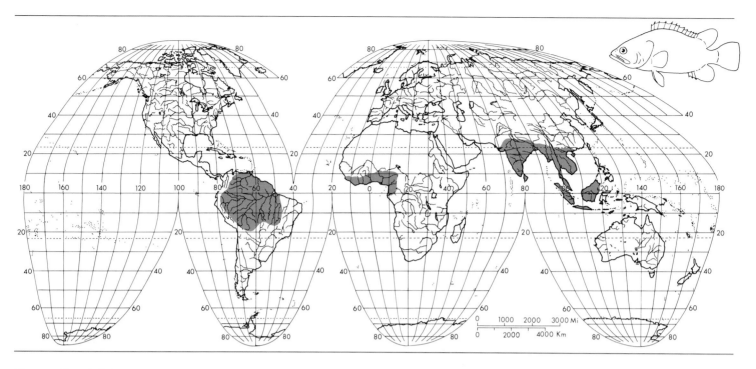

CLASS: Osteichthyes
  SUBCLASS: Actinopterygii
    SUPERORDER: Acanthopterygii

ORDER: Perciformes
  SUBORDER: Percoidei
    (1st) FAMILY: **NANDIDAE**—leaffishes (năn'-dĭ-dē)

Nandids are a primary division freshwater fish family with a tropical distribution in northern South America, west central Africa, and India to Borneo. There may be up to 7 genera and about 10 species. There are 1 or 2 endemic genera in each of the Neotropical (*Polycentrus, Monocirrhus*), Ethiopian (*Polycentropsis*), and Oriental (*Nandus, Badis*) regions. Another genus is the oriental *Pristolepis*, which some ichthyologists place in a separate family, the Pristolepidae (Barlow, Liem, and Wickler 1968, Gosline 1971). This interesting pattern of distribution could reflect a connection between the southern continents. The present assemblage is but a remnant of a once wider distribution. Nandids have an enormous, widely protrusible mouth and can "inhale" prey fishes two-thirds to three-fourths their own size. Their compressed body form and camouflage coloration resemble a leaf, and some species can advance toward potential prey with their head at a downward angle without any apparent fin movement. The dorsal fin is very long, with the spiny and soft portions joined. Size ranges from 6 to 25 cm, and these attractive fishes with interesting behavior are popular with tropical fish hobbyists. See Liem (1970) for a study of functional anatomy, Sterba (1966) and Hoedeman (1974) for aquarium care information and illustrations, and Nelson (1976) for classification.

Map references: Bartholomew, Clarke, and Grimshaw 1911*, Boulenger 1915, Darlington 1957, Gery 1969, Grzimek 1974*, Hoedeman 1974*, Innes 1966*, Meek 1916*, Nelson 1976*, Roberts 1975, Smith 1945, Sterba 1966*.

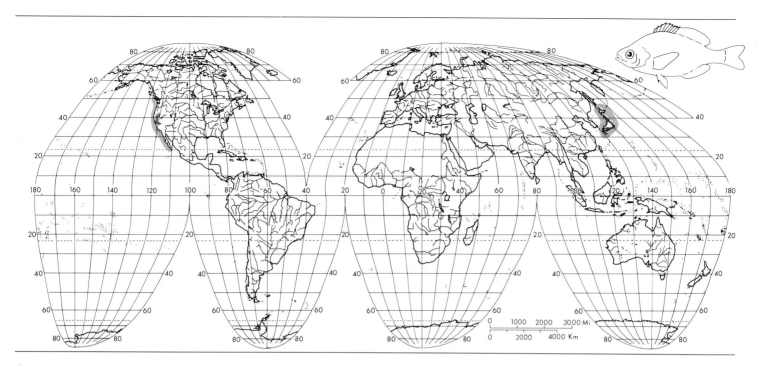

CLASS: Osteichthyes
  SUBCLASS: Actinopterygii
    SUPERORDER: Acanthopterygii

ORDER: Perciformes
  SUBORDER: Percoidei
    (Per) FAMILY: **EMBIOTOCIDAE**—surfperches
    (ĕm'-bĭ-ō-tŏs'-ĭ-dē)

This marine family is found along the Pacific coast of North America from Baja California to Alaska and Japan, although it appears to be absent from the intervening Aleutian Island chain. The greatest species diversity (20 of 23 species) occurs off California, where the group probably originated. The tuleperch, *Hysterocarpus traski*, the only consistently freshwater representative, is found in the Sacramento River drainage in central California, and *Cymatogaster aggregata* enters fresh water from Wrangell, Alaska to Baja California. This family is peculiar in that members give birth to live young. Such viviparity is very unusual among marine fishes. Surfperches may reach 45 cm and have a compressed body. The dorsal fin is long and undivided, and fits into a scaled groove on the side of the fin base. The anal fin is also elongated and modified in males to facilitate sperm transmission. Fossils date to the Miocene. See Hart (1973) for references and life history notes, Breder and Rosen (1966) for references to the unusual mode of reproduction, and Tarp (1952) for a revision of the family.

Map references: Bartholomew, Clarke, and Grimshaw 1911*, Eddy 1969, Hart 1973, Meek 1916, Morrow 1974, Moyle 1976, Rostlund 1952*, Schultz 1936.

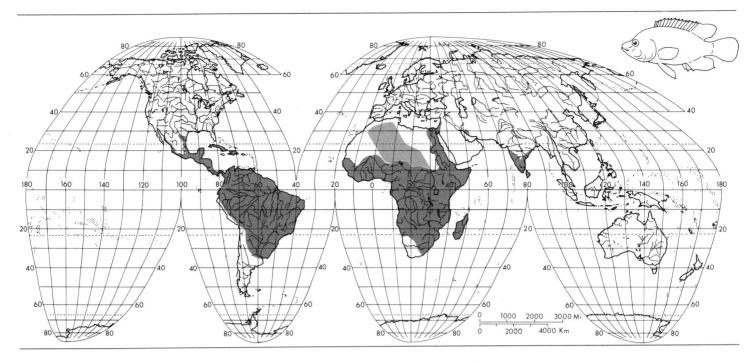

CLASS: Osteichthyes
   SUBCLASS: Actinopterygii
      SUPERORDER: Acanthopterygii

ORDER: Perciformes
   SUBORDER: Percoidei
      (2d) **FAMILY: CICHLIDAE**—cichlids (sĭk'-lĭ-dē)

This secondary division family ranges from the Rio Grande in southern Texas through Mexico, Central America, and South America to Río de la Plata. Cichlids are widely distributed throughout Africa except north of the Atlas Mountains and the extreme southern tip. Cichlids are native to Syria and Palestine, India, and such islands as Cuba, Hispaniola, Madagascar, and Ceylon. They obviously have some salt tolerance, and many are markedly euryhaline. The species diversity of this family is tremendous, especially in the African Great Lakes region, where hundreds of closely related forms occur sympatrically as species flocks. See Brooks (1950), Fryer and Iles (1972), Barbour and Brown (1974), Greenwood (1974), and Brichard (1978) for excellent expositions of this phenomenon. There are at least 700 species of cichlids, with Lake Malawi having more than 200, Lake Victoria 170, and Lake Tanganyika 126. Even more staggering is the fact that all but 4 of the Lake Malawi species are endemic. Of the 170 species from Lake Victoria, all save 6 are endemic, and all 126 Lake Tanganyika species are endemic. This family has members that have radiated to fill all types of niches, including isolated Saharan oases (Roberts 1975).

In the Americas there are about 200 species, only 1 of which (*Cichlasoma cyanoguttatum*) reaches northward into the United States. There is only 1 genus in India and Ceylon, *Etroplus*. Some species, especially those in the genus *Tilapia*, have been introduced into various parts of the world—New

Guinea, for example (Glucksman, West, and Berra 1976). Cichlids resemble centrarchids, which are their ecological equivalents in North America, but cichlids have a single nostril instead of the usual 2. Their lateral line is interrupted, and the spiny dorsal is long and joined to the soft dorsal fin. These fishes have elaborate nest-building, courtship, and parental care rituals. Some species incubate their eggs in their mouth. The South American discus, *Symphysodon discus*, secretes mucus which the young pick from the sides of the adults. Because of their attractive coloration and behavior, many species are imported as aquarium fishes. Other species are extensively pond-cultured for food. Most are small fishes, but some may reach 36 cm and 9 kg. Fossils date to the Eocene. See the above references for life history data and taxonomic information as well as Sterba (1966) for aquarium care and illustrations, Axelrod (1974) for habitat illustrations and color photographs, and Breder and Rosen (1966) for references to reproductive habits. Thompson (1979) published on the cytotaxonomy of 41 species of neotropical cichlids.

Map references: Bartholomew, Clarke, and Grimshaw 1911*, Darlington 1957, Eigenmann 1909a*, 1912*, Eigenmann and Allen 1942, Grzimek 1974*, Hoedeman 1974*, Innes 1966*, Kiener and Richard-Vidnard 1972, Lagler, Bardach, and Miller 1962*, Miller 1966*, Meek 1916*, Nelson 1976*, Norman and Greenwood 1975*, Roberts 1975, Rosen 1975*, Sterba 1966*, Trewavas 1942.

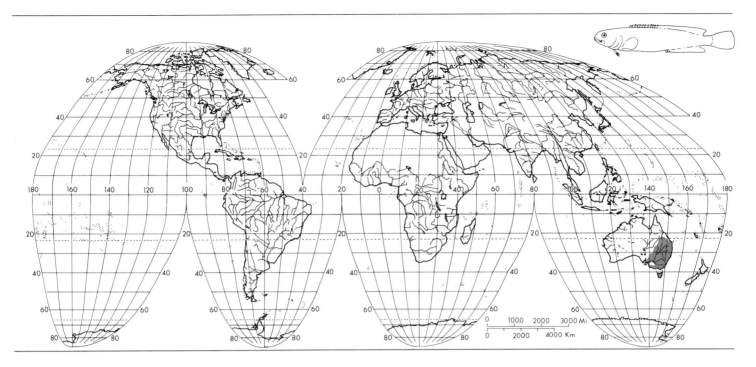

CLASS: Osteichthyes
  SUBCLASS: Actinopterygii
    SUPERORDER: Acanthopterygii

ORDER: Perciformes
  SUBORDER: Percoidei
    (Per) FAMILY: **GADOPSIDAE**—river blackfish
    [gā-dŏp'-sĭ-dē]

The Gadopsidae is restricted to southeast Australia and Tasmania. These unusual, slender percoids have a single long dorsal fin, long anal fin, and cycloid scales. The pelvic fins are reduced to a few rays and are located in the throat region anterior to the pectoral fins. There are, perhaps, 2 species. *Gadopsis marmoratus* is found in the upper reaches of coastal tributaries and the Murray-Darling river system, where gravel beds and snags are present. Its diet consists of insects, crustaceans, and molluscs, and it deposits eggs in hollow logs. It may grow to about 60 cm. A possible Tasmanian species, as yet undescribed, may reach a greater size. See Parrish (1966) for a review of the family, Lake (1971), Scott, Glover, and Southcott (1974), and McDowall (1980) for further information. Jackson (1978) provided information on spawning and early development. Rosen and Patterson (1969) and Gosline (1968) differ on its phylogenetic placement, which may be somewhere near the Blenniidae.

Map references: Lake 1971, Scott, Glover, and Southcott 1974.

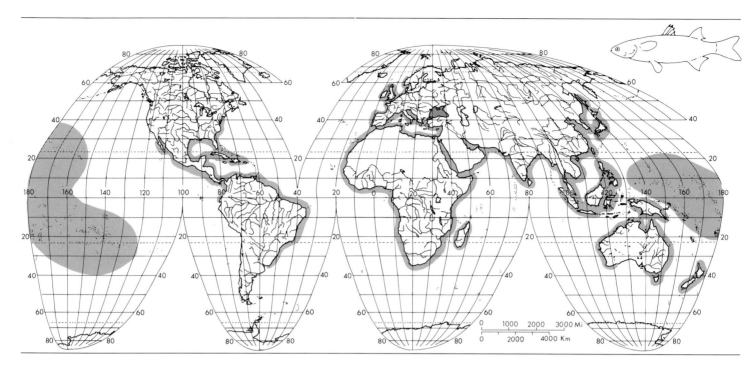

CLASS: Osteichthyes
   SUBCLASS: Actinopterygii
      SUPERORDER: Acanthopterygii

ORDER: Perciformes
   SUBORDER: Mugiloidei
      (Per) FAMILY: **MUGILIDAE**—mullets (mū-jīl'-ī-dē)

This cosmopolitan marine family of about 100 species has several members that enter fresh waters around the world: for example, the mountain mullet of the lower Mississippi Valley and Atlantic coastal streams, *Agonostomus monticola*. The striped mullet, *Mugil cephalus*, is widespread in coastal waters on both the Atlantic and Pacific coasts of the Americas, Europe, Africa, Asia, and Australia. Mullets have the spiny dorsal fin well separated from the soft dorsal. They have a fusiform body shape with adipose eyelids and large cycloid scales. The lateral line may be absent or reduced. Mullets usually travel in lively schools and feed on plankton and detritus which they extract and process from the bottom sedi-

ment via sievelike gill rakers, a gizzardlike stomach, and very long intestinal tract. Adults range in size from 30 to 90 cm and may be of considerable commercial importance. Their fossil record dates back to the Lower Oligocene of France. See Thomson (1964) for a bibliography of systematic references, and Schultz (1946) for a taxonomic review.

Map references: Berg 1949, Boulenger 1916, Eigenmann 1927, Fowler 1959, Grzimek 1974*, Herre 1953, Kiener and Richard-Vindard 1972, Lake 1971, La Monte 1952, Maitland 1977*, Miller 1966, Moore 1968, Smith 1965, Tinker 1978, Whitley 1968.

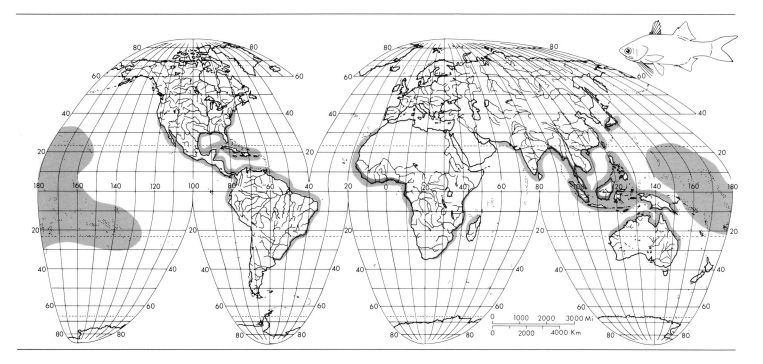

CLASS: Osteichthyes
SUBCLASS: Actinopterygii
SUPERORDER: Acanthopterygii

ORDER: Perciformes
SUBORDER: Polynemoidei
(Per) FAMILY: POLYNEMIDAE—threadfins
(pŏl'-ĭ-nĕm'-ĭ-dē) [pŏ-lē-nē'-mĭ-dē]

This marine family of 7 genera and about 35 nominal species occurs in coastal waters throughout the topics, but the majority of the genera and species are Malayan-oriental. Only a few species enter fresh water. *Polydactylus quadrifilis*, *Galeoides decadactylus*, and *Pentanemus quinquarius* enter African coastal rivers from the Senegal to the Congo, and *Polynemus paradiseus* occurs from Calcutta through Malaya to Bangkok and Sumatra and Borneo.

The threadfins take their name from the fact that the pectoral fin is divided into 2 separate sections. The ventral section consists of several filamentous, unconnected rays, which serve a tactile function. The upper portion of the pectoral fin is normal. There are 2 widely separate dorsal fins, and the caudal fin is deeply forked. The mouth is subterminal, and the teeth are small. Adipose eyelids are present as in mullets and,

along with the elongated pectoral feelers, are adaptations to a murky estuarine habitat. The body is compressed with weakly ctenoid scales, which extend onto the dorsal, anal, and caudal fins. Many species are eaten by man, and isinglass is produced from the swim bladders. Most threadfins are 30–60 cm; however, *Eleutheronema tetradactylum* of India may reach 1.8 m. Fossils date to the Upper Miocene. See Myers (1936) for a synopsis of the genera, and Kagwade (1970) for data on Indian species.

Map references: Boulenger 1916, Day 1878, Fitch and Lavenberg 1971, Fowler 1959, Herre 1953, Kagwade 1970*, Lake 1971, Munro 1967, Myers 1936, Smith 1945, Tinker 1978, Weber and De Beaufort 1922, Wheeler 1975.

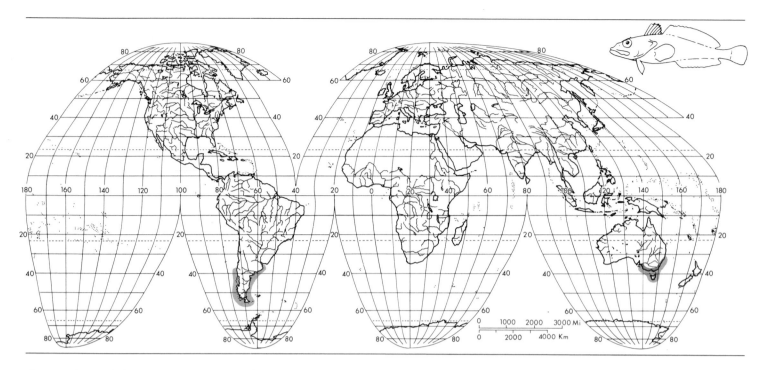

CLASS: Osteichthyes
 SUBCLASS: Actinopterygii
  SUPERORDER: Acanthopterygii

ORDER: Perciformes
 SUBORDER: Notothenioidei
  (Per) FAMILY: **BOVICHTHYIDAE** [bō-vĭk'-thĭ-ĭ-dē]

This coldwater marine family is found along the coasts of southern Chile, Argentina, southeast Australia, Tasmania, and New Zealand. One species, *Pseudaphritis urvilli*, which grows to 35 cm, enters rivers in Australia well above the zone of tidal influence, and Scott, Glover, and Southcott (1974) remark that specimens can be transferred from salt water directly to fresh water without noticeable adverse effects. These fishes have a depressed head and compressed body with a separate spiny and long soft dorsal fin. The anal fin is also elongate, and the pectoral fins are expanded. There are about 6 species in 4 genera.

Map references: Lake 1971, Norman 1966, Whitley 1968.

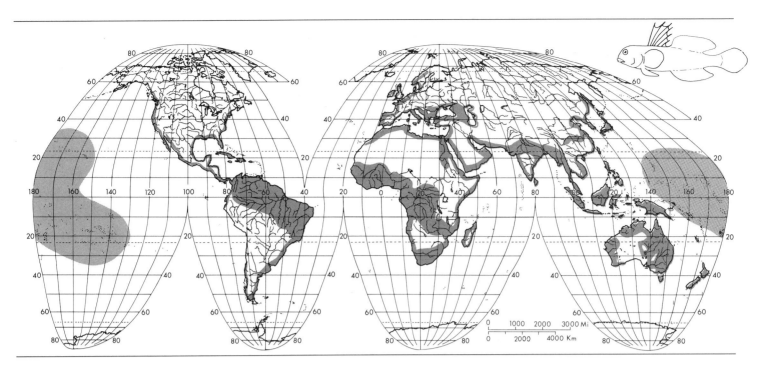

CLASS: Osteichthyes
   SUBCLASS: Actinopterygii
      SUPERORDER: Acanthopterygii

ORDER: Perciformes
   SUBORDER: Gobioidei
      (Per) FAMILY: **GOBIIDAE**—gobies and sleepers
      (gō-bī'-ĭ-dē) [gō-bē'-ĭ-dē]

The gobies are a very large, cosmopolitan, marine family of shallow coastal waters. Some members enter fresh waters and ascend rivers far inland from the sea. Most gobies from fresh or brackish waters have the left and right pelvic fins fused to form a suction disc. Sleepers, or gudgeons, which many authorities place in a separate family, the Eleotridae, do not have fused pelvic fins. In sleepers the base of the second dorsal fin is equal to or shorter than the distance from the end of the second dorsal fin to the base of the caudal fin. In gobies the second dorsal fin base is longer. Gobies (*sensu lato*) are cylindrical and lack a lateral line. The 2 dorsal fins are separate but close together, and are usually rather large, as is the anal fin. Scales may be present or absent. There are about 2,000 species (Birdsong 1975), which certainly makes this group the largest marine family and probably the largest of all fish families, as many gobies remain to be described. There are about 300 species of eleotrids. Most gobies are between 5 and 10 cm; however, the Philippine species *Pandaka pygmaea* is fully grown at 1.5 cm and is the smallest vertebrate known. Sleepers can be quite large, with 1 species reaching 90 cm, and many species are large enough to provide food for humans.

With such a great number of species one expects a concomitant diversity of habits. Some gobies burrow into bottom sand and mud; others live in coral crevices or the cavities of sponges. A few live in burrows dug by crustaceans. Some spawn in fresh water, others return to the sea for spawning, and most never leave the marine environment. Some gobies function as cleaning organisms. See Limbaugh (1961) for a review of cleaning symbiosis and Wickler (1968) for information on the related topic of mimicry in fishes. The Indo-Pacific mudskippers, *Periophthalmus*, which some put in a separate family, the Periopthalmidae, live on mudflats and mangrove swamps and can remain out of water for extended periods while foraging for insects and crustaceans. Some respiration may take place cutaneously and via water retained in the branchial chambers. These fishes may even perch on mangrove roots for elevated basking. See Polunin (1972) for photographs of this remarkable behavior.

Sleepers, such as the American *Dormitator* and the similar Australian *Mogurnda*, exhibit complex courtship behavior, color changes, and nest protection. Some gobies utilize their sucking disk in torrential mountain streams. Fossils date to the Eocene of Europe. See Zander (1974) for a general discussion of the suborder, Breder and Rosen (1966) for reproduction and references, and Sterba (1966) for aquarium information. Herre (1927) provided a major work on gobies.

Map references: Bartholomew, Clarke, and Grimshaw 1911*, Berg 1949, Boulenger 1916, Darlington 1957, Grzimek 1974*, Jubb 1967, Kiener and Richard-Vindard 1972, Lake 1971, Maitland 1977*, McDowall 1978*, Miller 1966, Tinker 1978, Whitaker 1968*, Whitley 1968.

149

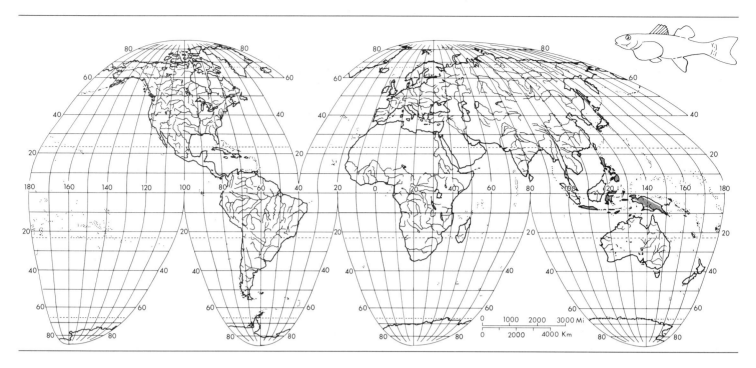

CLASS: Osteichthyes
  SUBCLASS: Actinopterygii
    SUPERORDER: Acanthopterygii

ORDER: Perciformes
  SUBORDER: Gobioidei
    (Per) FAMILY: **RHYACICHTHYIDAE**—loach goby
    [rȳ-ă-sĭk′-thĭ-ĭ-dē]

This monotypic family, composed of *Rhyacichthys aspro*, is found in torrential mountain streams of Java, the Celebes, the Philippines, New Guinea, and the Solomon Islands. Except for the presence of the spiny dorsal fin, *Rhyacichthys* resembles the homalopterid loaches of Asia. The head is flattened dorsally and ventrally, the pectoral fins are long and wide, and the pelvic fins are widely separated. These modifications allow the breast surface to form a broad, flat sucking disc with which the fish attaches to rocks. The 2 dorsal fins are relatively far apart for a gobioid fish. The mouth is small, protractile, inferior, and has fleshy lips. A lateral line is present. Maximum size is about 33 cm. See Herre (1927) for further information.

Map references: Darlington 1957, Herre 1927, Herre 1953, Munro 1967.

150

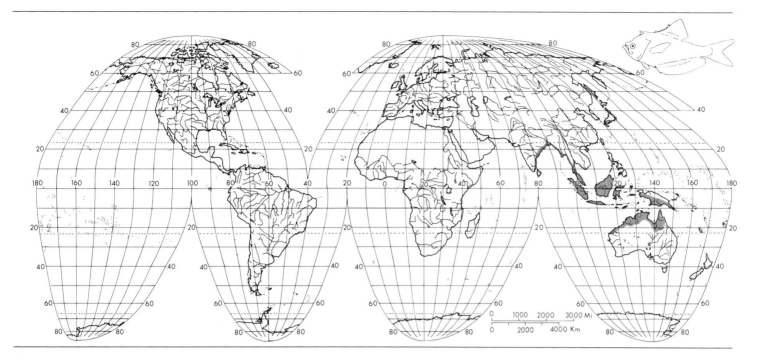

CLASS: Osteichthyes
  SUBCLASS: Actinopterygii
    SUPERORDER: Acanthopterygii

ORDER: Perciformes
  SUBORDER: Kurtoidei
    (Per) FAMILY: **KURTIDAE**—nurseryfishes
    [kŭr'-tĭ-dē]

The 2 species of nurseryfishes occur from the east coast of India into the Malay Archipelago, East Indies, southern New Guinea, and northern Australia. *Kurtus indicus* is Indo-Malayan, and *K. gulliveri* is Australian–New Guinean. Both species inhabit brackish water in large schools and may penetrate into fresh water. Males have an anteriorly pointed hook on top of the head formed from the supraoccipital crest. The eggs are attached at this point and remain until they hatch.

The anal fin is long, and the pelvic fins are thoracic. The dorsal fin is single, and its spines are reduced. The lateral line is short, and the opercular bones are very thin. These carnivorous fishes reach a maximum size of about 60 cm. See Lake (1971) for a color photograph of a male.

Map references: Cantor 1849, Lake 1971, Munro 1955, 1967.

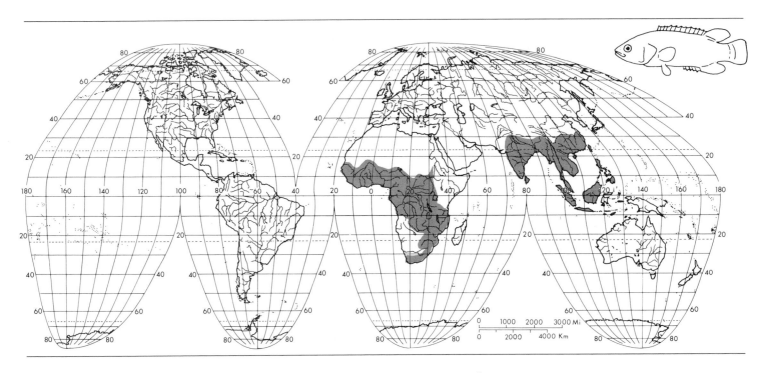

CLASS: Osteichthyes
  SUBCLASS: Actinopterygii
    SUPERORDER: Acanthopterygii

ORDER: Perciformes
  SUBORDER: Anabantoidei
    (1st) FAMILY: **ANABANTIDAE**—climbing perches
    (ăn'-ă-băn'-tĭ-dē)

The anabantids (about 20 species in 3 genera) occur in tropical Africa, India, Southeast Asia, East Indies, and the Philippines. All members of this suborder have an accessory air-breathing capability localized in highly vascularized bony convolutions above the gill chamber. This labyrinth organ enables these fishes to live in oxygen-poor habitats, and perhaps even to leave the water and ramble about on land. The body of anabantids is elongated and compressed, with a well-developed dorsal and anal fin. The paired fins are short. The labyrinth organ, pectoral, pelvic, and opercular spines, and a thick skin allow terrestrial locomotion, which has earned the name "climbing perch" for the oriental *Anabas testudineus*. *Ctenopoma* is an African genus of about 16 species of climbing perches. The extreme eastward distribution across Wallace's line to the Celebes and Halmahera of *Anabas* is probably the result of man carrying this hardy, air-breathing species from place to place (Myers 1951) and is not shown on the map. Males of this family build bubble nests, and maximum size is about 25 cm. Fossils date to the Pleistocene. See Meinken (1974) for a general discussion of the suborder and Sterba (1966) for aquarium information. Smith (1945) has an account of *Anabas*, and Nelson (1976) reviewed the controversy over the phylogenetic placement of this group.

Map references: Bartholomew, Clarke, and Grimshaw 1911*, Bertin and Arambourg 1958*, Boulenger 1916, Darlington 1957, Grzimek 1974*, Herre 1953, Hoedeman 1974*, Innes 1966*, Jubb 1967, Meek 1916*, Roberts 1975, Sterba 1966*.

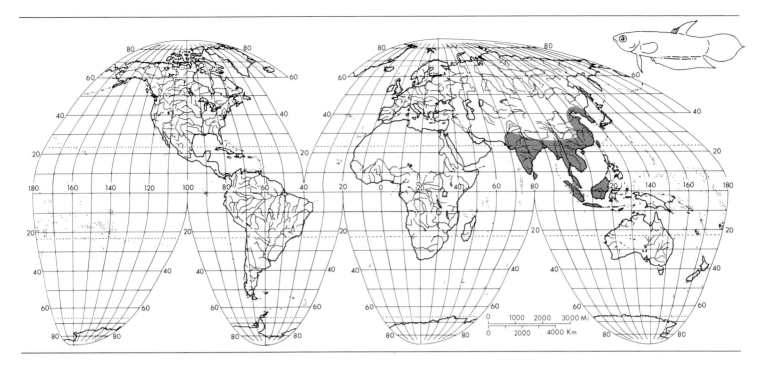

CLASS: Osteichthyes
  SUBCLASS: Actinopterygii
    SUPERORDER: Acanthopterygii

ORDER: Perciformes
  SUBORDER: Anabantoidei
    (1st) FAMILY: **BELONTIIDAE**—fighting fishes, gouramies [bĕ-lōn'-tĭ-ĭ-dē]

This family occurs in India, Southeast Asia, and the East Indies. It does not occur in Africa, as shown on other published maps. Most of these 30-odd species in 10 genera were previously classified with the Anabantidae. All have a labyrinth organ. Body form ranges from cylindrical to compressed. The anal fin is well developed, and the dorsal may be long or short. In some gouramies (*Trichogaster*) the first ray of the pelvic fins is elongated and functions as a tactile organ. Some species are extremely colorful, such as the paradise fish (*Macropodus*) and the fighting fishes (*Betta*), which are utilized in Southeast Asia for entertainment and gambling. Both groups build bubble nests, and the males tend the young. Interesting courtship, nest building, flowing fins, and gorgeous coloration have made these fishes one of the most popular aquarium families. Some larger belontiids, such as *T. pectoralis*, which

may reach 24 cm and 0.5 kg, have been introduced into other tropical areas such as New Guinea for pond culture (Glucksman, West, and Berra 1976), and 8 species of this suborder have escaped into the fresh waters of Florida from aquarium fish farms (Courtenay et al. 1974). See Smith (1945) for an extended discussion of fighting fishes, references, and life history notes for many species. Consult Sterba (1966) and Hoedeman (1974) for aquarium information and many illustrations and Liem (1963) for a review of the suborder.

Map references: Bartholomew, Clarke, and Grimshaw 1911*, Bertin and Arambourg 1958*, Darlington 1957, Grzimek 1974*, Herre 1953, Hoedeman 1974*, Innes 1966*, Meek 1916*, Smith 1945, Sterba 1966*.

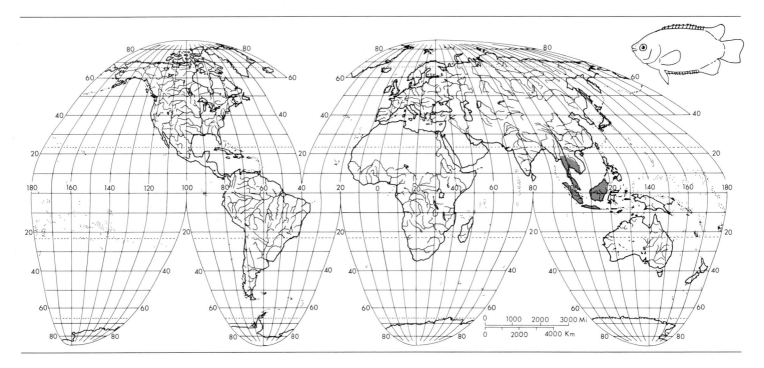

CLASS: Osteichthyes
  SUBCLASS: Actinopterygii
    SUPERORDER: Acanthopterygii

ORDER: Perciformes
  SUBORDER: Anabantoidei
    (1st) FAMILY: **HELOSTOMATIDAE**—kissing
    gourami [hē-lō-stō-mă'-tī-dē]

This monotypic family, composed of *Helostoma temmincki*, is found in the fresh waters of central Thailand, the Malay Peninsula, Sumatra, Java, and Borneo. It has a long dorsal and anal fin and compressed body, and the pelvic fins are not elongated as in *Trichogaster*. A labyrinth organ is present. *Helostoma* occurs in swamps, ponds, and sluggish waters, and feeds on algae. It may reach 30 cm. Two fish may widely extend their broad-lipped mouths and touch, earning their common name and a spot in the tropical fish hobbyist's menagerie. This may represent threat behavior between males. For an elementary discussion of fish behavior see Adler (1975), and Liem (1967a) for a study of the head anatomy of this species.

Map references: Grzimek 1974*, Nelson 1976*, Smith 1945.

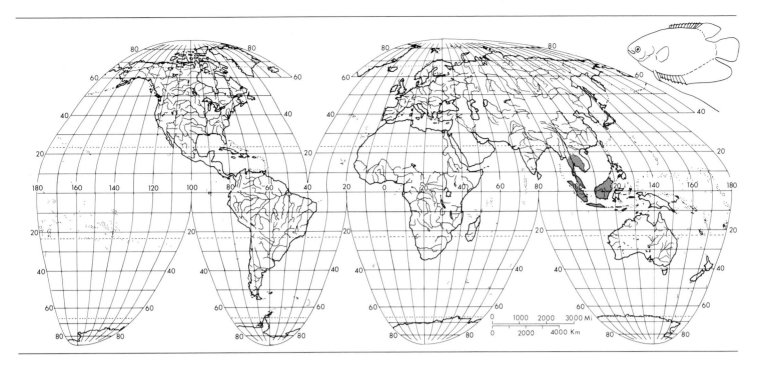

CLASS: Osteichthyes
    SUBCLASS: Actinopterygii
        SUPERORDER: Acanthopterygii

ORDER: Perciformes
    SUBORDER: Anabantoidei
        (1st) FAMILY: **OSPHRONEMIDAE**—giant gourami
        (ŏs'-frō-nĕm'-ĭ-dē) [ŏs-frō-nē'-mĭ-dē]

Osphronemus goramy, the only member of this family, was found originally in Sumatra, Borneo, Java, and probably Thailand and the Malay Peninsula. There are early reports of this fish from China and India, but this species is so hardy and has been transported by man to such an extent that the true native range of *Osphronemus* is difficult to determine (Smith 1945). This large gourami reaches 60 cm and 9 kg and thus is an important food fish in pond culture. It has long dorsal and anal fins, a compressed body, and filamentous pelvic rays which it uses as feelers. Fossils of this species date to the Upper Eocene of Sumatra.

Map references: Bartholomew, Clarke, and Grimshaw 1911*, Grzimek 1974*, Meek 1916*, Smith 1945.

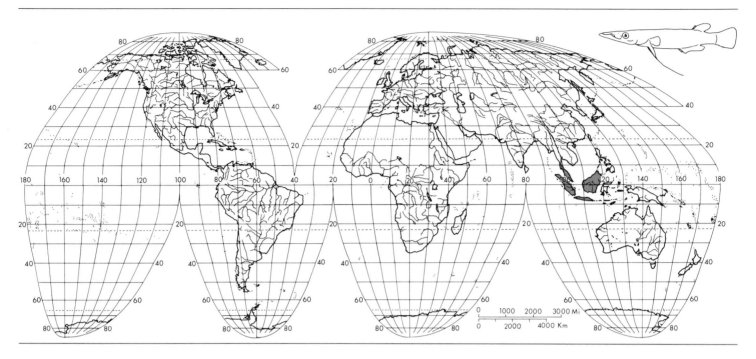

CLASS: Osteichthyes
   SUBCLASS: Actinopterygii
      SUPERORDER: Acanthopterygii

ORDER: Perciformes
   SUBORDER: Luciocephaloidei
      (1st) FAMILY: **LUCIOCEPHALIDAE**—pikehead
      [lū-sĭ-ō-sĕ-fă'-lĭ-dē]

The single species in this family, *Luciocephalus pulcher*, is found in the Malay Peninsula, Sumatra, Java, and Borneo. Its body form is *Esox*-like, with a peculiar funnellike mouth and short dorsal and anal fins set far back on an elongated body. The pelvic fins are produced into a long, filamentous ray, and the anal fin is notched. There is an accessory air breathing organ, but it is not labyrinthic as in the anabantoids. The swim bladder is absent. A jugular bony plate is present. This species grows to 18 cm and inhabits streams and feeds on insects and crustaceans. Liem (1967*b*) has studied this species.

Map references: Grzimek 1974*, Sterba 1966*.

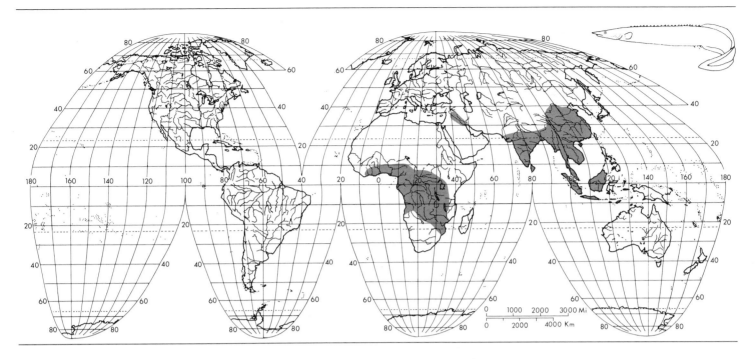

CLASS: Osteichthyes
  SUBCLASS: Actinopterygii
    SUPERORDER: Acanthopterygii

ORDER: Perciformes
  SUBORDER: Mastacembeloidei
    (1st) FAMILY: **MASTACEMBELIDAE**—spiny eels
    (măs'-tă-sĕm-bĕl'-ĭ-dē)

About 50 species of spiny eels, all but one in the genus *Mastacembelus*, are found in tropical west central Africa (34 species), the Tigris-Euphrates system of Iraq (1 species), and from India through the East Indies. These eellike fishes have a cartilaginous rostrum, at the end of which are the anterior nares. The posterior nares are near the eyes. There may be from 7 to 40 individual dorsal spines preceding the long dorsal fin. The dorsal, anal, and caudal fins are confluent in African species but separate in some oriental species. Pelvic fins are absent, and scales are tiny. The other genus is *Macrognathus*, which

is monotypic and found in the Orient. The largest spiny eels reach about 90 cm, but most are less than 35 cm. See Boulenger (1912, 1916) and Smith (1945) for details of various species.

Map references: Bartholomew, Clarke, and Grimshaw 1911*, Boulenger 1912, Boulenger 1916, Darlington 1957, Jubb 1967, Khalaf 1961, Meek 1916*, Nelson 1976*, Nichols 1943, Roberts 1975, Smith 1945, Sterba 1966*.

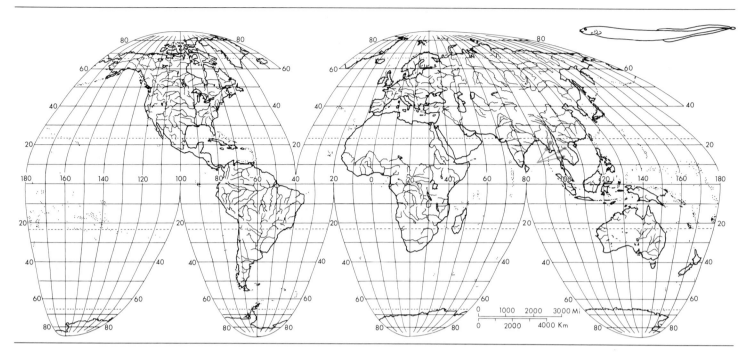

Class: Osteichthyes
   Subclass: Actinopterygii
      Superorder: Acanthopterygii

Order: Perciformes
   Suborder: Mastacembeloidei
      (1st) Family: **CHAUDHURIIDAE**
      [chŏwd-hū′-rĭ-ĭ-dē]

A single species, *Chaudhuria caudata*, is found in Lake Inle in Burma, near Bangkok, and in a Mekong tributary. It is similar to the mastacembelid eels but is smaller and lacks the fleshy rostrum and dorsal spines. Scales are small and embedded in the skin. The caudal region is compressed, and the pectoral fins are small. See Annandale (1918), Regan (1919), and Annandale and Hora (1923) for details. Yazdani (1976) has re-cently erected a new family, the Pillaiidae, composed of *Pillaia indica*, which is intermediate between the Mastacembelidae and the Chaudhuriidae and occurs in the same region as the latter.

Map references: Annandale 1918, Roberts 1971a.

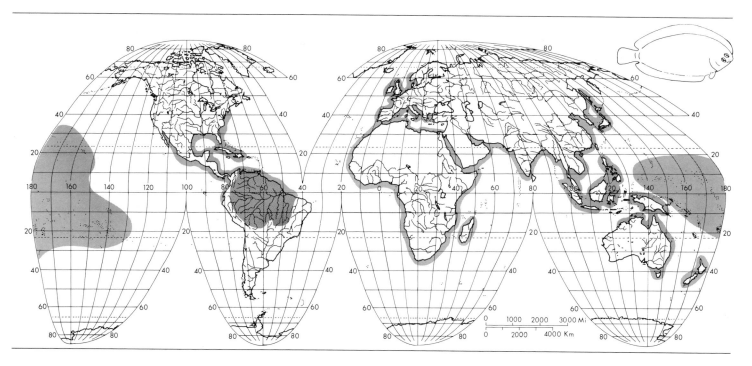

CLASS: Osteichthyes
    SUBCLASS: Actinopterygii
        SUPERORDER: Acanthopterygii

ORDER: Pleuronectiformes
    SUBORDER: Soleoidei
        (Per) FAMILY: SOLEIDAE—soles (sō-lē′-ĭ-dē)
        [sō-lĕ′-ĭ-dē]

This marine family of over 100 species is found in most tropic and temperate seas, and some species inhabit fresh waters. Soles are asymmetrical, oval, compressed fishes that lack spines in their fins. The dorsal fin extends onto the head. The eyes are small and have migrated to the right side of the head in adults. The upper jaw extends beyond the lower jaw. Pectoral fins are absent or poorly developed, and the preopercular margin is covered by skin and scales. The hogchoker, *Trinectes maculatus*, is common along coastal rivers from Cape Cod to Panama, and the genus *Achirus* can be found as far as 3,200 km up the Amazon into Peru. Fossils of this suborder date to the middle Eocene of Egypt. Refer to Kyle (1913, 1921) and Norman (1934) for major works on flatfishes and their metamorphosis.

Map references: Day 1878, Eigenmann and Allen 1942, Fowler 1959, Gery 1969, Grzimek 1974*, Herre 1953, Lake 1971, Miller 1966, Smith 1965, Tinker 1978, Whitaker 1968*.

159

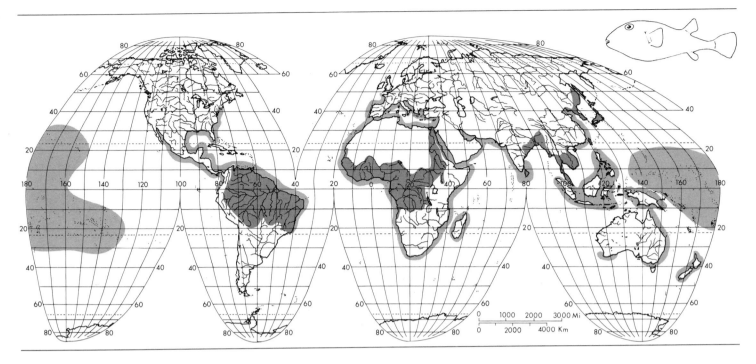

CLASS: Osteichthyes
  SUBCLASS: Actinopterygii
    SUPERORDER: Acanthopterygii

ORDER: Tetraodontiformes
  SUBORDER: Tetraodontoidei
    (Per) FAMILY: **TETRAODONTIDAE**—puffers
    (tĕt′-ră-ō-dŏn′-tĭ-dē)

This worldwide marine family of perhaps 90 species has a few representatives in fresh waters of South America, Africa, and southeast Asia. The genera *Chonerhinus* (Southeast Asia, Africa), *Colomesus* (South America) and *Tetraodon* (Asia and Africa) have freshwater species. Puffers get their names from the ability to gulp air and water into an expansible, thin-walled diverticulum of the gut. This gives the fish a balloon shape and erects the body spines, which are an impressive defense mechanism. An inflated fish is unable to swim and floats upside down. Puffers lack pelvic fins and a first dorsal fin. They have a parrotlike beak with a median suture. Such a crushing beak is suitable for hard-shelled prey like crustaceans and molluscs. The organs, especially the skin, gonads, and liver contain tetrodotoxin, a deadly neurotoxic poison, yet in Japan puffers are considered a delicacy. Licensed fugu chefs learn to prepare the flesh in a way that avoids contamination with poisonous tissues; however, about 50 cases of puffer poisoning are reported each year, of which 60 per-

cent are fatal. First aid before the onset of paralysis should include the use of an emetic. After paralysis, mouth-to-mouth respiration may be necessary to maintain life until medical help can be obtained. Captain Cook nearly died of puffer poisoning during his second voyage when he ate a small amount of liver and roe in New Caledonia in 1774.

The largest puffers reach 90 cm, but most are less than half that size. The small freshwater species are used as aquarium animals. Fossils of this suborder date to the Lower Eocene of Europe. See Halstead (1967) and Edmonds (1975) for a review of poisonous fishes, Sterba (1966) for aquarium information, and Winterbottom (1974) for the familial phylogeny of the order.

Map references: Barnard No Date, Berg 1949, Boulenger 1916, Breder 1929, Day 1878, Eigenmann and Allen 1942, Fowler 1959, Gery 1969, Lake 1971, Miller 1966, Munro 1955, Smith 1945, Sterba 1966, Tinker 1978, Wheeler 1969*.

Glossary

These words are defined as used in this book. They may have different meanings when used in a different context

adipose fin. The fleshy fin on the back behind the dorsal fin as found in trout and catfish

aestivate. To pass the unfavorable conditions of summer in a state of torpor

ammocoete. Larval lamprey

anadromous. Of fish that ascend rivers to spawn, as salmons do

anterior. The front end

autochthonous. Native in the sense of having evolved in a given place

axillary process. Bony splint at base of pelvic fin

barbels. Fleshy projection near mouth, chin or snout as in catfish or cod

benthic. A term that refers to the bottom of a body of water

biconcave. Concave on both ends

branchial. Pertaining to the gills

buccal. Pertaining to the mouth

cartilage. Tough, resilient, white skeletal tissue

catadromous. Of fish that descend rivers to spawn in the sea, as do the American and European eels

caudal peduncle. The fleshy tail end of the body between the anal and caudal fin

circumpolar. Surrounding either pole of the earth

compressed. Flattened from side to side

conspecific. A term applied to individuals or populations of the same species

cosmopolitan. Worldwide distribution

countershading. Coloration with parts normally in shadow being light or parts normally illuminated being dark

ctenoid. Of scales whose posterior margin has teethlike projections, as in perciform fishes

cycloid. Of scales whose posterior margin is smooth, as in cypriniform fishes

deciduous. Of scales easily shed, not firmly attached

depauperate. Including few kinds of organisms, impoverished

depressed. Flattened from top to bottom

detritus. Organic debris

dextral. Right

dimorphism. Two body forms in the same species

disjunct. Separated

disseminule. That part of an organism which is capable of dispersal

dorsal. Of, on, or near the back

ecological equivalent. Unrelated groups that occupy similar niches in different geographical regions

elver. A young eel chiefly found along shores or in estuaries

endangered. Actively threatened with extinction

endemic. Restricted to a particular area

estuary. Wide brackish mouth of a river where tide meets current

family. A group of phylogenetically related genera or a single genus forming a taxonomic category ranking between the order and the genus

forage. Food

fusiform. Cigar-shaped, rounded, broadest in the middle, and tapering at each end

ganoid scale. Hard, glossy, enameled scales, as in gars

genus, pl. **genera.** A group of phylogenetically related species or a single species forming a taxonomic category ranking between the family and the species

gill raker. Bony projection on anterior edge of gill arch

Gondwanaland. A single prehistoric immense southern continent composed of Africa, South America, Antarctica, Australia, New Zealand, and peninsular India

gonopodium. Intromittent organ of male poecilids formed from modified anal rays

gular. Behind chin and between the sides of the lower jaw

hermaphroditic. Having both testes and ovaries in one body

heterocercal. Having vertebral column extend up into larger lobe of caudal fin

holarctic. Northern parts of Old and New World

ichthyology. The branch of zoology that deals with the scientific study of fishes, especially their taxonomy, zoogeography, evolution, and ecology

keel. A sharp ridge on the ventral midline

kype. Curved or hooked lower jaw of a male salmon

lanceolate. Spear-shaped

lateral line. Series of openings to sensory canals along the sides of a fish

leptocephalus. Larval eel

mandible. Lower jaw

maxillary. Lateral part of upper jaw

medial. Towards the midline of the body

metamorphosis. A change in structure due to development

molariform. Molarlike crushing teeth as in the Sparidae

monotypic. Having only a single representative as a family with 1 genus or a genus with 1 species

naked. Without scales

nape. Dorsal surface immediately behind head

niche. The role of an organism in its environment

nomen dubium. Term used to indicate insufficient evidence exists to allow recognition of a nominal (named) species

nuptial. Referring to courtship or breeding

operculum. Bony gill cover

opisthocoelous. Having vertebrae convex anteriorly and concave posteriorly, as in the gars

osmoregulation. The control of osmotic pressure of body fluids within an organism

ostariophysan. A fish of the order Ostariophysi (characoids, cyprinoids, and siluroids) having the anterior 4 or 5 vertebrae modified as Weberian ossicles which connect the swim bladder with the inner ear

oviparous. Egg-laying

peripheral division. The division of fishes very tolerant of salty water, such as salmon, plotosid catfish, sticklebacks, and gobies

pharyngeal teeth. Toothlike projections from the pharyngeal gill arches as in the Cyprinidae

phytoplankton. Microscopic algae, plant plankton

piscivorous. Fish-eating

poikilothermic. Cold-blooded, body temperature approximates that of the environment

population. All the individuals of the same species living in a given area

posterior. The tail end

primary division. The division of strictly freshwater fishes, having little salt tolerance, such as bowfins, pikes, most Ostariophysi, sunfishes, and darters

primitive. Early in a given evolutionary sequence

protractile. Protrusible

protrusible. Having mouth that can be extended forward

pungent. Sharp

ray. Usually branched and flexible rod that supports fin membrane

relict. A survivor that continues to exist after extinction of other members of its group

rheotaxis. Movement toward or away from current

secondary division. The division of freshwater fishes which have some salt tolerance, such as gars, cyprinodonts, and cichlids

sensu lato. In the broadest sense

sinistral. Left

species, pl. **species.** A group of actually or potentially interbreeding natural populations which are reproductively isolated from other such groups

species flock. Concentration of large numbers of distinct but related species in an isolated area, as cichlids in African Great Lakes

specific epithet. The second name of the scientific binomial

spermatophore. Small packet of sperm produced by males and inserted into females, as in the Poeciliidae and the Horaichthyidae

spine. Sharp, hardened, unbranched fin rays

spiracle. Dorsally located remnant of the first gill slit

spiral valve. Spiral fold of mucous membrane projecting into the intestines

subtropical. Nearly tropical, bordering tropical zone

suctorial. Adapted for sucking

superior mouth. Mouth that opens upward, with lower jaw more anterior than upper jaw

sympatric. Occurring in the same area

synonymy. A term referring to the existence of two or more different scientific names for the same taxon

tactile. Relating to the sense of touch

taxonomy. The science of classification

terminal mouth. Mouth that opens at anterior end of head with upper and lower jaws equal

territory. Any area defended by an animal

tropical. Referring to the region of the earth between the Tropic of Cancer and the Tropic of Capricorn

tubercle. Temporary epidermal projection on head, body, or fins of males of some species which facilitates contact with females during spawning or which is used for defense of territories, common among the Cyprinoidei

vagility. Inherent power of movement of individuals or its disseminules

vascularized. Supplied with blood vessels

venomous. Able to inject a toxin by biting or stinging

ventral. Of, on, or near the lower surface

viviparous. Giving birth to live young

Wallace's line. Hypothetical line between Bali and Lombok, Borneo and the Celebes, and the Philippines and the Moluccas which separates the characteristic Asian fauna from the Australian, thereby marking the boundary of the Oriental and Australian biogeographic realms

Weberian apparatus or **ossicles.** Series of 4 or 5 modified vertebrae which connect the swim bladder to the inner ear of Ostariophysian fishes

Weber's line. Hypothetical line lying approximately along the Australo-Papuan Shelf which separates the islands that have a majority of Oriental animals from those which have a majority of Australian ones, a line of faunal balance sometimes preferred to Wallace's line as the boundary between the Oriental and Australian realms

Principal Rivers of the World

River	Countries of Transit	Outflow	Length in KM and (MI)		Rank
Alabama	United States	Mobile R.	507	(315)	161
Albany	Canada	Hudson Bay	982	(610)	105
Aldan	Soviet Union	Lena R.	2,414	(1,500)	34
Allegheny	United States	Ohio R.	523	(325)	158
Amazon	Peru–Brazil	Atlantic O.	6,276	(3,900)	3
Amu Darya	Soviet Union	Aral Sea	2,253	(1,400)	38
Amur	China–Soviet Union	Tatar Strait	4,345	(2,700)	10
Angara	Soviet Union	Yenisei R.	1,852	(1,151)	57
Araguaia	Brazil	Tocantins R.	1,770	(1,100)	59
Arkansas	United States	Mississippi R.	2,334	(1,450)	36
Athabasca	Canada	Lake Athabasca	1,231	(765)	84
Back	Canada	Arctic O.	974	(605)	106
Big Black	United States	Mississippi R.	531	(330)	156
Bighorn	United States	Yellowstone R.	540	(336)	154
Black	United States	White R.	451	(280)	175
Brahmaputra	China–India–Bangladesh (East Pakistan)	Bay of Bengal	2,736	(1,700)	29
Brazos	United States	Gulf of Mexico	1,400	(870)	77
Bug (Southern)	Soviet Union	Dnieper Estuary	853	(530)	115
Bug (Western)	Soviet Union–Poland	Vistula R.	724	(450)	128
Canadian	United States	Arkansas R.	1,458	(906)	73
Cedar	United States	Iowa R.	529	(329)	157
Cheyenne	United States	Missouri R.	805	(500)	119
Chiangjiang. See Yanzi					
Churchill	Canada	Hudson Bay	1,609	(1,000)	64
Cimarron	United States	Arkansas R.	966	(600)	108
Colorado	United States–Mexico	Gulf of California	2,334	(1,450)	37
Colorado (Texas)	United States	Gulf of Mexico	1,352	(840)	78
Columbia	Canada–United States	Pacific O.	1,955	(1,215)	47
Congo	Zaire–Republic of Congo	Atlantic O.	4,828	(3,000)	5
Coosa	United States	Alabama R.	460	(286)	173
Cumberland	United States	Ohio R.	1,106	(687)	94
Dakota	United States	Missouri R.	1,143	(710)	89
Danube	West Germany–Austria–Czechoslovakia–Hungary–Yugoslavia–Rumania–Bulgaria–Soviet Union	Black Sea	2,776	(1,725)	27
Darling	Australia	Murray R.	1,867	(1,160)	56
Delaware	United States	Delaware Bay	476	(296)	169

RIVER	COUNTRIES OF TRANSIT	OUTFLOW	LENGTH IN KM AND (MI)		RANK
Deschutes	United States	Columbia R.	402	(250)	185
Des Moines	United States	Mississippi R.	853	(530)	116
Dnieper	Soviet Union	Black Sea	2,253	(1,400)	39
Dniester	Soviet Union	Black Sea	1,408	(875)	76
Don	Soviet Union	Sea of Azov	1,931	(1,200)	50
Donets	Soviet Union	Don R.	1,046	(650)	98
Drava	Austria–Yugoslavia–Hungary	Danube R.	724	(450)	129
Dvina, Northern	Soviet Union	White Sea	756	(470)	125
Dvina, Western	Soviet Union	Baltic Sea	1,030	(640)	100
Ebro	Spain	Mediterranean Sea	756	(470)	126
Elbe	Czechoslovakia–East Germany–West Germany	North Sea	1,167	(725)	88
Euphrates	Turkey–Syria–Iraq	Persian Gulf	2,736	(1,700)	28
Flint	United States	Apalachicola R.	426	(265)	180
Fly	Papua New Guina	Coral Sea	1,127	(700)	90
Fraser	Canada	Pacific O.	1,118	(695)	92
Gambia	Guinea–Senegal–Gambia	Atlantic O.	805	(500)	120
Ganges	India	Bay of Bengal	2,494	(1,550)	33
Garonne	France	Gironde R.	563	(350)	150
Gila	United States	Colorado R.	1,014	(630)	101
Godavari	India	Bay of Bengal	1,448	(900)	74
Grand	United States	Lake Michigan	418	(260)	181
Green	United States	Colorado R.	1,175	(730)	87
Green (Kentucky)	United States	Ohio R.	579	(360)	147
Hsi. *See* Xijiang					
Huanghe. *See* Yellow					
Hudson	United States	New York Bay	492	(306)	164
Humboldt	United States	Humboldt Lake	467	(290)	171
Illinois	United States	Mississippi R.	439	(273)	178
Indus	Pakistan	Arabian Sea	3,058	(1,900)	21
Iowa	United States	Mississippi R.	468	(291)	170
Irrawaddy	Burma	Bay of Bengal	2,012	(1,250)	45
Irtysh	Soviet Union	Ob R.	2,961	(1,840)	22
James (Virginia)	United States	Chesapeake Bay	547	(340)	152
Japura	Colombia–Brazil	Amazon R.	2,816	(1,750)	25
John Day	United States	Columbia R.	452	(281)	174
Jordan	Lebanon–Israel–Jordan	Dead Sea	322	(200)	191
Jurua	Peru–Brazil	Amazon R.	1,931	(1,200)	51
Kama	Soviet Union	Volga R.	1,931	(1,200)	49
Kentucky	United States	Ohio R.	417	(259)	183
Klamath	United States	Pacific O.	402	(250)	186
Kolyma	Soviet Union	Arctic O.	1,609	(1,000)	65
Kootenay	Canada–United States	Columbia R.	644	(400)	141
Lena	Soviet Union	Arctic O.	4,506	(2,800)	6
Little Colorado	United States	Colorado R.	483	(300)	166
Little Missouri	United States	Missouri R.	901	(560)	111
Loire	France	Atlantic O.	1,006	(625)	102
Mackenzie	Canada	Beaufort Sea	4,064	(2,525)	13
Madeira	Brazil	Amazon R.	3,380	(2,100)	18
Magdalena	Columbia	Caribbean Sea	1,706	(1,060)	61
Marañon	Peru	Amazon R.	1,609	(1,000)	66
Marne	France	Seine R.	523	(325)	159
Mekong	China–Burma–Thailand–Laos–Kampuchea (Cambodia)	South China Sea	4,184	(2,600)	11
Meuse	France–Belgium–Netherlands	North Sea	925	(575)	109
Milk	United States	Missouri R.	1,004	(624)	103
Minnesota	United States	Mississippi R.	534	(332)	155
Mississippi	United States	Gulf of Mexico	3,975	(2,470)	15
Missouri	United States	Mississippi R.	4,382	(2,723)	9
Missouri–Mississippi	United States	Gulf of Mexico	6,418	(3,988)	2
Mureşul	Rumania–Hungary	Tisza R.	644	(400)	142
Murray	Australia	Indian O.	1,931	(1,200)	52
Narmada	India	Arabian Sea	1,287	(800)	80

River	Countries of Transit	Outflow	Length in km and (mi)		Rank
Neches	United States	Sabine Lake	451	(280)	176
Negro, Rio	Argentina	Atlantic O.	1,127	(700)	91
Negro, Rio	Colombia–Brazil	Amazon R.	2,253	(1,400)	40
Nelson	Canada	Hudson Bay	644	(400)	143
Neosho	United States	Arkansas R.	740	(460)	127
Neuse	United States	Pamlico Sound	418	(260)	182
New	United States	Kanawha R.	410	(255)	84
Niger	Guinea–Mali–Niger–Benin (Dahomey)–Nigeria	Gulf of Guinea	4,184	(2,600)	12
Nile	Uganda–Sudan–Egypt	Mediterranean Sea	6,437	(4,000)	1
Niobrara	United States	Missouri R.	694	(431)	132
North Platte	United States	Platte R.	995	(618)	104
Nueces	United States	Corpus Christi Bay	544	(338)	153
Ob	Soviet Union	Gulf of Ob	4,023	(2,500)	14
Oder	Poland–East Germany	Baltic Sea	885	(550)	112
Ohio	United States	Mississippi R.	1,579	(981)	69
Oka	Soviet Union	Volga R.	1,529	(950)	71
Orange	Lesotho–South Africa–Namibia (South West Africa)	Atlantic O.	2,092	(1,300)	42
Orinoco	Venezuela–Colombia	Atlantic O.	2,575	(1,600)	32
Osage	United States	Missouri R.	805	(500)	121
Ottawa	Canada	Saint Lawrence R.	1,102	(685)	95
Ouachita	United States	Red R.	974	(605)	107
Owyhee	United States	Snake R.	402	(250)	187
Paraguay	Brazil–Paraguay–Argentina	Paraná R.	2,414	(1,500)	35
Paraná	Brazil–Paraguay–Argentina	Río de la Plata	3,943	(2,450)	16
Parnaíba	Brazil	Atlantic O.	1,448	(900)	75
Peace	Canada	Slave R.	1,690	(1,050)	62
Pearl	United States	Gulf of Mexico	781	(485)	122
Pechora	Soviet Union	Arctic O.	1,770	(1,100)	60
Pecos	United States	Rio Grande	1,183	(735)	86
Pee Dee	United States	Atlantic O.	700	(435)	131
Pilcomayo	Bolivia–Argentina–Paraguay	Paraguay R.	1,609	(1,000)	67
Plata, Río de la	Argentina–Uruguay	Atlantic O.	298	(185)	192
Platte	United States	Missouri R.	499	(310)	163
Po	Italy	Adriatic Sea	673	(418)	138
Potomac	United States	Chesapeake Bay	462	(287)	172
Powder	United States	Yellowstone R.	604	(375)	146
Purus	Brazil	Amazon R.	3,219	(2,000)	19
Red	United States	Mississippi R.	1,931	(1,200)	53
Red (of the North)	United States–Canada	Lake Winnipeg	877	(545)	113
Republican	United States	Kansas R.	679	(422)	136
Rhine	Switzerland–West Germany–France–Netherlands	North Sea	1,320	(820)	79
Rhone	Switzerland–France	Mediterranean Sea	811	(504)	118
Rio Grande	United States–Mexico	Gulf of Mexico	2,897	(1,800)	23
Roanoke	United States	Albemarle Sound	612	(380)	145
Rock	United States	Mississippi R.	483	(300)	167
Roosevelt, Río	Brazil	Madeira R.	1,529	(950)	72
Sabine	United States	Gulf of Mexico	649	(403)	140
Sacramento	United States	San Francisco Bay	615	(382)	144
Saguenay	Canada	Saint Lawrence R.	201	(125)	193
Saint Francis	United States	Mississippi R.	684	(425)	134
Saint John	United States–Canada	Bay of Fundy	673	(418)	139
Saint Johns	United States	Atlantic O.	444	(276)	177
Saint Lawrence	United States–Canada	Gulf of Saint Lawrence	1,223	(760)	85
Saint Maurice	Canada	Saint Lawrence R.	523	(325)	160
Salado, Río	Argentina	Paraná R.	1,931	(1,200)	54
Salmon	United States	Snake R.	676	(420)	137
Salween	China–Burma	Bay of Bengal	2,816	(1,750)	26
San Joaquin	United States	San Francisco Bay	563	(350)	151
San Juan	United States	Colorado R.	579	(360)	148
São Francisco	Brazil	Atlantic O.	2,897	(1,800)	24
Saskatchewan	Canada	Lake Winnipeg	1,939	(1,205)	48

River	Countries of Transit	Outflow	Length in km and (mi)		Rank
Savannah	United States	Atlantic O.	505	(314)	162
Seine	France	English Channel	772	(480)	123
Senegal	Mali–Mauritania–Senegal	Atlantic O.	1,609	(1,000)	68
Shannon	Ireland	Atlantic O.	386	(240)	189
Si. *See* Xijiang					
Smoky Hill	United States	Kansas R.	869	(540)	114
Snake	United States	Columbia R.	1,670	(1,038)	63
South Platte	United States	Platte R.	682	(424)	135
Sungari	China	Amur R.	1,287	(800)	81
Susquehanna	United States	Chesapeake Bay	715	(444)	130
Syr Darya	Soviet Union	Aral Sea	2,092	(1,300)	43
Tagus	Spain–Portugal	Atlantic O.	911	(566)	110
Tallahatchie	United States	Yazoo R.	484	(301)	165
Tallapoosa	United States	Alabama R.	431	(268)	179
Tennessee	United States	Ohio R.	1,049	(652)	97
Thames	United Kingdom	North Sea	336	(209)	190
Tiber	Italy	Mediterranean Sea	393	(244)	188
Tigris	Turkey–Syria–Iraq	Euphrates R.	1,851	(1,150)	58
Tisza	Hungary–Yugoslavia	Danube R.	1,287	(800)	82
Tobol	Soviet Union	Irtysh R.	1,287	(800)	83
Tocantins	Brazil	Para R.	2,736	(1,700)	30
Tombigbee	United States	Mobile R.	845	(525)	117
Trinity	United States	Galveston Bay	579	(360)	149
Ucayali	Peru	Amazon R.	1,931	(1,200)	55
Ural	Soviet Union	Caspian Sea	2,253	(1,400)	41
Uruguay	Brazil–Argentina–Uruguay	Río de la Plata	1,579	(981)	70
Vistula	Poland	Baltic Sea	1,046	(650)	99
Volga	Soviet Union	Caspian Sea	3,742	(2,325)	17
Wabash	United States	Ohio R.	764	(475)	124
Weser	West Germany	North Sea	483	(300)	168
White	United States	Mississippi R.	1,110	(690)	93
Wisconsin	United States	Mississippi R.	692	(430)	133
Xijiang (Hsi)	China	South China Sea	2,012	(1,250)	46
Xingu	Brazil	Amazon R.	2,092	(1,300)	44
Yangzi (Chiangjiang)	China	East China Sea	5,150	(3,200)	4
Yellow (Huanghe)	China	Gulf of Chihli (Bohaiwan)	4,506	(2,800)	8
Yellowstone	United States	Missouri R.	1,080	(671)	96
Yenisei	Soviet Union	Arctic O.	4,506	(2,800)	7
Yukon	Canada–United States	Bering Sea	3,219	(2,000)	20
Zambezi	Angola–Zambia–southern Zimbabwe (Rhodesia)– Mozambique	Indian O.	2,655	(1,650)	31

Modified from *The Random House Dictionary of the English Language, Webster's New Geographical Dictionary*, and other sources.

Principal Lakes of the World

Lake	Countries	Locality	Area in km² and (mi²)		Rank
Albert	Zaire–Uganda	East Africa	5,343	(2,064)	32
Aral Sea	Soviet Union	western Turkestan	67,741	(26,166)	4
Athabasca	Canada	northeast Alberta and northwest Saskatchewan	7,767	(3,000)	24
Baikal	Soviet Union	southern Siberia	34,173	(13,200)	7
Balaton	Hungary	western Hungary	595	(230)	54
Balkhash	Soviet Union	Kazakhstan	18,420	(7,115)	16
Bangweulu	Zambia	northeastern Zambia	4,323	(1,670)	41
Caspian Sea	Iran–Soviet Union	southwest Asia	437,521	(169,000)	1
Cayuga	United States	central New York State	171	(66)	67
Chad	Chad–Niger–Nigeria	northwest central Africa	25,889	(10,000)	12
Champlain	Canada–United States	between New York and Vermont	1,553	(600)	50
Como	Italy	Lombardy (Italian Lake District)	145	(56)	68
Constance, Lake (Boden See)	Austria–Switzerland–West Germany	between southwest West Germany and northeast Switzerland	536	(207)	58
Dead Sea	Israel–Jordan	near eastern end of Mediterranean	958	(370)	52
Dongtinghu (Tung-T'ing)	China	Hunan Province	3,754	(1,450)	47
Dubawnt	Canada	southwestern Keewatin District	4,282	(1,654)	42
Erie	Canada–United States	Great Lakes, between Ontario and Ohio	25,733	(9,940)	13
Eyre	Australia	northeastern South Australia	8,880	(3,430)	21
Gairdner	Australia	southern South Australia	3,883	(1,500)	44
Garda	Italy	eastern Lombardy (Italian Lake District)	370	(143)	60
Geneva, Lake (Lake Leman)	France–Switzerland	eastern France and southwest Switzerland	582	(225)	56
Great Bear	Canada	central Mackenzie District	33,138	(12,800)	8
Great Salt	United States	northwestern Utah	5,954	(2,300)	27
Great Slave	Canada	southern Mackenzie District	28,923	(11,172)	10
Helmand	Iran	eastern Iran	5,178	(2,000)	34
Huron	Canada–United States	Great Lakes between Ontario and Michigan	59,570	(23,010)	5
Issyk-Kul	Soviet Union	northeastern Kirghizia	5,825	(2,250)	29
Kariba	Zimbabwe (Rhodesia)	south central Africa	5,307	(2,050)	33

169

Lake	Countries	Locality	Area in KM² AND (MI²)		Rank
Khanka	China–Soviet Union	between Manchuria and maritime Siberia	4,401	(1,700)	39
Kyoga	Uganda	south central Uganda	2,589	(1,000)	48
Ladoga	Soviet Union	northwestern Soviet Union	18,122	(7,000)	17
Lake of the Woods	Canada–United States	Minnesota–southwestern Manitoba–southwestern Ontario	3,844	(1,485)	45
Leopold II	Zaire	western Congo	4,401	(1,700)	40
Maggiore	Italy–Switzerland	Lombardy (Italian Lake District)	215	(83)	63
Manitoba	Canada	southern Manitoba	4,704	(1,817)	37
Maracaibo	Venezuela	along coast of northwest Venezuela	16,310	(6,300)	18
Mead	United States	northwest Arizona and southeast Nevada	588	(227)	55
Michigan	United States	Great Lakes between Michigan and Wisconsin	57,991	(22,400)	6
Murray	Papua New Guinea	Papua	777	(300)	53
Mweru	Zaire–Zambia	central Africa	4,194	(1,620)	43
Nettiling	Canada	Baffin Island	5,064	(1,956)	36
Neuchatel, Lake of	Switzerland	western Switzerland	220	(85)	62
Nicaragua	Nicaragua	southwest Nicaragua	7,922	(3,060)	23
Nipigon	Canada	southern Ontario	4,479	(1,730)	38
Nyasa	Mozambique–Malawi–Tanzania	southeastern Africa	28,478	(11,000)	11
Okeechobee	United States	southern Florida	1,890	(730)	49
Onega	Soviet Union	northwestern Soviet Union	9,745	(3,764)	19
Oneida	United States	central New York State	207	(80)	64
Ontario	Canada–United States	Great Lakes between Ontario and New York	19,520	(7,540)	15
Pontchartrain	United States	southeast Louisiana	1,553	(600)	51
Qinghai (Tsinghai, Koko Nor)	China	Northeastern Qinghai Province	5,954	(2,300)	28
Reindeer	Canada	northern part of Manitoba-Saskatchewan boundary	6,327	(2,444)	25
Rudolf	Kenya–Ethiopia–Sudan	East Africa	9,061	(3,500)	20
Seneca	United States	western New York State	173	(67)	66
Superior	Canada–United States	Great Lakes, between Ontario and Michigan	82,378	(31,820)	2
Tahoe	United States	on California-Nevada boundary	518	(200)	59
Tanganyika	Burundi–Zaire–Zambia–Tanzania	central Africa	32,879	(12,700)	9
Titicaca	Bolivia–Peru	Altiplano, Andes Mts.	8,284	(3,200)	22
Torrens	Australia	Eastern South Australia	6,213	(2,400)	26
Tsing Hai (Koko Nor). See Qinghai					
Tung-T'ing. See Dongtinghu					
Urmia	Iran	northwestern Iran	5,178	(2,000)	35
Van	Turkey	eastern Turkey in Asia	3,764	(1,454)	46
Vänern	Sweden	southern Sweden	5,543	(2,141)	30
Victoria	Kenya–Tanzania–Uganda	East Africa	69,454	(26,828)	3
Winnebago	United States	east central Wisconsin	557	(215)	57
Winnipeg	Canada	southern Manitoba	24,077	(9,300)	14
Winnipegosis	Canada	southwestern Manitoba	5,400	(2,086)	31
Winnipesaukee	United States	central New Hampshire	184	(71)	65
Yellowstone	United States	Yellowstone National Park, northwestern Wyoming	362	(140)	61
Zurich, Lake of	Switzerland	northern Switzerland	88	(34)	69

Modified from *Ti   .dom House Dictionary of the English Language*, *Webster's New Geographical Dictionary*, and other sources.

Geological Time Chart

Era	Period	Epoch	Biological Events	Years Before Present	Continental Movements and Associated Developments
Cenozoic	Quaternary	Recent	Modern man	11 thousand	
		Pleistocene	Early man	0.5 to 3 million	Wide-spread glaciation.
	Tertiary	Pliocene	Large carnivores; many modern genera of birds and mammals	7 million	Arctic ice begins forming. Major uplift of Rocky Mountain region. Baja California separates from mainland, forming Gulf of California.
		Miocene	Abundant grazing mammals	25 million	Antarctic ice sheet reaches maximum. Isthmus of Panama rises from the sea. Mediterranean isolated, dries up. Rapid growth of Himalayas. Red Sea begins to open. Antarctic ice sheet forming. Northerly motion of Africa produces the Alps.
		Oligocene	Rise of modern families of birds and mammals	40 million	Main Pacific plate touches North America, altering mountain formation in western states.
		Eocene	Radiation of placentals	60 million	Intensive volcanic activity in western North America. India begins impinging on Asia. Australia separates from Antarctica.
		Paleocene	First placental mammals; teleosts abundant in sea	70 million	Land bridge between the Americas submerges.

Era	Period	Epoch	Biological Events	Years Before Present	Continental Movements and Associated Developments
Mesozoic	Cretaceous		Holostei exceeded by Teleostei; climax of giant land and marine reptiles, followed by extinction; flowering plants; decline of gymnosperms	135 million	North America and Europe separate. India breaks from Australia and Antarctica. Africa and South America separate in breakup of Gondwanaland.
	Jurassic		First birds; first mammals; dinosaurs abundant; Holostei abundant	180 million	Andes forming. Africa and South America moving apart, splitting Pangaea. Sierra Nevada batholiths forming.
	Triassic		First dinosaurs; mammallike reptiles; conifers dominate plants	230 million	Closure of ocean between Europe and Asia, formation of Urals.
Paleozoic	Permian		Chondrostei abundant; radiation of reptiles; displacement of amphibians; extinction of many marine invertebrates	280 million	Final closure of ancient Atlantic.
	Carboniferous	Pennsylvanian	First reptiles; giant insects; great conifer forests	310 million	
		Mississippian	Radiation of amphibians; abundant sharks; scale trees and seed ferns	345 million	Development of the Appalachians.
	Devonian		First amphibians; freshwater fishes abundant; bryozoans and corals; Sarcopterygii dominant	405 million	
	Silurian		First jawed fishes (Placoderms)	425 million	
	Ordovician		Ostracoderms (first vertebrates); abundant marine invertebrates; first land plants	500 million	Ancient Atlantic begins to shrink.
	Cambrian		Origin of many invertebrate phyla and classes; trilobites dominant; marine algae	600 million	
Precambrian	Precambrian		Fossil algae; other fossils extremely rare; evidence of sponges and worm burrows Fossil filamentous chains of bacteriumlike cells have been found in 3.5 billion year old rocks from northwestern Australia		

Combined from: Hickman, Hickman, and Hickman (1974), Sullivan (1974), and Orr (1976). Information on the relative time of origin of fish families can be found in Andrews et al. (1967) and Romer (1966).

National Geographic Magazine Articles on Fishes

National Geographic Magazine is renowned for its beautiful photographs. Back issues can be obtained for a few cents each at old book fairs. If the bibliophiles among us were to assemble the articles listed below and have them bound, they would possess a unique fish book with dramatic illustrations found no where else.

Clark, E. 1972. The Red Sea's garden of eels. 142:724–34 (November).

———. 1974. The Red Sea's sharkproof fish. 146:718–27 (November).

———. 1975. Into the lair of "sleeping" sharks. 147:570–84 (April).

———. 1978. Flashlight fish of the Red Sea. 154:718–28 (November).

Davidson, T. 1958. Freezing the trout's lightning leap. 113:525–30 (April).

Faulkner, D. 1965. Finned doctors of the deep. 128:867–73 (December).

Greenberg, J. 1962. Florida's coral city beneath the sea. 121:71–90 (January).

Houot, G. S. 1958. Four years of diving to the bottom of the sea. 113:715–32 (May).

Idyll, C. P. 1968. The incredible salmon. 134:195–219 (August).

———. 1969. Grunion, the fish that spawn on land. 135:714–23 (May).

———. 1969. New Florida resident, the walking catfish. 135:847–51 (June).

Kenney, N. T. 1968. Sharks: wolves of the sea. 133:222–57 (February).

Libby, E. L. 1959. Miracle of the mermaid's purse. 116:413–20 (September).

Polunin, I. 1972. Who says fish can't climb trees? 141:85–91 (January).

Sisson, R. F. 1950. Lake Sunapee's golden trout. 98:529–36 (October).

———. 1976. Adrift on a raft of sargassum. 149:188–99 (February).

Voss, G. 1956. Solving life secrets of the sailfish. 109:859–72 (June).

Wolfsheimer, G. 1960. The discus fish yields a secret. 117:675–81 (May).

Zahl, P. A. 1953. Fishing in the whirlpool of Charybdis. 104:579–618 (November).

———. 1954. Night life in the Gulf Stream. 105:391–418 (March).

———. 1958. Hatchfish: torchbearers of the deep. 113:713–14 (May).

———. 1959. Little horses of the sea. 115:131–53 (January).

———. 1970. Seeking the truth about the feared piranha. 138:715–34 (November).

———. 1973. Those outlandish goldfish. 143:514–33 (April).

———. 1978. The four-eyed fish sees all. 153:390–94 (March).

———. 1978. Dragons of the deep. 153:838–45 (June).

Scientific American Articles on Fishes

The following is a selection of recent *Scientific American* articles which make excellent supplemental reading for many college level fish courses.

Agranoff, B. W. 1967. Memory and protein synthesis. 216:115–23 (June).

Applegate, V. C., and Moffett, J. W. 1955. The sea lamprey. 192: 36–41 (April).

Brett, J. R. 1965. The swimming energetics of salmon. 213:80–85 (August).

Brown, J. H. 1971. The desert pupfish. 225:104–10 (November).

Carey, F. G. 1973. Fish with warm bodies. 228:36–44 (February).

Denton, E. 1960. The buoyancy of marine animals. 203:118–29 (July).

———. 1971. Reflectors in fishes. 224:64–72 (January).

Fish, M. P. 1956. Animal sounds in the sea. 194:93–104 (April).

Fuhrman. F. A. 1967. Tetrodotoxin. 217:60–71 (August).

Gilbert, P. W. 1962. The behavior of sharks. 207:60–68 (July).

Gray, J. 1957. How fishes swim. 197:48–54 (August).

Grundfest, H. 1960. Electric fishes. 203:115–24 (October).

Hasler, A. D. and Larsen, J. A. 1955. The homing salmon. 193: 72–76 (August).

Hickling, C. F. 1963. The cultivation of tilapia. 208:143–52 (May).

Holt, S. J. 1969. The food resources of the ocean. 221:178–97 (September).

Idyll, C. P. 1973. The anchovy crisis. 228:22–29 (June).

Isaacs, J. D. 1975. Active animals of the deep-sea floor. 233:84–91 (October).

Jensen, D. 1966. The hagfish. 214:82–90 (February).

Johansen, K. 1968. Air-breathing fishes. 219:102–11 (October).

Leggett, W. C. 1973. The migrations of the shad. 228:92–98 (March).

Limbaugh, C. 1961. Cleaning symbiosis. 205:42–49 (August).

Lissmann, H. W. 1963. Electric location by fishes. 208:50–59 (March).

Llano, G. A. 1957. Sharks v. men. 196:54–61 (June).

Luhling, K. H. 1963. The archer fish. 209:100–108 (July).

McCosker, J. E. 1977. Flashlight fishes. 236:106–14 (March).

Millot, J. 1955. The coelacanth. 193:34–39 (December).

Ruud, J. T. 1965. The ice fish. 213:108–14 (November).

Scholander, P. F. 1957. The wonderful net. 196:96–107 (April).

Shaw, E. 1962. The schooling of fishes. 206:128–38 (June).

Tinbergen, N. 1952. The curious behavior of the stickleback. 187: 22–26 (December).

Todd, J. H. 1971. The chemical languages of fishes. 224:98–108 (May).

Guides to the Freshwater Fishes of North America

ALABAMA
Smith-Vaniz, W. F. 1968. *Freshwater fishes of Alabama*. Auburn: Auburn Univ. Agric. Exp. Sta. 211 pp.

ALASKA
McPhail, J. D., and Lindsey, C. C. 1970. *Freshwater fishes of northwestern Canada and Alaska*. Fish. Res. Bd. Can. Bull. no. 173. Ottawa. 381 pp.
Morrow, J. E. 1974. *Illustrated keys to the freshwater fishes of Alaska*. Anchorage: Alaska Northwest Publ. Co. 78 pp.

ALBERTA
Paetz, M. J., and Nelson, J. S. 1970. *The fishes of Alberta*. Edmonton: Queen's Printer. 282 pp.

APPALACHIA
Jenkins, R. E.; Lachner, E. A.; and Schwartz, F. J. 1972. Fishes of the central Appalachian drainages: their distribution and dispersal. In *The distributional history of the biota of the Southern Appalachians*, part 3, pp. 43–117. Res. Div. Monogr. no. 4. Va. Polytech. Inst. St. Univ., Blacksburg.

ARCTIC
Wynne-Edward, V. C. 1952. Fishes of the Arctic and Subarctic. In *Freshwater vertebrates of the Arctic and Subarctic*, pp. 5–24. Fish. Res. Bd. Can. Bull. no. 94.

ARIZONA
Minckley, W. L. 1973. *Fishes of Arizona*. Phoenix: Ariz. Game and Fish Dept. 293 pp.

ARKANSAS
Buchanan, T. M. 1973. *Key to the fishes of Arkansas*. Little Rock: Ark. Game and Fish Comm. 68 pp. 198 maps.

BRITISH COLUMBIA
Carl, G. C.; Clemens, W. A.; and Lindsey, C. C. 1959. *The fresh-water fishes of British Columbia*. B.C. Provincial Mus. Hdbk. no. 5. 3d ed. 192 pp.

CALIFORNIA
Moyle, P. B. 1976. *Inland fishes of California*. Berkeley: University of California Press. 405 pp.
Stoltz, D. L., and Naiman, R. J. 1978. *The natural history of native fishes in the Death Valley system*. Nat. Hist. Mus. Los Angeles Co. Sci. Ser. no. 30. 76 pp.

CANADA
Scott, W. B. 1967. *Freshwater fishes of eastern Canada*. 2d ed. Toronto: University of Toronto Press. 137 pp.
Scott, W. B., and Crossman, E. J. 1973. *Freshwater fishes of Canada*. Fish. Res. Bd. Can. Bull. no. 184. Ottawa. 966 pp.
See also ALASKA

COLORADO
Beckman, W. C. 1963. *Guide to the fishes of Colorado*. Boulder: Univ. Colo. Mus. 110 pp.
Everhart, W. H., and Seaman, W. R. 1971. *Fishes of Colorado*. Denver: Colo. Game, Fish, and Park Div. 75 pp.

CONNECTICUT
Whitworth, W. R.; Berrien, P. L.; and Keller, W. T. 1968. *Freshwater fishes of Connecticut*. State Geol. and Nat. Hist. Surv. Bull. no. 101. 134 pp.

DELAWARE
Lee, D. S.; Norden, A.; Gilbert, C. R.; and Frank, R. 1976. A list of the freshwater fishes of Maryland and Delaware. *Chesapeake Sci.* 17, no. 3:205–11.

FLORIDA
Briggs, J. C. 1958. A list of Florida fishes and their distribution. *Bull. Fla. St. Mus.* 2, no. 8:223–318.
Carr, A., and Goin, C. J. 1959. *Guide to the reptiles, amphibians, and freshwater fishes of Florida*. Gainesville: University of Florida Press. 341 pp.
Stevenson, H. M. 1976. *Vertebrates of Florida*. Gainesville: University Presses of Florida. 607 pp.

GEORGIA
Dahlberg, M. D., and Scott, D. C. 1971. *The freshwater fishes of Georgia*. Bull. Ga. Acad. Sci. no. 29. 64 pp.

GREAT LAKES   Hubbs, C. L., and Lagler, K. F. 1958. *Fishes of the Great Lakes region*. Ann Arbor: University of Michigan Press. 213 pp.

HAWAII   Marita, C. M. 1963. *Freshwater fishing in Hawaii*. Honolulu: Dept. Land and Nat. Res. 22 pp.
See also Guides to Marine Fishes

ILLINOIS   Forbes, S. A., and Richardson, R. E. 1920. *The Fishes of Illinois*. Rev. ed. Ill. Nat. Hist. Surv. no. 3. 357 pp. Atlas. 103 maps.
Smith, P. 1979. *Fishes of Illinois*. Urbana: University of Illinois Press. 314 pp.

INDIANA   Gerking, S. D. 1945. *The distribution of the fishes of Indiana*. Invest. Ind. Lakes and Streams 3, no. 1. 137 pp. 113 maps.
———. 1955. Key to the fishes of Indiana. *Invest. Ind. Lakes and Streams* 4:49–86.
Nelson, J. S., and Gerking, S. D. 1968. *Annotated key to the fishes of Indiana*. Bloomington: Dept. of Zoology, Indiana Univ. 84 pp.

IOWA   Harlan, J. R., and Speaker, E. B. 1951. *Iowa fish and fishing*. 4th ed. Reprint 1969. Des Moines: Iowa Conservation Comm. 365 pp.

KANSAS   Cross, F. B. 1967. *Handbook of fishes of Kansas*. Univ. Kans. Mus. Nat. Hist. Misc. Publ. no. 45. Lawrence. 357 pp.
Cross, F. B., and Collins, J. T. 1975. *Fishes in Kansas*. Univ. of Kans. Mus. Nat. Hist. Public Ed. Ser. no. 3. 189 pp.

KENTUCKY   Clay, W. M. 1975. *The fishes of Kentucky*. Frankfort: Ky. Dept. Fish and Wildlife Resources. 416 pp.

LABRADOR   Backus, R. H. 1957. The fishes of Labrador. Bull. Amer. Mus. Nat. Hist. 113, no. 4: 273–338.

LOUISIANA   Douglas, N. H. 1974. *Freshwater fishes of Louisiana*. Baton Rouge, La.: Claitor's Publ. 443 pp.
Gowanloch, J. N. 1933. *Fishes and fishing in Louisiana*. Bull. La. Dept. Cons. no. 23. 638 pp. Reprinted with addenda, 1965.

MAINE   Everhart, W. H. 1958. *Fishes of Maine*. Augusta, Maine: Dept. of Inland Fish and Game. 94 pp.

MANITOBA   Fedoruk, A. N. 1969. *Checklist of and key to the freshwater fishes of Manitoba*. Manitoba Dept. Mines and Nat. Res., Canada Land Inventory Project Rep. no. 6. 98 pp.

MARYLAND   *See* DELAWARE

MASSACHUSETTS   Mugford, P. S. 1969. *Illustrated manual of Massachusetts freshwater fish*. Mass. Div. Fish and Game. 127 pp.

MEXICO   Alvarez, J. 1950. *Claves para la determinacion de especies en los peces de las aquas continentales Mexicanas*. Mex. Secretaria de Marina. 144 pp.
———. *Peces mexicanos*. Inst. Nacional de Invest. Biol. Pesquerias, Mexico.

MICHIGAN   *See* GREAT LAKES

MINNESOTA   Eddy, S., and Underhill, J. C. 1974. *Northern fishes*. Minneapolis: University of Minnesota Press. 414 pp.

MISSISSIPPI   Cook, F. A. 1959. *Freshwater fishes in Mississippi*. Jackson: Miss. Game and Fish Comm. 239 pp.

MISSOURI   Pflieger, W. L. 1971. A distributional study of Missouri fishes. *Univ. Kans. Publ. Mus. Nat. Hist.* 20, no. 3:225–570. 193 maps.
———. 1975. *The fishes of Missouri*. Columbia: Mo. Dept. Cons. 343 pp.

MONTANA   Brown, C. J. D. 1971. *Fishes of Montana*. Bozeman: Montana State Univ. 207 pp.
Weisel, G. F. 1957. *Fish guide for inter-mountain Montana*. Missoula: Montana State University Press. 88 pp.

NEBRASKA   Morris, J.; Morris, L.; and Witt, L. 1972. *The fishes of Nebraska*. Nebr. Game and Parks. Comm. 98 pp.

NEVADA   LaRivers, I. 1962. *Fishes and fisheries of Nevada*. Carson City: Nev. State Fish and Game Comm. 782 pp.

NEWFOUNDLAND   Scott, W. B., and Crossman, E. J. 1954. *Fishes occurring in the freshwaters of insular Newfoundland*. Ottawa: Dept. Fish. 124 pp.

NEW HAMPSHIRE   Scarola, J. F. 1973. *Freshwater fishes of New Hampshire*. Concord: N.H. Fish and Game Dept. 131 pp.

NEW JERSEY   Fowler, H. W. 1945. *A study of the fishes of the southern Piedmont and coastal plain*. Acad. Nat. Sci. Phila. Mono. no. 7. 40 pp.
Stiles, E. W. 1978. *Vertebrates of New Jersey*. Somerset, N.J.: E. W. Stiles Publ. 148 pp.

NEW MEXICO   Koster, W. J. 1957. *Guide to the fishes of New Mexico*. Albuquerque: University of New Mexico Press. 116 pp.

NEW YORK   Bean, T. H. 1903. *Catalogue of the fishes of New York*. N.Y. State Mus. Bull. no. 60. 784 pp.
Greeley, J. R. 1927–40. Watershed survey reports on fishes of New York rivers. Supplements to the 16th–29th Ann. Repts. of N.Y. State Conservation Dept. Albany.

NORTH CAROLINA   Fish, F. F. 1967. *Some North Carolina freshwater fishes*. Raleigh: St. Mus. Div. N.C. Dept. Agr. and N.C. Wildlife Resour. Comm. 49 pp.
Menhinick, E. F.; Burton, T. M.; and Bailey, J. R. 1974. An annotated checklist of the freshwater fishes of North Carolina. *J. Elisha Mitchell Sci. Soc.* 90, no. 1:24–50.
Smith, H. M. 1907. *The fishes of North Carolina*. Raleigh: North Carolina Geol. and Econ. Survey. vol. 2. 453 pp.

NORTH DAKOTA   Hankinson, T. L. 1929. Fishes of North Dakota. *Pap. Mich. Acad. Sci. Arts. Lett.* 10:439–60.

NOVA SCOTIA   Livingstone, D. A. 1953. *The freshwater fishes of Nova Scotia*. Proc. Nova Scotia Inst. of Sci. 23, no. 1. 90 pp.

OHIO   Trautman, M. B. 1957. *The fishes of Ohio*. Columbus: Ohio State University Press. 683 pp. 2d ed. forthcoming.

OKLAHOMA   Miller, R. J., and Robison, H. W. 1973. *The fishes of Oklahoma*. Stillwater: Oklahoma State University Press. 246 pp.

ONTARIO   MacKay, H. H. 1963. *Fishes of Ontario*. On-
            tario: Dept. Lands and Forests. 300 pp.
OREGON   Bond, C. E. 1961. *Keys to Oregon freshwater
            fishes*. Agric. Exp. Sta. Oregon State Univ.,
            Tech. Bull. no. 38. 42 pp.
            See also WASHINGTON
QUEBEC   Legendre, V. 1953. The freshwater fishes of the
            Province of Quebec. *Ninth Rep. Biol. Bur.
            Game Fish Dept. Quebec, 1951–52*, pp.
            190–294.
            ————. 1954. *Key to Game and Commercial
            Fishes*. Montreal: Soc. Can. d'Écol. 180 pp.
SOUTH DAKOTA Bailey, R. M., and Allum, M. O. 1962. *Fishes
            of South Dakota*. Univ. of Mich. Mus. Zool.
            Misc. Publ. no. 119. 131 pp.
TENNESSEE   Etnier, D. A., and Starnes, W. C. 1981. *The
            fishes of Tennessee*. Knoxville: University of
            Tennessee Press. In press.
            Kuhne, E. R. 1939. *A guide to the fishes of Ten-
            nessee and the mid-South*. Nashville: Tenn.
            Dept. of Conservation. 124 pp.
TEXAS   Hubbs, C. 1976. *A checklist of Texas freshwater
            fishes*. Texas Parks and Wildlife Dept. Tech. Ser.
            no. 11. 12 pp.
            Knapp, F. T. 1953. *Fishes found in the fresh-
            water of Texas*. Brunswick, Ga.: Ragland Stu-
            dio. 166 pp.
UNITED STATES Eddy, S., and Underhill, J. C. 1978. *How to
            know the freshwater fishes*. 3d ed. Dubuque,
            Iowa: Brown. 215 pp.
            Jordan, D. S., and Evermann, B. W.

            1896–1900. *The fishes of North and Middle
            America*. Bull. U.S. Nat. Mus. no. 47. Wash.,
            D.C. Reprint, 4 vols. Neptune City, N.J.: T.F.H.
            Publ., 1963.
            Moore, G. A. 1968. Fishes. In *Vertebrates of
            the United States*, ed. W. F. Blair et al., pp.
            22–165. 2d ed. New York: McGraw-Hill.
UTAH   Sigler, W. F., and Miller, R. R. 1963. *Fishes of
            Utah*. Salt Lake City: Utah State Dept. Fish and
            Game. 203 pp.
VIRGINIA   Martin, R. G. 1960. *A list of the fishes of Vir-
            ginia*. Virginia Wildlife. Richmond: Va. Comm.
            Game and Inland Fish. 4 pp.
WASHINGTON Schultz, L. P. 1936. Keys to the fishes of Wash-
            ington, Oregon, and closely adjoining regions.
            Univ. Wash. Publ. Biol. 2, no. 4:103–228.
WEST VIRGINIA Denoncourt, R. F.; Raney, E. C.; Hocutt, C. H.;
            and Stauffer, J. R. 1975. A checklist of the fishes
            of West Virginia. *Va. J. Sci. 26*, no. 3:117–20.
WISCONSIN   Greene, C. W. 1935. *The distribution of
            Wisconsin fishes*. Madison: Wis. Cons. Comm.
            235 pp.
            Johnson, M., and Becker, G. C. 1970. Anno-
            tated list of the fishes of Wisconsin. *Wis. Acad.
            Sci., Arts, and Lett. 58*:265–300.
WYOMING   Baxter, G. T., and Simon, J. R. 1970. *Wyoming
            Fishes*. Wyo. Fish. Dept. Bull. no. 4.
            Cheyenne. 168 pp.
            Simon, J. R. 1946. *Wyoming Fishes*. Wyo.
            Game and Fish Dept. Bull. 129 pp.

Guides to the Marine Fishes of North America

ATLANTIC COAST

Leim, A. H., and Scott, W. B. 1966. *Fishes of the Atlantic coast of Canada*. Fish. Res. Bd. Can. Bull. no. 155. Ottawa. 485 pp.

WESTERN NORTH ATLANTIC

Sears Found. for Marine Res. 1948–77. *Fishes of the western North Atlantic*. 7 pts. New Haven.

ATLANTIC AND GULF OF MEXICO

Breder, C. M., Jr. 1945. *Field book of marine fishes of the Atlantic Coast from Labrador to Texas*. 2d ed. New York: Putnam's. 332 pp.

Dahlberg, M. D. 1975. *Guide to coastal fishes of Georgia and nearby states*. Athens: University of Georgia Press. 186 pp.

Hoese, H. D., and Moore, R. H. 1977. *Fishes of the Gulf of Mexico*. College Station: Texas A&M University Press. 327 pp.

Walls, J. G. 1975. *Fishes of the northern Gulf of Mexico*. Neptune City, N.J.: T.F.H. Publ. 432 pp.

GULF OF MAINE

Bigelow, H. B., and Schroeder, W. C. 1953. *Fishes of the Gulf of Maine*. Fish. Bull. 74, Vol. 53. Reprint (MCZ, 1966). 577 pp.

CHESAPEAKE BAY

Hildebrand, S. F., and Schroeder, W. C. 1928. *Fishes of Chesapeake Bay*. U.S. Bur. Fish Bull. vol. 53, pt. 1. Reprint. Neptune City, N.J.: T.F.H. Publ., 1972. 388 pp.

BERMUDA AND WEST INDIES

Beebe, W. M., and Tee-van, J. 1933. *Field book of the shore fishes of Bermuda*. New York: Putnam's. Reprint. Dover, 1970. 337 pp.

CARIBBEAN

Randall, J. F. 1968. *Caribbean reef fishes*. Jersey City, N.J.: T.F.H. 318 pp.

BAHAMAS

Böhlke, J. F., and Chaplin, C. C. G. 1968. *Fishes of the Bahamas*. Wynnewood, Pa.: Livingstone. 771 pp.

PACIFIC

Clemens, W. A., and Wilby, G. V. 1961. *Fishes of the Pacific coast of Canada*. Fish. Res. Bd. Can. Bull. no. 68. Ottawa. 443 pp.

Hart, J. L. 1973. *Pacific fishes of Canada*. Fish. Res. Bd. Can. Bull. no. 180. Ottawa. 740 pp.

Miller, D. J., and Lea, R. N. 1972. *Guide to the coastal fishes of California*. Fish Bull. no. 157. Calif. Dept. of Fish and Game. 249 pp.

GULF OF CALIFORNIA

Thomson, D. A.; Findley, L. T.; and Kerstitch, A. N. 1979. *Reef fishes of the Sea of Cortez: the rocky-shore fishes of the Gulf of California*. New York: Wiley. 302 pp.

HAWAII

Gosline, W. A., and Brock, V. E. 1960. *Handbook of Hawaiian fishes*. Honolulu: University Press of Hawaii. 372 pp.

Tinker, S. W. 1978. *Fishes of Hawaii*. Honolulu: Hawaiian Services. 532 pp.

OLDER IDENTIFICATION SOURCES

Lagler, K. F. 1956. *Freshwater fishery biology*. 2d ed. Dubuque, Iowa: Brown. Pp. 62–74.

WORLDWIDE SOURCES

Blackwelder, R. E. 1972. *Guide to the taxonomic literature of vertebrates*. Ames: Iowa State University Press. Pp. 19–105.

Lindberg, G. V. 1974. *Fishes of the world*. New York: Wiley. Pp. 446–510.

Ricker, W. F., ed. 1968. *Methods of assessment of fish production in freshwaters*. Oxford: Blackwell. Pp. 62–77.

Reading List

Serious ichthyology students would be well advised to read and acquire the following informative and enjoyable books for their personal libraries.

Alexander, R. McN. 1967. *Functional design in fishes*. London: Hutchinson University Library. 160 pp.

Bond, C. E. 1979. *Biology of fishes*. Philadelphia: Saunders. 514 pp.

Curtis, B. 1961. *The life story of the fish*. New York: Dover. 284 pp.

Greenfield, D. W., ed. 1971. *Systematic ichthyology: a collection of readings*. New York: MSS Educational Pub. Co. 297 pp.

Herald, E. S. 1962. *Living fishes of the world*. Garden City, N.Y.: Doubleday. 304 pp.

Lagler, K. F.; Bardach, J. E.; Miller, R. R.; and Passino, D. R. M. 1977. *Ichthyology*. 2d ed. New York: Wiley. 506 pp.

Love, M., and Cailliet, G. M., eds. 1979. *Readings in ichthyology*. Santa Monica, Calif.: Goodyear Publ. Co. 525 pp.

Marshall, N. B. 1965. *The life of fishes*. London: Weidenfeld and Nicholson.

Nikolsky, G. V. 1963. *The ecology of fishes*. London and New York: Academic Press. 352 pp.

Norman, J. R., and Greenwood, P. H. 1975. *The history of fishes*. 3d ed. New York: Wiley. 467 pp.

Ommanney, F. D. 1964. *The fishes*. Life Nature Library. New York: Time. 192 pp.

Schultz, L. P., and Stern, E. M. 1948. *The ways of fishes*. Princeton, N.J.: Van Nostrand. 264 pp.

Fish Classification, Embryology, and Physiology References

Fish Classification

Berg, L. S. 1940. Classification of fishes both recent and fossil. *Trav. Inst. Zool. Acad. Sci. URSS 5, no. 2:87–517*. Lithoprint. Ann Arbor, Mich.: J. W. Edwards, 1947.

Gosline, W. A. 1971. *Functional morphology and classification of teleostean fishes*. Honolulu: University Press of Hawaii. 208 pp.

Greenwood, P. H.; Rosen, D. E.; Weitzman, S. H.; and Myers, G. S. 1966. Phyletic studies of teleostean fishes, with a provisional classification of living forms. *Bull. Amer. Mus. Nat. Hist.* 131, no. 4:339–456.

Jordan, D. S. 1963. *The genera of fishes and a classification of fishes*. Stanford, Calif.: Stanford University Press. 800 pp. Reprint of 1917–20 and 1923 works.

Lindberg, D. U. 1974. *Fishes of the world*. New York: Wiley. 545 pp.

McAllister, D. E. 1968. *Evolution of branchiostegals and classification of teleostome fishes*. Nat. Mus. Can. Bull. no. 221. 239 pp.

Nelson, J. S. 1976. *Fishes of the world*. New York: Wiley. 416 pp.

Norman, J. R. 1966. *A draft synopsis of the orders, families, and genera of recent fishes and fish-like vertebrates*. London: British Museum (Nat. Hist.) 649 pp. Photolithograph of author's 1939–44 manuscript.

Fish Embryology

Fish and Wildlife Service. 1978. *Development of fishes of the mid-Atlantic bight—an atlas of egg, larval, and juvenile stages*. 6 vols. Washington, D.C.: U.S. Government Printing Office. 2,288 pp. 1,241 illus.

Fish Physiology

Hoar, W. S., and Randall, D. J., eds. 1969–79. *Fish physiology*. 8 vols. New York: Academic Press.

References

Adler, H. E. 1975. *Fish behavior: why fishes do what they do.* Neptune City, N.J.: T.F.H. Publ.

Alfred, E. R. 1969. The Malayan cyprinoid fishes of the family Homalopteridae. *Zool. Meded.* 43, no. 18:213–37.

Allen, G. R. 1978. A review of the archerfishes (family Toxotidae). *Rec. West. Aust. Mus.* 6, no. 4:355–78.

———. 1980. A generic classification of rainbowfishes (Melanotaeniidae). *Rec. West. Aust. Mus.* 8, no. 3:449–90.

Allen, K. R. 1951. *The Horokiwi Stream.* New Zealand Marine Dept. Fish. Bull. no. 10.

Alexander, R. McN. 1964. The structure of the Weberian apparatus in the Siluri. *Proc. Zool. Soc. Lond.* 142, no. 3:419–40.

American Zoologist. 1977. Recent advances in the biology of sharks. *American Zoologist* 17, no. 2:287–515.

Andrews, A. P. 1976. A revision of the family Galaxiidae (Pisces) in Tasmania. *Aust. J. Mar. Freshwater Res.* 27:297–349.

Andrews, S. M.; Gardiner, B. G.; Miles, R. S.; and Patterson, C. 1967. Pisces. In *The fossil record,* ed. W. B. Harland et al., pp. 637–83. London: Geological Soc.

Annandale, N. 1918. Fish and fisheries of the Inle Lake. *Rec. Indian Mus.* 14:33–64.

Annandale, N., and Hora, S. L. 1923. The systematic position of the Burmese fish *Chaudhuria. Ann. Mag. Nat. Hist.,* 9th ser. 11:327–33.

Axelrod, H. R. 1974. *African cichlids of Lakes Malawi and Tanganyika.* Neptune City, N.J.: T.F.H. Publ.

Bailey, R. J. 1936. The osteology and relationships of the phallostethid fishes. *J. Morph.* 59:453–83.

Bailey, R. M. 1971. Pisces (Zoology). In *McGraw-Hill Encyclopedia of Science and Technology,* 10:281–82. 3d ed.

Bailey, R. M., et al. 1970. *A list of common and scientific names of fishes from the United States and Canada.* 3d edition. Amer. Fish. Soc. Spec. Publ. no. 6.

Baldridge, H. D. 1974. *Shark attack: a program of data reduction and analysis.* Contri. Mote Mar. Lab., vol. 1, no. 2. Reprint. New York: Berkley Publ. Corp.

Balon, E. K., ed. 1980. *Charrs: salmonid fishes of the genus "Salvelinus."* The Hague: Junk.

Banarescu, P. 1973. Carp. In *Grzimek's animal life encyclopedia* 4:305–55. New York: Van Nostrand Reinhold Co.

Banister, K. E. 1970. The anatomy and taxonomy of *Indostomus paradoxus* Prashad and Mukerji. *Bull. Br. Mus. Nat. Hist. (Zool.)* 19:179–209.

Barbour, C. D. 1973. A biogeographical history of *Chirostoma* (Pisces: Atherinidae): a species flock from the Mexican plateau. *Copeia,* no. 3, pp. 533–56.

Barbour, C. D., and Brown, J. H. 1974. Fish species diversity in lakes. *Amer. Nat.* 108:473–89.

Barlow, G. W.; Liem, K. F.; and Wickler, W. 1968. Badidae, a new fish family—behavioural, osteological, and developmental evidence. *J. Zool.* 156:415–47.

Barnard, K. H. N.d. A pictorial guide to South African fishes. Cape Town: Maskew Miller.

———. 1943. Revision of the indigenous freshwater fishes of the S.W. Cape region. *Ann. South African Mus.* 36:101–262.

Bartholomew, J. G.; Clarke, W. E.; and Grimshaw, P. H. 1911. *Atlas of zoogeography.* Edinburgh: Bartholomew.

Beamish, R. J.; Merriles, M. J.; and Crossman, E. J. 1971. Karyotypes and DNA values for members of the suborder Esocoidei (Osteichthyes: Salmoniformes). *Chromosoma* 34:436–47.

Behnke, R. J. 1972. The systematics of salmonid fishes of recently glaciated lakes. *J. Fish. Res. Bd. Can.* 29:639–71.

———. 1974. Salmoniformes. In *Encyclopaedia Britannica macropaedia* 16:185–92.

Bell, J. D., et al. 1981. Recent records of the Australian grayling *Prototroctes maraena* Gunther (Pisces: Prototroctidae) with notes on its distribution. *Aust. Zool.* In press.

Bell, M. A. 1976. Evolution of phenotypic diversity in *Gasterosteus aculeatus* superspecies on the Pacific coast of North America. *Syst. Zool.* 25:211–27.

Bell-Cross, G. 1968. *The distribution of fishes in central Africa.* Fish. Res. Bull. Zambia no. 4.

Bennett, G. W. 1971. *Management of lakes and ponds.* 2d ed. New York: Van Nostrand.

Bennett, M. V. L. 1971a. Electric organs. In *Fish physiology,* ed.

W. S. Hoar and D. J. Randall, 5:347–491. New York: Academic Press.

———. 1971b. Electroreception. In *Fish physiology*, ed. W. S. Hoar and D. J. Randall, 5:493–574. New York: Academic Press.

Berg, L. S. 1940. Classification of fishes, both recent and fossil. *Trav. Inst. Zool. Acad. Sci. URSS* 5(2):87–517. Lithoprint. Ann Arbor, Mich.: J. W. Edwards, 1947.

———. 1949. Freshwater fishes of the USSR and adjacent countries. 4th ed. 3 vols. Jerusalem: Israel Program for Scientific Translation.

Berggren, W. A., and Hollister, C. D. 1974. Paleogeography, paleobiology, and the history of circulation in the Atlantic Ocean. In *Studies in paleo-oceanography*, ed. W. Hay, pp. 126–86. Spec. Publ. Soc. Econ. Paleont. Mineral. no. 20.

Berra, T. M. 1973. A home range study of *Galaxias bongbong* in Australia. *Copeia*, no. 2, pp. 363–66.

Berra, T. M., and Berra, R. M. 1977. A temporal and geographical analysis of new teleost names proposed at twenty-five year intervals from 1869–1970. *Copeia*, no. 4, pp. 640–47.

Berra, T. M., and Gunning, G. E. 1972. Seasonal movements and home range of the longear sunfish, *Lepomis megalotis* (Rafinesque), in Louisiana. *Amer. Midl. Nat.* 88:368–75.

Berra, T. M.; Moore, R.; and Reynolds, L. F. 1975. The freshwater fishes of the Laloki River system of New Guinea. *Copeia*, no. 2, pp. 316–26.

Berra, T. M., and Weatherley, A. H. 1972. A systematic study of the Australian freshwater serranid fish genus *Maccullochella*. *Copeia*, no. 1, pp. 53–64.

Berry, F. H. 1964. Review and emendation of "Family Clupeidae," by Samuel F. Hildebrand. *Copeia*, no. 4, pp. 720–30.

Bertin, L. 1956. *Eels: a biological study*. London: Cleaver-Hume.

Bertin, L., and Arambourg, C. 1958. Ichthyogeographie. In *Traité de zoologie*, ed. P. P. Grasse, 13, fasc. 3:1944–66.

Bertmar, G. 1968. Lungfish phylogeny. In *Current problems of lower vertebrate phylogeny*, ed. T Ørvig, pp. 259–83. New York: Wiley.

Bigelow, H. B., and Schroeder, W. C. 1948. Sharks. In *Fishes of the western North Atlantic*, 1(1):59–576. New Haven, Conn.: Mem. Sears Found. Mar. Res.

———. 1963. Family Osmeridae. In *Fishes of the western North Atlantic*, 1(3):553–97. New Haven, Conn.: Mem. Sears Found. Mar. Res.

Birdsong, R. S. 1975. The osteology of *Microgobius signatus* Poey (Pisces: Gobiidae), with comments on other gobioid fishes. *Bull. Fla. State Mus., Biol. Sci.* 19, no. 3:135–87.

Birkhead, W. S. 1972. Toxicity of stings of ariid and ictalurid catfishes. *Copeia*, no. 4, pp. 790–807.

Bishop, K. A., and Bell, J. D. 1978. Observations on the fish fauna below Tallowa Dam (Shoalhaven River, New South Wales) during river flow stoppages. *Aust. J. Mar. Freshwat. Res.* 29:1–7.

———. 1979. Aspects of the biology of the Australian grayling *Prototroctes maraena* Gunther (Pisces: Prototroctidae). *Aust. J. Mar. Freshwat. Res.* 29:743–61.

Blackburn, M. 1950. The Tasmanian whitebait, *Lovettea seali* (Johnston), and the whitebait fishery. *Aust. J. Mar. Freshwat. Res.* 1:155–98.

Boeseman, M. 1956. Fresh-water sawfishes and sharks in Netherlands New Guinea. *Science* 123:222–23.

———. 1964. Notes on the fishes of western New Guinea III: the fresh water shark of Jamoer Lake. *Zool. Meded.* 40:9–22.

Böhlke, J. 1955. Studies on fishes of the family Characidae—no. 10: notes on the coloration of the species of *Hemiodus*, *Pterohemiodus*, and *Anisitria*, with the description of a new *Hemiodus* from the Rio Negro at the Brazil-Colombia Border. *Notulae Naturae*, no. 278.

Böhlke, J., and Myers, G. S. 1956. Studies on fishes of the family Characidae—no. 11: a new genus and species of hemiodontins from the Rio Orinoco in Venezuela. *Notulae Naturae*, no. 286.

Borror, D. J. 1960. *Dictionary of word roots and combining forms*. Palo Alto, Calif.: Mayfield Publ. Co.

Boulenger, G. A. 1909–16. Catalogue of the fresh-water fishes of Africa. 4 vols. London: British Museum (Nat. Hist.).

———. 1912. A synopsis of the fishes of the genus *Mastacembelus*. *J. Acad. Nat. Sci. Philadelphia*, 2d ser. 15:197–203.

Branson, B. A., and Moore, G. A. 1962. The lateralis components of the acoustico-lateralis system in the sunfish family Centrarchidae. *Copeia*, pp. 1–108.

Breder, C. M., Jr. 1929. *Field book of marine fishes of the Atlantic coast*. New York: Putnam's.

Breder, C. M., Jr., and Rosen, D. E. 1966. Modes of reproduction in fishes. Garden City, N.Y.: Natural History Press.

Brichard, P. 1978. Fishes of Lake Tanganyika. Neptune City, N.J., T.F.H. Publ.

Briggs, J. C. 1974. Operation of zoogeographic barriers. *Syst. Zool.* 23:248–56.

———. 1979. Ostariophysan zoogeography: an alternative hypothesis. *Copeia*, no. 1, pp. 111–18.

Brooks, J. L. 1950. Speciation in ancient lakes. *Quart. Rev. Biol.* 25:131–76.

Brown, T. W. 1973. *Sharks: the silent savages*. Boston: Little, Brown and Co.

Brundin, L. 1975. Circum-antarctic distribution patterns and continental drift. *Mem. Mus. natn. hist. nat.*, 88:19–27.

Bruun, A. F. 1963. The breeding of the North Atlantic freshwater eels. *Adv. Mar. Biol.* 1:137–70.

Budker, P. 1971. *The life of sharks*. New York: Columbia University Press.

Cantor, T. E. 1849. Catalogue of Malayan fishes. *J. of Asiatic Society of Bengal* 18, no. 2:983–1443.

Carl, G. C.; Clemens, W. A.; and Lindsey, C. C. 1959. *The freshwater fishes of British Columbia*. British Columbia Provincial Museum Handbook no. 5. 3d ed.

Carlander, K. D. 1977. *Handbook of freshwater fishery biology*. 2d ed. Ames: Iowa State University Press.

Casey, J. G. 1964. *Angler's guide to sharks of the northeastern United States, Maine to Chesapeake Bay*. Bureau of Sport Fish. and Wildlife Circular no. 179. Washington, D.C.

Castex, M. N. 1967. Fresh water venomous rays. In *Animal Toxins*, ed. F. E. Russell and P. R. Saunders, pp. 167–76. Oxford: Pergamon Press.

Cavender, T. M. 1969. *An Oligocene mudminnow (family Umbridae) from Oregon with remarks on relationships within the Esocoidei*. Occas. Pap. Mus. Zool. Univ. Mich. no. 660.

———. 1978. Taxonomy and distribution of the bull trout, *Salvelinus confluentus* (Suckey), from the American Northwest. *Calif. Fish and Game*. 64, no. 3:139–74.

Chardon, M. 1967. Réflexions sur la dispersion des Ostariophysi à la lumière de recherches morphologiques nouvelles. *Ann. Soc. R. Zool. Belg.* 97, no. 3:175–86.

———. 1968. Anatomie comparée de l'appareil de Weber et des

structures connexes chez les Siluriformes. *Mus. R. Afr. Cent. Ann.*, 8th ser. (Zool.) 169:1–277.

Clausen, H. S. 1959. Denticipitidae, a new family of primitive isopondylous teleosts from West African freshwater. *Vidensk Meddr. Dansk Naturh. Foren.* 121:141–51.

Clemens, W. A., and Wilby, G. V. 1961. *Fishes of the Pacific Coast of Canada.* Fish Res. Bd. Can. Bull. no. 68. Ottawa.

Cohen, D. M. 1970. How many recent fishes are there? *Proc. Calif. Acad. Sci.* 38:341–46.

Cohen, D. M., and Nielson, J. G. 1978. *Guide to the identification of genera of the fish order Ophidiiformes with a tentative classification of the order.* NOAA Technical Report, NMFS Circular no. 417.

Cohen, D. M., and Robins, C. R. 1970. A new ophidioid fish (Genus *Lucifuga*) from a limestone sink: New Providence Island, Bahamas. *Proc. Biol. Soc. Wash.* 83, no. 11:133–44.

Colbert, E. H. 1973. *Wandering lands and animals.* New York: Dutton.

Coleman, N. 1974. *Australian marine fishes in colour.* Sydney: Reed.

Collette, B. B. 1963. The subfamilies, tribes, and genera of the Percidae (Teleostei). *Copeia*, no. 4, pp. 615–23.

———. 1965. Hemiramphidae (Pisces, Synentognathi) from Tropical West Africa. *Atlantide Report*, no. 8, pp. 218–35.

———. 1966. "Belonion," a new genus of fresh-water needlefishes from South America. Amer. Mus. Novitates no. 2274.

———. 1966. A review of the venomous toadfishes, subfamily Thalassophryninae. *Copeia*, no. 4, pp. 846–64.

———. 1967. The taxonomic history of the darters (Percidae: Etheostomatini). *Copeia*, no. 4, pp. 814–19.

———. 1973. *Daector quadrizonatus,* a valid species of freshwater venomous toadfish from the Rio Truando, Colombia, with notes on additional material of other species of *Daector. Copeia*, no. 2, pp. 355–57.

———. 1974a. *Potamorrhaphis petersi,* a new species of freshwater needlefish (Belonidae) from the upper Orinoco and Rio Negro. *Proc. Biol. Soc. Wash.* 87:31–40.

———. 1974b. *Strongylura hubbsi,* a new species of freshwater needlefish from the Usumacinta Province of Guatemala and Mexico. *Copeia*, no. 3, pp. 611–19.

———. 1974c. South American freshwater needlefishes (Belonidae) of the genus *Pseudotylosurus. Zool. Meded.* 48, no. 16:169–86.

———. 1974d. The garfishes (Hemiramphidae) of Australia and New Zealand. *Rec. Aust. Mus.* 29:11–105.

———. 1976. Indo–west Pacific halfbeaks (Hemiramphidae) of the genus *Rhynchorhampus,* with descriptions of two new species. *Bull. Mar. Sci.* 26, no. 1:72–98.

———. 1977. Epidermal breeding tubercles and bony contact organs in fishes. *Symp. Zool. Soc. Lond.* no. 39, pp. 225–68.

Collette, B. B., et al. 1977. Biology of the percids. *J. Fish. Res. Board Can.* 34:1890–99.

Collette, B. B., and Banarescu, P. 1977. Systematics and zoogeography of the fishes of the family Percidae. *J. Fish. Res. Board. Can.* 34:1450–63.

Collette, B. B., and Knapp, L. W. 1966. Catalog of type specimens of the darters (Pisces, Percidae, Etheostomatini). *Proc. U.S. Nat. Mus.* 119, no. 3550.

Collette, B. B., and Parin, N. V. 1970. Needlefishes (Belonidae) of the eastern Atlantic Ocean. *Atlantide Report*, no. 11, pp. 7–60.

Cooper, A. 1971. Fishes of the World. New York: Grosset & Dunlap.

Cooper, J. E., and Kuehne, R. A. 1974. *Speoplatyrhinus poulsoni,* a new genus and species of subterranean fish from Alabama. *Copeia*, no. 2, pp. 486–93.

Coppleson, V. M. 1958. *Shark attack.* Sydney: Angus and Robertson.

Courtenay, W. R., Jr.; Sahlman, H. F.; Miley, W. W., II; and Herrena, D. J. 1974. Exotic fishes in fresh and brackish waters of Florida. *Biol. Cons.* 6, no. 4:292–302.

Cousteau, J.-Y., and Cousteau, P. 1970. *The shark: splendid savage of the sea.* New York: Doubleday.

Cox, C. B. 1974. Vertebrate paleodistributional patterns and continental drift. *Jour. Biogeogr.* 1:75–94.

Cracraft, J. 1974. Continental drift and vertebrate distribution. *Ann. Rev. Ecol. Syst.* 5:215–61.

———. 1975. Mesozoic dispersal of terrestrial faunas around the southern end of the world. *Mem. Mus. nat. hist. nat.* 88:29–54.

Crass, R. S. 1964. *Freshwater fishes of natal.* Pietermaritzburg: Shuter & Shooter.

Cressy, R. F., and Collette, B. B. 1971. Copepods and needlefishes: a study in host-parasite relationships. *Fish. Bull.* 68:347–432.

Croizat, L.; Nelson, G.; and Rosen, D. E. 1974. Centers of origin and related concepts. *Syst. Zool.* 23:265–87.

Crossman, E. J. 1966. A taxonomic study of *Esox americanus* and its subspecies in eastern North America. *Copeia*, no. 1, pp. 1–20.

———. 1978. Taxonomy and distribution of North American esocids. In *Selected coolwater fishes of North America*, ed. R. L. Kendall, pp. 13–26. Amer. Fish. Soc. Spec. Publ. no. 11.

Darlington, P. J., Jr. 1957. *Zoogeography.* New York: Wiley.

Davies, D. H. 1963. *Shark attack and its relation to temperature beach patronage and the seasonal abundance of dangerous sharks.* South African Assn. Mar. Biol. Res. Investigational Report no. 6.

———. 1964. *About sharks and shark attack.* Durban: Brown, Davis and Platt.

Dawson, C. E. 1972. Nektonic pipefishes (Syngnathidae) from the Gulf of Mexico off Mississippi. *Copeia*, no. 4, pp. 844–48.

———. 1978. *Syngnathus parvicarinatus,* a new Australian pipefish, with notes on *S. sauvagei* (Whitley) and *Leptonotus caretta* (Klunzinger). *Copeia*, no. 2, pp. 288–93.

Day, F. 1878. *The fishes of India.* Vol 1. Reprint. New Delhi: Today & Tomorrow's Book Agency, 1971.

de V. Pienaar, U. 1968. *The freshwater fishes of the Kruger National Park.* National Parks Board of South Africa.

DeWitt, H. H. 1969. A second species of the family Cottidae from the New Zealand region. *Copeia*, no. 1, pp. 30–34.

Dietz, R. S., and Holden, J. C. 1970. Reconstruction of Pangeaea: breakup and dispersion of continents, Permian to present. *J. Geophys. Res.* 75:4939–56.

Druzhinin, A. D. 1974. On distribution and biology of drums (or croakers)—Sciaenidae family—throughout the world ocean. *Ichthyologica* 6:37–47.

Dymond, J. R. 1963. Family Salmonidae. In *Fishes of the western North Atlantic*, pp. 457–502. Mem. Sears Found. Mar. Res. no. 1, pt. 3. New Haven.

Eastman, J. T. 1977. The pharyngeal bones and teeth of catostomid fishes. *Amer. Midl. Nat.* 97:68–88.

Eddy, S. 1969. *How to know the freshwater fishes.* 2d ed. Dubuque, Iowa: Brown.

Eddy, S., and Underhill, J. C. 1974. *Northern fishes.* Minneapolis: University of Minnesota Press.

Edmonds, C. 1975. *Dangerous marine animals of the Indo-Pacific region*. Newport, Victoria, Australia: Wedneil Publ.

Edwards, H., ed. 1975. *Sharks and shipwrecks*. New York: New York Times Book Co.

Ege, W. 1939. A revision of the genus *Anguilla* Shaw: a systematic, phylogenetic, and geographical study. *Dana Rep.* 16:1–256.

Eigenmann, C. H. 1909a. The fresh-water fishes of Patagonia and an examination of the Archiplata-Archhelenis theory. In *Reports of Princeton University Expedition to Patagonia, 1896–1899*, 3, pt. 3:225–374.

———. 1909b. *Cave vertebrates of America*. Carnegie Inst. Wash. Publ. no. 104.

———. 1910. Catalogue of the fresh-water fishes of tropical and south temperate America. In *Reports of Princeton University Expedition to Patagonia 1896–1899*, 3, pt. 4:375–511.

———. 1912. The freshwater fishes of British Guiana, including a study of the ecological grouping of species and the relation of the fauna of the plateau to that of the lowlands. *Mem. Carnegie Mus.* 5.

———. 1918. The Pygidiidae: a family of South American catfish. *Mem. Carnegie Mus.* 7, no. 5:259–398.

———. 1922. The fishes of western South America, pt. 1: the fishes of northwestern South America. *Mem. Carnegie Mus.* 9, no. 1:1–350.

———. 1927. The fresh-water fishes of Chile. *Mem. Nat. Acad. Sci.* 22, no. 2:1–63.

Eigenmann, C. H., and Allen, W. R. 1942. Fishes of western South America. Lexington, Ky.: University of Kentucky.

Eigenmann, C. H., and Eigenmann, R. S. 1889. A revision of the edentulouse genera of Curimatinae. *Ann. N.Y. Acad. Sci.* 4:409–40.

———. 1892. A catalogue of the fresh-water fishes of South America. *Proc. U.S. Nat. Mus.* 14:1–81.

Eigenmann, C. H., and Myers, G. S. 1917–29. *The American Characidae*. Mem. Mus. Comp. Zool. no. 43, 5 parts.

Ellis, M. M. 1913. The gymnotid eels of tropical America. *Mem. Carnegie Mus.* 6:109–204.

Ellis, R. 1975. *The book of sharks*. New York: Grosset and Dunlap.

Ferris, S. D., and Whitt, G. S. 1978. Phylogeny of tetraploid catostomid fishes based on the loss of duplicate gene expression. *Syst. Zool.* 27:189–206.

Fitch, J. S., and Lavenberg, J. 1971. *Marine food and game fishes of California*. Berkeley: University of California Press.

Fitzsimons, J. M. 1972. A revision of two genera of goodeid fishes (Cyprinodontiformes, Osteichthyes) from the Mexican Plateau. *Copeia*, no. 4, 728–56.

———. 1976. Ethological isolating mechanisms in goodeid fishes of the genus *Xenotoca* (Cyprinodontiformes, Osteichthyes). *Bull. South. Calif. Acad. Sci.* 75:84–99.

Forey, P. L. 1973. *A revision of the elopiform fishes, fossil and recent. Bull. Br. Mus. Nat. Hist. (Geol.)*, suppl. no. 10.

Fowler, H. W. 1932. A synopsis of the fishes of China, part IV: the cats, lizard fishes, green gars, half beaks, and flying fishes. *Hong Kong naturalist* 3:247–79. Reprinted in H. W. Fowler, *A synopsis of the fishes of China*, vol. 1. Lochem, Netherlands: Antiquariaat Junk, 1972.

———. 1934. A synopsis of the fishes of China, part V, continued. *Hong Kong naturalist* 5:304–19. Reprinted in H. W. Fowler, *A synopsis of the fishes of China*, vol. 1. Lochem, Netherlands: Antiquariaat Junk, 1972.

———. 1956. *Fishes of the Red Sea and southern Arabia*. Vol. 1. Jerusalem: Weizmann Science Press of Israel.

———. 1959. *Fishes of Fiji*. Suva: Government of Fiji.

———. 1972. *A Synopsis of the Fishes of China*. 2 vols. Lochem, Netherlands: Antiquariaat Junk.

Frankenberg, R. 1969. Studies on the evolution of galaxiid fishes with particular reference to the Australian fauna. Ph.D. dissertation, Univ. of Melbourne.

———. 1974. Native freshwater fish. In *Biogeography and Ecology in Tasmania*, ed. W. D. Williams, pp. 113–40. Monographiae Biologicae no. 25. The Hague: Junk.

Fraser-Brunner, A. 1950. A revision of the fishes of the family Gasteropelecidae. *Ann. Mag. Nat. Hist.*, 12th ser. 3:959–70.

Freihofer, W. C., and Lin, M. W. 1974. Perciformes. In *Encyclopaedia Britannica macropaedia*, 14:46–58.

Freihofer, W. C., and Neil, E. H. 1967. Commensalism between midge larvae (Diptera:Chironomidae) and catfishes of the family Astroblepidae and Loricariidae. *Copeia*, no. 1, pp. 39–45.

Fryer, G., and Iles, T. D. 1972. *The cichlid fishes of the Great Lakes of Africa*. Neptune City, N.J.: T.F.H. Publ.

Fuiman, L. A. 1979. Descriptions and comparisons of catostomid fish larvae: Northern Atlantic drainage species. *Trans. Amer. Fish. Soc.* 108:560–603.

Fuiman, L. A., and Witman, D. C. 1979. Descriptions and comparisons of catostomid fish larvae: *Catostomus catastomus* and *Moxostoma erythrurum*. *Trans. Amer. Fish. Soc.* 108:604–19.

Garman, S. 1913. *The Plagiostomia (sharks, skates, and rays)*. Mem. Mus. Comp. Zool. no. 36.

Garrick, J. A. F. 1967. A broad view of *Carcharinus* species, their systematics and distribution. In *Sharks, skates, and rays*, ed. P. W. Gilbert, R. F. Mathewson, and D. P. Rall, pp. 85–91. Baltimore: Johns Hopkins University Press.

Garrick, J. A. F., and Schultz, L. P. 1963. A guide to the kinds of potentially dangerous sharks. In *Sharks and survival*, ed. P. W. Gilbert, pp. 3–60. Boston: Heath & Co.

Gehringer, V. W. 1959. Early development and metamorphosis of the ten-pounder *Elops saurus* Linnaeus. *U.S. Fish and Wild. Serv. Bull.* 59, no. 155:619–47.

Gery, J. 1969. The freshwater fishes of South America. In *Biogeography and Ecology in South America*, ed. E. J. Fittkau et al., pp. 828–48. Monographiae Biologicae no. 19. The Hague: Junk.

———. 1972. *Poissons characoides des Guyanes, I: generalites; II: famille des Serrasalmidae*. Zoologische Verhandelingen no. 122. Leiden.

———. 1973a. Order: mormyrids. In *Grzimek's animal life encyclopedia*, 4:205–12. New York: Van Nostrand Reinhold.

———. 1973b. Characins and electric eels. In *Grzimek's animal life encyclopedia*, 4:276–304. New York: Van Nostrand Reinhold.

Gilbert, C. R. 1976. Composition and derivation of the North American freshwater fish fauna. *Fla. Scientist* 39, no. 2:104–11.

———. 1978. Type catalogue of the North American cyprinid fish genus *Notropis*. *Bull. Fla. State Mus. Biol. Sci.* 23, no. 1:1–104.

Gilbert, P. W., ed. 1963. *Sharks and survival*. Boston: Heath and Co.

Gilbert, P. W.; Mathewson, R. F.; and Rall, D. P., eds. 1967. *Sharks, skates, and rays*. Baltimore: Johns Hopkins University Press.

Glen, W. 1975. *Continental drift and plate tectonics*. Columbus, Ohio: Merrill.

Glucksman, J.; West, G.; and Berra, T. M. 1976. The introduced fishes of Papua New Guinea with special reference to *Tilapia mossambica*. *Biol. Cons.* 9:37–44.

Gordon, B. L. 1977. *The secret lives of fishes*. New York: Grosset and Dunlap.

Gosline, W. A. 1966. The limits of the fish family Serranidae with notes on other lower percoids. *Proc. Calif. Acad. Sci.* 33:91–112.

——. 1968. The suborders of perciform fishes. *Proc. U.S. Nat. Mus.* no. 124, pp. 1–78.

——. 1971. *Functional morphology and classification of teleostean fishes.* Honolulu: University Press of Hawaii.

——. 1973. Considerations regarding the phylogeny of Cypriniform fishes, with special reference to structures associated with feeding. *Copeia*, no. 4, pp. 761–76.

——. 1975. The palatine-maxillary mechanism in catfishes, with comments on the evolution and zoogeography of modern siluroids. *Occ. Pap. Calif. Acad. Sci.*, no. 120, pp. 1–31.

——. 1978. *Unbranched dorsal-fin rays and subfamily classification in the fish family Cyprinidae.* Occ. Pap. Mus. Zool. Univ. Mich. no. 684.

Gosztonyi, A. E., and McDowall, R. M. 1974. Zoogeography of *Galaxias maculatus* in South America. *Copeia*, no. 4, pp. 978–79.

Graham, J. B. 1972. Aerial vision in amphibious fishes. *Fauna* 3:14–23.

Graham, K., and Bonislawsky, P. 1978. *An indexed bibliography of the paddlefish ("Polydon spathula").* Columbia: Missouri Dept. of Conservation.

Greenwood, P. H. 1968. The osteology and relationships of the Denticipitidae, a family of clupeomorph fishes. *Bull. Br. Mus. Nat. Hist. (Zool.)* 16:213–73.

——. 1974a. *The cichlid fishes of Lake Victoria, East Africa: the biology and evolution of a species flock.* Bull. Br. Mus. Nat. Hist. (Zool.), suppl. no. 6.

——. 1974b. Review of the Cenozoic freshwater fish faunas in Africa. *Ann. Geol. Surv. Egypt.* 4:211–32.

——. 1974c. Osteoglossomorpha. In *Encyclopaedia Britannica macropaedia*, 13:763–65.

——. 1976. A review of the family Centropomidae (Pisces, Perciformes). *Bull. Br. Mus. Nat. Hist. (Zool.)* 29, no. 1:1–81.

——. 1977. Notes on the anatomy and classification of elopomorph fishes. *Bull. Br. Mus. Nat. Hist. (Zool.)* 32, no. 4:65–102.

Greenwood, P.H.; Rosen, D. E.; Weitzman, S. H.; and Myers, G. S. 1966. Phyletic studies of teleostean fishes, with a provisional classification of living forms. *Bull. Amer. Mus. Nat. Hist.* 131, no. 4:339–456.

Greenwood, P. H., and Thomson, K. S. 1960. The pectoral anatomy of *Pantodon buchholzi* (a freshwater flying fish) and the related Osteoglossidae. *Proc. Zool. Soc. London.* 135:283–301.

Gregory, W. K., and Conrad, G. M. 1938. The phylogeny of the characin fishes. *Zoologica* 23:319–60.

Gruchy, I. M., and McAllister, D. E. 1972. *A bibliography of the smelt family, Osmeridae.* Fish. Res. Bd. Can. Tech. Rept. no. 368.

Grundfest, H. 1960. Electric fishes. *Sci. Amer.* 203:115–24.

Grzimek, B., ed. 1973. *Grzimek's Animal Life Encyclopedia.* Vol. 4. *Fishes.* New York: Van Nostrand Reinhold.

——, ed. 1974. *Grzimek's animal life encyclopedia.* Vol. 5. *Fishes II: Amphibians.* New York: Van Nostrand Reinhold.

Gudger, E. W. 1930. *The Candiru—the only vertebrate parasite of man.* New York: Hoeber.

Gunter, G. 1938. Notes on invasion of fresh water by fishes of the Gulf of Mexico, with special reference to the Mississippi-Atchafalaya river system. *Copeia*, no. 1, pp. 69–72.

Gunther, A. 1870. *Catalogue of fishes in the British Museum.* Vol. 8. London: British Museum.

Hagen, D. W., and McPhail, J. D. 1970. The species problem within *Gasterosteus aculeatus* in the Pacific coast of North America. *J. Fish. Res. Bd. Can.* 27:147–155.

Haig, J. 1950. Studies on the classification of the catfishes of the Oriental and Palaearctic family Siluridae. *Rec. Indian Mus.* 48:59–116.

Halstead, B. W. 1967–70. *Poisonous and venomous marine animals of the world.* Vols. 2 and 3. *Vertebrates.* Washington, D.C.: U.S. Govt. Print. Office.

Harden-Jones, F. R. 1968. *Fish migration.* London: Arnold.

Hardisty, M. W., and Potter, I. C., eds. 1971. *The biology of lampreys.* Vol. 1. New York: Academic Press.

Harrington, R. W., Jr. 1961. Oviparous hermaphroditic fish with internal self-fertilization. *Science* 134:1749–50.

Harry, R. R. 1953. A contribution to the classification of the African catfishes of the family Amphiliidae, with description of collections from Cameroon. *Revue de zoologie et de botanique africaines* 47, nos. 3–4:177–232.

Hart, J. L. 1973. *Pacific Fishes of Canada.* Fish. Res. Bd. Canada Bull. no. 180.

Hasler, A. D. 1966. *Underwater guideposts.* Madison: University of Wisconsin Press.

Herald, E. S. 1959. From pipefish to seahorse—a study of phylogenetic relationships. *Proc. Calif. Acad. Sci.* 29, no. 13:465–73.

——. 1962. *Living fishes of the world.* Garden City, New York: Doubleday.

Herre, A. W. 1927. *Gobies of the Philippines and the China Sea.* Philippine Bureau of Science Monograph no. 23.

——. 1939. The genera of Phallostethidae. *Proc. Biol. Soc. Wash.* 52:139–44.

——. 1942. New and little known phallostethids with keys to the genera of Philippine species. *Stanford Ichthyol. Bull.* 2:137–56.

——. 1944. A review of the halfbeaks or Hemiramphidae of the Philippines and adjacent waters. *Stanford Univ. Publ. Biol. Sci.* 9, no. 2:41–86.

——. 1953. *Check list of Philippine fishes.* Fish and Wildlife Res. Rept. no. 20. Washington, D.C.

Hickman, C. P., Sr.; Hickman, C. P., Jr.; and Hickman, F. M. 1974. *Integrated principles of zoology.* 5th ed. St. Louis: Mosby.

Hildebrand, S. F. 1925. Fishes of the Republic of El Salvador. *Bull. Bureau Fisheries* 41:237–87.

——. 1943. A review of the American anchovies (family Engraulidae). *Bull. Bingham Oceanographic Collection* 8, no. 2:1–165.

——. 1963a. Family Elopidae. In *Fishes of the western North Atlantic*, pp. 111–37. Mem. Sears Found. Mar. Res. no. 1, pt. 3. New Haven, Conn.

——. 1963b. Family Engraulidae. In *Fishes of the western North Atlantic*, pp. 152–249. Mem. Sears Found. Mar. Res. no. 1, pt. 3. New Haven, Conn.

Hildebrand, F. S.; Rivas, L. R.; and Miller, R. R. 1963. Family Clupeidae. In *Fishes of the western North Atlantic*, pp. 257–452. Mem. Sears Found. for Mar. Res. no. 1, pt. 3. New Haven, Conn.

Hoedeman, J. J. 1974. *Naturalists' guide to freshwater aquarium fish.* New York: Sterling Pub. Co.

Hora, S. L. 1932. Classification, bionomics, and evolution of homalopterid fishes. *Mem. Indian Mus.* 12:263–330.

——. 1933. Siluroid fishes of India, Burma, and Ceylon, I: loach-like fishes of the genus *Amblyceps* Blyth. *Rec. Indian Mus.* 35:607–21.

————. 1936. Siluroid fishes of India, Burma, and Ceylon, II: fishes of the genus *Akysis* Bleeker. *Rec. Indian Mus.* 38:194–209.

————. 1952. Functional divergence, structural convergence, and predaptation exhibited by the fishes of the cyprinoid family Psilorhynchidae Hora. *J. Bombay Nat. Hist. Soc.* 50:880–84.

Horn, M. H. 1972. The amount of space available for marine and freshwater fishes. *Fish. Bull.* 70:1295–97.

Howden, H. F. 1974. Problems in interpreting dispersal of terrestrial organisms related to continental drift. *Biotropica* 6:1–6.

Howes, G. J. 1976. The cranial musculature and taxonomy of characoid fishes of the tribes Cynodontini and Characini. *Bull. Br. Mus. Nat. Hist. (Zool.)* 29, no. 4:203–48.

Hubbs, C. L. 1930. *Material for revision of the catostomid fishes of eastern North America.* Misc. Publ. Mus. Zool. Univ. Michigan. no. 20.

————. 1938. Fishes from the caves of Yucatan. *Carnegie Inst. Washington Publ.*, no. 491, pp. 261–95.

————. 1941. A new family of fishes. *J. Bombay Nat. Hist. Soc.* 42:446–47.

Hubbs, C. L.; Hubbs, L. C.; and Johnson, R. E. 1943. *Hybridization in nature between species of catostomid fishes.* Contri. Lab. Vert. Biol. Univ. Mich. no. 22.

Hubbs, C. L., and Lagler, K. F. 1958. *Fishes of the Great Lakes region.* Ann Arbor: University of Michigan Press.

Hubbs, C. L., and Potter, I. C. 1971. Distribution, phylogeny, and taxonomy. In *Biology of lampreys*, ed. M. W. Hardesty and D. C. Potter, pp. 1–65. New York: Academic Press.

Hubbs, C. L., and Turner, C. L. 1939. *Studies of the fishes of the order cyprinodontes: XVI: a revision of the Goodeidae.* Misc. Publ. Mus. Zool. Univ. Michigan no. 42.

Idyll, C. P. 1969a. Grunion, the fish that spawns on land. *Nat. Geog. Mag.* 135:714–23 (May).

————. 1969b. New Florida resident: the Walking Catfish. *Nat. Geog. Mag.* 135:847–51 (June).

Innes, W. T. 1966. Exotic aquarium fishes. Jersey City, N.J.: T.F.H. Publ.

Jackson, P. B. N. 1961. *The fishes of northern Rhodesia.* Lusaka: Govt. Printer.

Jackson, P. D. 1976. A note on the food of the Australian grayling, *Prototroctes maraena* Gunther (Galaxioidei:Prototroctidae). *Aust. J. Mar. Freshwat. Res.* 27:525–28.

————. 1978. Spawning and early development of the river blackfish, *Gadopsis marmoratus* Richardson (Gadopsiformes:Gadopsidae), in the McKenzie River, Victoria. *Aust. J. Mar. Freshwat. Res.* 29:293–98.

Jarvik, E. 1968. The systematic position of the Dipnoi. In *Current problems of lower vertebrate phylogeny*, ed. T. Ørvig, pp. 223–45. New York: Wiley.

Jayaram, K. C. 1956. Taxonomic status of the Chinese catfish family Cranoglanididae, Myers, 1931. *Proc. Natl. Inst. Sci. India* 21B, no. 6:256–63.

————. 1974. Ecology and distribution of freshwater fishes, amphibia and reptiles. In *Ecology and Biogeography in India*, ed. M. S. Mani, pp. 517–84. Monographiae Biologicae no. 23. The Hague: Junk.

————. 1977. Zoogeography of Indian freshwater fishes. *Proc. Indian Acad. Sci.* 86B:265–74.

Jayaram, K. C., and Majumbar, N. 1964. Siluroid fishes of India, Burma, and Ceylon: 15: fishes of the genus *Chaca* Gray, 1831. *Proc. Zool. Soc. India* 17, no. 2:177–81.

Jenkins, R. E. 1976. A list of undescribed freshwater fish species of continental United States and Canada, with additions to the 1970 Checklist. *Copeia*, no. 3, pp. 642–44.

Jensen, N. H. 1976. Reproduction of the bull shark, *Carcharhinus leucas*, in the Lake Nicaragua–Rio San Juan system. In *Investigations of the ichthyofauna of Nicaraguan lakes*, ed. T. B. Thorson, pp. 539–59.

Jordan, D. S., and Hubbs, C. L. 1919. *A monographic review of the family Atherinidae, or silversides.* Stanford Univ. Publ. Univ. Ser., Studies in Ichthyology.

Jordan, D. S., and Seale, A. 1926. Review of the Engraulidae, with descriptions of new and rare species. *Bull. Mus. Comp. Zool.* 67:335–418.

Jubb, R. A. 1967. *Freshwater fishes of southern Africa.* Cape Town: Bolkema.

Kagwade, P. V. 1970. The polynemid fishes of India. *Bull. Cent. Mar. Fish. Res. Inst.* no. 18, pp. 1–69.

Kahsbauer, K. 1974. Pipefishes and Seahorses. In *Grzimek's animal life encyclopedia*, 5:34–43. New York: Van Nostrand Reinhold.

Karbe, L. 1973. Suborder: salmonids. In *Grzimek's animal life encyclopedia*, 4:213–49. New York: Van Nostrand Reinhold.

Kelly, W. E., and Atz, J. W. 1964. A pygidiid catfish that can suck blood from goldfish. *Copeia*, no. 4, pp. 702–4.

Khalaf, K. T. 1961. *The marine and freshwater fishes of Iraq.* Baghdad: Univ. of Baghdad.

Kiener, A., and Richard-Vindard, G. 1972. Fishes of the continental waters of Madagascar. In *Biogeography and ecology in Madagascar*, ed. R. Battistini and G. Richard-Vindard, pp. 477–99. Monographiae Biologicae no. 21. The Hague: Junk.

Koelz, W. 1929. Coregonid fishes of the Great Lakes. *Bull. Bureau Fisheries* 43:297–643.

Kozhov, M. 1963. *Lake Baikal and its life.* Monographical Biologica no. 11. The Hague: Junk.

Krekorian, C. O'N. 1976. Field observations in Guyana on the reproductive biology of the spraying characid, *Copeina arnoldi* Regan. *Amer. Midl. Nat.* 96, no. 1:88–97.

Krueger, W. H. 1961. Meristic variation in the fourspine stickleback, *Apeltes quadraeus. Copeia*, no. 4, pp. 442–50.

Kyle, H. M. 1913. Flat-fishes (Heterosomata). *Rep. Danish Exped. Medit.* 2:1–156.

————. 1921. The asymmetry, metamorphosis and origin of flatfishes. *Phil. Trans. Royal Soc.*, ser. B, 211:75–129.

Kulkarni, C. V. 1940. On the systematic position, structural modification, bionomics, and development of a remarkable new family of cyprinodont fishes from the province of Bombay. *Rec. Indian Mus.* 42, no. 2:379–423.

Lachner, E. A.; Robins, C. R.; and Courtenay, W. R., Jr. 1970. *Exotic fishes and other acquatic organisms introduced into North America.* Smithsonian Contri. Zool., no. 59.

Ladiges, W. 1973. Order: Bonytongues. In *Grzimek's animal life encyclopedia*, 4:202–4. New York: Van Nostrand Reinhold.

Lagler, K. F. 1956. *Freshwater fishery biology.* 2d ed. Dubuque, Iowa: Brown Co.

Lagler, K. F.; Bardach, J. E.; and Miller, R. R. 1962. *Ichthyology.* New York: Wiley.

Lake, J. S. 1971. *Freshwater fishes and rivers of Australia.* Melbourne: Nelson.

————. 1978. *Australian freshwater fishes.* Melbourne: Nelson.

La Monte, F. 1952. *Marine game fishes of the world.* Garden City, N.Y.: Doubleday.

Liem, K. F. 1963. *The comparative osteology and phylogeny of the*

Anabantoidei (Teleostei, Pisces). Illinois Biol. Monogr. no. 30.

———. 1967 a. Functional morphology of the head of the anabantoid teleost fish *Helostoma temmincki*. *J. Morph.* 121:135–58.

———. 1967 b. A morphological study of *Luciocephalus pulcher*, with notes on gular elements in other recent teleosts. *J. Morph.* 121:103–33.

———. 1970. Comparative functional anatomy of the Nandidae (Pisces:Teleostei). *Fieldiana (Zool.)* 56:1–166.

Limbaugh, C. 1961. Cleaning symbiosis. *Sci. Amer.* 205:42–49 (August).

Lineaweaver, T. H., III, and Backus, R. H. 1973. *The natural history of sharks.* New York: Doubleday.

Linnaeus, C. 1758. *Systema naturae: regnum animale.* 10th ed. Facsimile reprint. Leipzig: Engelmann, 1894.

Lissmann, H. W. 1958. On the function and evolution of electric organs in fish. *J. Exp. Biol.* 35, no. 1:156–91.

Llewellyn, L. C. 1974. Spawning, development, and distribution of the southern pigmy perch *Nannoperca australis australis* Gunther from Inland Waters in Eastern Australia. *Aust. J. Mar. Freshwat. Res.* 25:121–49.

Lowe-McConnell, R. H. 1975. *Fish communities in tropical freshwaters.* London: Longman.

Luling, Karl H. 1974. Dipnoi. In *Encyclopaedia Britannica macropaedia*, 5:813–15.

Lundberg, J. G., and Baskin, J. N. 1969. *The caudal skeleton of the catfishes, order: Siluriformes.* Amer. Mus. Novititates no. 2398.

McAllister, D. E. 1963. *A revision of the smelt family, Osmeridae.* Bull. Nat. Mus. Can. no. 191.

McCormick, H. W.; Allen, T.; and Young, W. E. 1963. *Shadows in the sea.* Philadelphia: Chilton Co.

McCulloch, A. R. 1929–30. *A checklist of the fishes recorded from Australia.* Aust. Mus. Mem. no. 5.

MacDonald, C. M. 1978. Morphological and biochemical systematics of Australian freshwater and estuarine percichthyid fishes. *Aust. J. Mar. Freshwat. Res.* 29:667–98.

McDowall, R. M. 1969. Relationships of galaxioid fishes with a further discussion of Salmoniform classification. *Copeia,* no. 4, pp. 796–824.

———. 1970 a. Comments on a new taxonomy of *Retropinna* (Galaxioidei:Reptropinnidae). *N.Z. J. Mar. Freshwat. Res. 4,* no. 3:312–24.

———. 1970 b. The galaxiid fishes of New Zealand. *Bull. Mus. Comp. Zool.* 139, no. 7:341–432.

———. 1971 a. The galaxiid fishes of South America. *J. Linn. Soc.* 50, no. 1:33–73.

———. 1971 b. Fishes of the family Aplochitonidae. *J. Roy. Soc. N.Z. J,* no. 1:31–52.

———. 1972. The species problem in freshwater fishes and the taxonomy of diadromous and lacustrine populations of *Galaxias maculatus* (Jenyns). *J.Roy. Soc. N.Z. 2,* no. 3:325–67.

———. 1973 a. The status of the South African galaxiid (Pisces: Galaxiidae). *Ann. Cape Prov. Mus. (Nat. Hist.)* 9, no. 5:91–101.

———. 1973 b. *Galaxias indicus* Day, 1888—a *nomen dubium. J. Roy. Soc. N.Z.* 3, no. 2:191–92.

———. 1974. Specialization in the dentition of the southern graylings—genus *Prototroctes* (Galaxioidei: Prototroctidae). *J. Fish Biol.* 6:209–13.

———. 1976. Fishes of the family Prototroctidae (Salmoniformes). *Aust. J. Mar. Freshwat. Res.* 27:641–59.

———. 1978 a. Generalized tracks and dispersal in biogeography. *Syst. Zool.* 27:88–104.

———. 1978 b. *New Zealand freshwater fishes.* Auckland: Heinemann.

———. 1979. Fishes of the family Retropinnidae (Pisces: Salmoniformes)—a taxonomic revision and synopsis. *J. Roy. Soc. N.Z.* 9, no. 1:85–121.

———, ed. 1980. *Freshwater fishes of south-eastern Australia.* Sydney: Reed.

McDowall, R. M., and Frankenberg, R. S. In press. The galaxiid fishes of Australia (Salmoniformes: Galaxiidae). *Rec. Aust. Mus.*

McDowall, R. M., and Fulton, W. 1978. A revision of the genus *Paragalaxias* Scott (Salmoniformes: Galaxiidae). *Aust. J. Mar. Freshwat. Res.* 29:93–108.

McPhail, J. D. 1963. Geographic variation in North American ninespine sticklebacks, *Pungitius pungitius. J. Fish. Res. Bd. Canada* 20, no. 1:27–44.

McPhail, J.D., and Lindsey, C. C. 1970. *Freshwater fishes of northwestern Canada and Alaska.* Fish. Res. Bd. Can. Bull. no. 173.

Mago Leccia, F. 1970. *Lista de los peces de Venezuela incluyendo un estudio preliminar sobre la ictiogeografia del pais.* Caracas: Ministerio de Agricultura y Cria.

Mahdi, Nuri. N.d. *Fishes of Iraq.* Ministry of Education.

Maitland, P. S. 1977. Freshwater fishes of Britain and Europe. London: Hamlyn.

Mansueti, A. J. 1963. Some changes in morphology during ontogeny in the pirate perch, *Aphredoderus s. sayanus. Copeia,* no. 3, pp. 546–57.

Masters, C. O. 1968. The most dreaded fish in the Amazon River. *Carolina Tips* 31, no. 2:5–6.

Matthew, E. D. 1915. Climate and evolution. *Ann. N.Y. Acad. Sci.* 24:171–318.

Mayr, E. 1944. Wallace's Line in light of recent zoogeographic studies. *Quart. Rev. Biol.* 19:1–14.

———, ed. 1952. The problem of land connections across the south Atlantic with special reference to the Mesozoic. *Bull. Amer. Mus. Nat. Hist.* 99:79–258.

Meek, A. 1916. *The migrations of fish.* London: Arnold.

Mees, G. F. 1961. Description of a new fish of the family Galaxiidae from Western Australia. *J. Roy. Soc. West. Aust.* 44:33–38.

Meinken, H. 1974. *Suborder labyrinth fishes.* In *Grzimek's animal life encyclopedia,* 5:212–13. New York: Van Nostrand Reinhold Co.

Mendis, A. S. 1954. Fishes of Ceylon. Fisheries Research Stations Bull. no. 2. Ceylon: Dept. of Fisheries.

Messtorff, H. J. 1973. Codfishes. In *Grzimek's animal life encyclopedia,* 4:405–25. New York: Van Nostrand Reinhold.

Midgley, S. H. 1968. *A study of Nile perch in Africa and its suitability for Australian conditions.* Winston Churchill Memorial Trust (Australia) Fellowship Report no. 3.

Miles, R. S. 1977. Dipnoan (lungfish) skulls and the relationships of the group: a study based on new species from the Devonian of Australia. *Zool. J. Linn. Soc.* 61:1–328.

Miller, D. J., and Lea, R. N. 1972. *Guide to the coastal marine fishes of California.* Calif. Dept. of Fish and Game Fish Bull. no. 157.

Miller, R. J., and Evans, H. E. 1965. External morphology of the brain and lips in catostomid fishes. *Copeia,* no. 4, pp. 467–87.

Miller, R. R. 1958. Origin and affinities of the freshwater fish fauna of western North America. In *Zoogeography,* ed. C. L. Hubbs, pp. 187–222. Washington, D.C.: AAAS. Reprint. New York: Arno Press, 1974.

———. 1961. Speciation rates in some freshwater fishes of western

North America. In *Vertebrate Speciation*, ed. F. Blair, pp. 537–60. Austin: University of Texas Press.

———. 1966. Geographical distribution of Central American freshwater fishes. *Copeia*, no. 4, pp. 773–802.

———. 1979. Ecology, habits, and relationships of the Middle American cuatro ojos, *Anableps dowi* (Pisces: Anablepidae). *Copeia*, no. 1, pp. 82–91.

Miller, R. R., and Fitzsimons, J. M. 1971. *Ameca splendens*, a new genus and species of goodeid fish from western Mexico, with remarks on the classification of the Goodeidae. *Copeia*, no. 1, pp. 1–13.

Mitchell, R. W.; Russell, W. H.; and Elliott, W. R. 1977. Mexican eyeless characin fishes, genus *Astyanax*: environment, distribution, and evolution. Texas Tech. Univ. Mus. Spec. Publ. no. 12. Lubbock: Texas Tech. Univ.

Mong, S. J., and Berra, T. M. 1979. The effects of increasing dosages of X-radiation on the chromosomes of the central mudminnow, *Umbra limi* (Kirtland) (Salmoniformes: Umbridae). *J. Fish. Biol.* 14:523–27.

Moore, G. A. 1968. Fishes. In *Vertebrates of the United States*, ed. W. F. Blair et al., pp. 22–165. 2d ed. New York: McGraw-Hill.

Moore, W. S.; Miller, R. R.; and Schultz, R. J. 1970. Distribution, adaptation, and probable origin of an all-female form of *Poeciliopsis* (Pisces: Poeciliidae) in northwestern Mexico. *Evolution* 24:789–95.

Moriarty, C. 1978. *Eels: a natural and unnatural history*. New York: Universe Books.

Morrow, J. E. 1974. *Illustrated keys to the fresh-water fishes of Alaska*. Anchorage: Alaska Northwest Publ. Co.

Morton, W. M. 1980. Goodbye Dolly. *Fisheries* 5, no. 3:17–21.

Moyle, P. B. 1976. *Inland fishes of California*. Berkeley: University of California Press.

Munro, I. S. R. 1938. Handbook of Australian fishes no. 10. *Fisheries Newsletter* 16, no. 4:71–75.

———. 1955. *The marine and fresh water fishes of Ceylon*. Canberra: Dept. of External Affairs.

———. 1967. *The fishes of New Guinea*. Port Moresby, New Guinea: Dept. of Agr. Stock and Fish.

Myers, G. S. 1935. A new phallostethid fish from Palwan. *Proc. Biol. Soc. Washington* 48:5–6.

———. 1936. A new polynemid fish collected in the Sadong River, Sarawak, by Dr. William T. Hornaday, with notes on the genera of Polynemidae. *J. Wash. Acad. Sci.* 26:376–82.

———. 1937. Notes on phallostethid fishes. *Proc. U.S. Nat. Mus.* 84:137–43.

———. 1938. Fresh-water fishes and West Indian zoogeography. *Ann. Rep. Smithsonian Inst. for 1937*, pp. 339–64.

———. 1944. Two extraordinary new blind nematognath fishes from the Rio Negro, representing a new subfamily of Pygidiidae, with a rearrangement of the genera of the family and illustrations of some previously described genera and species from Venezuela and Brazil. *Proc. California Acad. Sci.*, 4th ser. 23:591–602.

———. 1949. Salt-tolerance of fresh-water fish groups in relation to zoogeographical problems. *Bijdr. Dierk.* 28:315–22.

———. 1951. Freshwater fishes and East Indian zoogeography. *Stanford Ichthyol. Bull.* 4, no. 1:11–21.

———. 1952. Sharks and sawfishes in the Amazon. *Copeia*, no. 4, pp. 268–69.

———. 1960. The genera and ecological geography of the South American banjo catfishes, family Aspredinidae. *Stanford Ichthyol. Bull.* 7, no. 4:132–39.

———. 1966. Derivation of the freshwater fish fauna of Central America. *Copeia*, no. 4, pp. 766–73.

———. 1967. Zoogeographical evidence of the age of the South Atlantic Ocean. *Studies in tropical oceanography*, no. 5, pp. 614–21.

———, ed. 1972. *The piranha book*. Neptune City, N.J.: T.F.H. Publ.

———. 1979. A freshwater sea horse. *Tropical fish hobbyist* 28:29–34 (June).

Nalbant, T. 1973. Loaches. In *Grzimek's animal life encyclopedia*, 4:355–60. New York: Van Nostrand Reinhold.

Nelson, E. M. 1948. The comparative morphology of the Weberian apparatus of the Catostomidae and its significance in systematics. *J. Morph.* 83, no. 2:225–51.

———. 1976. Some notes on the Chinese sucker *Myxocyprinus*. *Copeia*, no. 3:594–95.

Nelson, G. J. 1969. *Infraorbital bones and their bearing on the phylogeny and geography of Osteoglosomorph fishes*. Amer. Mus. Novitiates no. 2394.

———. 1970. *The hyobranchial apparatus of teleostean fishes of the families Engraulidae and Chirocentridae*. Amer. Mus. Novitiates no. 2410.

———. 1972. *Cephalic sensory canals, pitlines, and the classification of esocoid fishes, with notes on galaxiids and other teleosts*. Amer. Mus. Novititates no. 2492.

———. 1974. Paracanthopterygii. In *Encyclopaedia Britannica macropaedia*, 13:979–82.

———. 1978. From Candolle to Croizat: comments on the history of biogeography. *J. Hist. Biol.* 11, no. 2:269–305.

Nelson, G. J., and Rothman, M. N. 1973. The species of gizzard shads (Dorosomatinae) with particular reference to the Indo-Pacific region. *Bull. Amer. Mus. Nat. Hist.* 150:133–203.

Nelson, J. S. 1971. Comparison of the pectoral and pelvic skeletons and of some other bones and their phylogenetic implications in the Aulorhynchidae and Gasterosteidae (Pisces). *J. Fish. Res. Bd. Can.* 28:427–42.

———. 1976. *Fishes of the world*. New York: Wiley.

Netboy, A. 1974. *The salmon: their fight for survival*. Boston: Houghton Mifflin Co.

Nichols, J. T. 1943. *The freshwater fishes of China*. Natural History of Central Asia, vol. 9.

Norden, C. R. 1961. Comparative osteology of representative salmonid fishes, with particular reference to the grayling (*Thymallus arcticus*) and its phylogeny. *J. Fish. Res. Bd. Can.* 18, no. 5:679–781.

Norman, J. R. 1934. *A systematic monograph of the flatfishes (Heterosomata)*. Vol. 1. London: British Museum (Nat. Hist.).

———. 1966. A draft synopsis of the orders, families, and genera of recent fishes and fish-like vertebrates. London: British Museum (Nat. Hist.).

Norman, J. R., and Greenwood, P. H. 1975. *A history of fishes*. 3d ed. New York: Wiley.

Novacek, M. J., and Marshall, L. G. 1976. Early biogeographic history of ostariophysean fishes. *Copeia*, no. 1, pp. 1–12.

Orr, R. T. 1976. *Vertebrate biology*. 4th ed. Philadelphia: Saunders.

Ovchynnyk, M. M. 1967. *Freshwater fishes of Ecuador*. Latin American Studies Center Monograph Series no. 1. East Lansing: Mich. St. Univ.

Parrish, R. H. 1966. A review of the Gadopsidae, with a description of a new species from Tasmania. Master's thesis, Oregon State University.

Patterson, C. 1974. Atheriniformes. In *Encyclopaedia Britannica macropaedia*, 2:269–74.

———. 1975. The distribution of Mesozoic freshwater fishes. *Mem. Mus. Natn. hist. nat.* 88:156–73.

Patterson, C., and Rosen, D. E. 1977. Review of ichthyodectiform and other Mesozoic teleost fishes and the theory and practice of classifying fossils. *Bull. Amer. Mus. Nat. Hist.* 158, no. 2:81–172.

Pelseneer, P. 1904. La "Ligne de Weber": limite zoologique de l'Asie et de l'Australie. *Bull. Classe Sci. Acad. R. Belgique*, pp. 1001–22.

Peters, N. 1973. Gonorynchiformes. In *Grzimek's animal life encyclopedia*, 4: pp. 269–75. New York: Van Nostrand Reinhold.

Pflieger, W. L. 1971. A Distributional Study of Missouri fishes. *Univ. of Kans. Mus. Nat. Hist.* 20, no. 3:225–570.

Platnick, N. I., and Nelson, G. 1978. A method of analysis for historical biogeography. *Syst. Zool.* 27:1–16.

Poll, M. 1973. Nombre et distribution geographique des poissons d'eau douce africains. *Bull. Mus. natn. hist. nat.*, 3d ser. no. 150, *Écologie generale* 6:113–28.

Poll, M., and Gosse, J. P. 1969. Revision des Malapteruridae (Pisces, Siluriformes) et description d'une deuxième espèce de silvre electrique: *Malapterurus microstoma. Bull. Inst. R. Sci. Nat. Belg.* 45, no. 38:1–12.

Polunin, I. 1972. Who says fish can't climb trees. *Nat. Geog. Mag.* 141:85–91 (January).

Pope, P. 1973. *A dictionary of sharks*. St. Petersburg, Fla.: Great Outdoors Publ. Co.

Prashad, B., and Mukerji, D. D. 1929. The fish of the Indawgyi Lake and the streams of the Myitkina District (Upper Burma). *Rec. Indian Mus.* 31:161–223.

Ramaswami, L. S. 1957. Skeleton of cyprinoid fishes in relation to phylogenetic studies, 8: The skull and Weberian ossicles of Catostomidae. *Proc. Zool. Soc. Calcutta, Mookerjee Mem. Vol.*, pp. 293–303.

Randall, J. E. 1963. Dangerous sharks of the western Atlantic. In *Sharks and survival*, ed. P. W. Gilbert, pp. 339–61. Boston: Heath.

Regan, C. T. 1909. A revision of the fishes of the genus *Elops. Ann. Mag. Nat. Hist.*, 3d ser. 8:37–40.

———. 1911. The classification of the teleostean fishes of the order Ostariophysi, I: Cyprinoidae. *Ann. Mag. Nat. Hist.*, 8th ser. 8:13–32.

———. 1919. Note of Chaudhuria, a teleostean fish of the order Opisthomi. *Ann. Mag. Nat. Hist.*, 9th ser. 3:198–99.

Ricciuti, E. R. 1973. *Killers of the seas*. New York: Walker & Co.

Roberts, T. R. 1969. Osteology and relationships of characoid fishes, particularly the genera *Hepsetus, Salminus, Hoplias, Ctenolucius,* and *Acestrorhynchus. Proc. Calif. Acad. Sci.*, 4th ser. 36, no. 15:391–500.

———. 1971a. The fishes of the Malaysian family Phallostethidae (Atheriniformes). *Breviora*, no. 374, pp. 1–27.

———. 1971b. Osteology of the Malaysian phallostethoid fish *Ceratostethus bicornis*, with a discussion of the evolution of remarkable structural novelties in its jaws and external genitalia. *Bull. Mus. Comp. Zool.* 142, no. 4:393–418.

———. 1971c. *Micromischodus sugillatus*, a new hemiodontid characin fish from Brazil, and its relationship the Chilodontidae. *Breviora*, no. 367, pp. 1–25.

———. 1972. Ecology of fishes in the Amazon and Congo basins. *Bull. Mus. Comp. Zool.* 143, no. 2:117–47.

———. 1973. Osteology and relationships of the Prochilocontidae, a South American family of characoid fishes. *Bull. Mus. Comp. Zool.* 145, no. 4:213–35.

———. 1974a. Dental polymorphism and systematics in *Saccodon*, a neotropical genus of freshwater fishes (Parodontidae, Characoidei). *J. Zool.* 173, no. 3:303–21.

———. 1974b. Osteology and classification of the neotropical characoid fishes of the families Hemiodontidae (including Anodontidae) and Parodontidae. *Bull. Mus. Comp. Zool.* 146, no. 9:411–72.

———. 1975. Geographical distribution of African freshwater fishes. *Zool. J. Linn. Soc.* 57:249–319.

Romer, A. S. 1966. *Vertebrate paleontology*. 3d ed. Chicago: University of Chicago Press.

Rosen, D. E. 1962. *Comments on the relationships of the North American cave fishes of the family Amblyopsidae.* Amer. Mus. Novitates no. 2109.

———. 1964. The relationships and taxonomic position of the halfbeaks, killifishes, silversides and their relatives. *Bull. Amer. Mus. Nat. Hist.* 127:219–67.

———. 1973. Suborder Cyprinodontoidei. In *Fishes of the western North Atlantic*, pp. 229–62. Mem. Sears Found. for Mar. Res. 1, part 6. New Haven, Conn.

———. 1974. Phylogeny and zoogeography of salmoniform fishes and relationships of *Lepidogalaxias salmondroides. Bull. Amer. Mus. Nat. Hist.* 153, no. 2:265–326.

———. 1975. A vicariance model of Caribbean biogeography. *Syst. Zool.* 24:431–64.

———. 1978. Vicariant patterns and historical explanation in biogeography. *Syst. Zool.* 27:159–88.

———. 1979. Fishes from the uplands and intermontane basins of Guatemala: revisionary studies and comparative geography. *Bull. Amer. Mus. Nat. Hist.* 162, no. 5:267–376.

Rosen, D. M., and Bailey, R. M. 1963. The Poeciliid fishes (Cyprinodontiformes), their structure, zoogeography, and systematics. *Bull. Amer. Mus. Nat. Hist.* 126, no. 1:1–176.

Rosen, D. M., and Greenwood, P. H. 1970. *Origin of the Weberian apparatus and the relationships of the ostariophysan and gonorynchiform fishes.* Amer. Mus. Novitates no. 2428.

———. 1976. A fourth neotropical species of synbrachid eel and the phylogeny and systematics of synbranchiform fishes. *Bull. Amer. Mus. Nat. Hist.* 157:1–70.

Rosen, D. M., and Patterson, C. 1969. The structure and relationships of the paracanthopterygian fishes. *Bull. Amer. Mus. Nat. Hist.* 141, no. 3:357–474.

Rostlund, E. 1952. *Freshwater fish and fishing in native North America*. Univ. of Cal. Publ. in Geography no. 9. Berkeley.

Roughley, T. C. 1966. *Fish and fisheries of Australia*. Sydney: Angus & Robertson.

Runcorn, S. K., ed. 1962. *Continental drift*. New York: Academic Press.

Sazima, I. 1980. Behavior of two Brasilian species of parodontid fishes, *Apareiodon piracicabae* and *A. ibitiensis. Copeia*, no. 1, pp. 166–69.

Schmidt, J. 1922. The breeding places of the eel. *Phil. Trans. Roy. Soc.*, ser. B, 211:179–208.

———. 1925. The breeding places of the eel. *Ann. Rep. Smithson. Inst. 1924*, pp. 279–316.

Schubert, K. 1973. Order: Herring. In *Grzimek's animal life encyclopedia*, 4:172–201. New York: Van Nostrand Reinhold.

Schultz, L. P. 1963. Keys to the fishes of Washington, Oregon, and closely adjourning regions. *Univ. of Wash. Publ. in Biol.* 2, no. 4:103–228.

———. 1944. The catfishes of Venezuela with descriptions of thirty-eight new forms. *Proc. U.S. Nat. Mus.* 94:173–338.

———. 1946. A revision of the genera of mullets, fishes of the family Mugilidae, with descriptions of three new genera. *Proc. U.S. Nat. Mus.* 96:377–95.

———. 1948. A revision of six subfamilies of atherine fishes, with descriptions of new genera and species. *Proc. U.S. Nat. Mus.* 98:1–48.

Schultz, R. J. 1973. Unisexual fish: laboratory synthesis of a "species." *Science* 179:180–81.

Schwassmann, H.O., and Kruger, L. 1965. Experimental analysis of the visual system of the four-eyed fish *Anableps microlepis*. *Vision Research* 5:269–81.

Scientific American. 1973. *Continents adrift*. San Francisco: Freeman.

Scott, T. D.; Glover, C. J. M.; and Southcott, R. V. 1974. The marine and freshwater fishes of South Australia. South Aust.: Govt. Print.

Scott, W. B., and Crossman, E. J. 1973. *Freshwater fishes of Canada*. Fish. Res. Bd. Can. Bull. no. 184. Ottawa.

Smith, A. G., and Briden, J. C. 1977. Mesozoic and Cenozoic paleocontinental maps. Cambridge: Cambridge University Press.

Smith, H. M. 1936. The archer fish. *Nat. Hist.* 38:3–11.

———. 1945. The freshwater fishes of Siam, or Thailand. *Bull. U.S. Nat. Mus.* no. 188.

Smith, J. L. B. 1965. The sea fishes of southern Africa. 5th ed. South Africa: Central News Agency.

Soltz, D. L., and Naiman, R. J. 1978. *The natural history of native fishes in the Death Valley system*. Nat. Hist. Mus. Los Angeles Co. Sci. Ser. no. 30.

Springer, V. G., and Fraser, T. H. 1976. *Synonymy of the fish families Cheilobranchidae (=Alabetidae) and Gobiesocidae, with descriptions of two new species of "Alabes."* Smithsonian Contri. Zool. no. 234.

Stead, D. G. 1963. Sharks and rays of Australian seas. Sydney: Angus and Robertson.

Sterba, G. 1966. Freshwater fishes of the world. Rev. ed. London: Studio Vista.

Sullivan, W. 1974. Continents in motion. New York: McGraw-Hill.

Suttkus, R. D. 1963. Order Lepisostei. In *Fishes of the western North Atlantic*, pp. 61–88. Mem. Sears Found. for Mar. Res. no. 1, pt. 3. New Haven, Conn.

Svetovidov, A. N. 1962. *Gadiformes*. Fauna of the U.S.S.R. 9, no. 4. Translation of 1948 Russian edition. Nat. Sci. Found., Israel Program for Scientific Translations.

Tarling, D., and Tarling, M. 1975. *Continental drift*. Garden City, N.Y.: Anchor Books.

Tarp, F. H. 1952. A revision of the family Embiotociade (the surfperches). *Calif. Dept. Fish and Game Fish Bull.* no. 112.

Taylor, W. R. 1969. *A revision of the catfish genus Noturus Rafinesque with an analysis of higher groups in the Ictaluridae*. Bull. U.S. Nat. Mus. no. 282.

Tesch, F. W. 1977. *The eel*. London: Chapman and Hall.

Thomerson, J. E., and Thorson, T. B. 1977. The bull shark, *Carcharhinus leucas*, from the upper Mississippi River, near Alton, Illinois. *Copeia*, no. 1, pp. 166–68.

Thompson, K. W. 1979. Cytotaxonomy of forty-one species of Neotropical Cichlidae. *Copeia*, no. 4, pp. 679–91.

Thomson, D. A.; Findley, L. T.; and Kerstitch, A. N. 1979. *Reef fishes of the Sea of Cortez*. New York: Wiley.

Thomson, J. M. 1964. *A bibliography of systematic references of the grey mullets (Mugilidae)*. CSIRO Divisions of Fisheries & Oceanography. Technical Paper no. 16. Melbourne.

Thorson, T. B. 1971. Movement of bull sharks, *Carcharinus leucas*, between Caribbean Sea and Lake Nicaragua demonstrated by tagging. *Copeia*, no. 2, pp. 336–38.

———. 1976a. The status of the Lake Nicaragua shark: an updated appraisal. In *Investigations of the ichthyofauna of Nicaraguan lakes*, ed. T. B. Thorson, pp. 561–74.

———, ed. 1976b. *Investigations of the ichthyofauna of Nicaraguan lakes*. Lincoln: School of Life Sciences, Univ. Nebr.–Lincoln.

Thorson, T. B.; Cowan, C. M.; and Watson, D. E. 1967. *Potamotrygon* spp. Elasmobranchs with low urea content. *Science* 158:375–77.

Thorson, T. B., and Gerst, J. W. 1972. Comparison of some parameters of serum and uterine fluid of pregnant, viviparous sharks (*Carcharhinus leucas*) and serum of the near-term young. *Comp. Biochem. Physiol.* 42A:33–40.

Thorson, T. B., and Watson, D. E. 1975. Reassignment of the African freshwater stingray, *Potamotrygon garouaensis*, to the genus *Dasyatis*, on physiologic and morphologic grounds. *Copeia*, no. 4, pp. 701–12.

Thorson, T. B.; Watson, D. E.; and Cowan, C. M. 1966. The status of the freshwater shark of Lake Nicaragua. *Copeia*, no. 4, pp. 385–402.

Thys van den Audenaerde, D. F. E. 1961. L'anatomie de *Phractolaemus ansorgei* Blgr et la position systematique des Phractolaemidae. *Annls Mus r. Afr. cent.* 103:101–67.

Tinbergen, N. 1952. The curious behavior of the sticklebacks. *Sci. Amer.* 187:22–26.

Tinker, S. W. 1978. Fishes of Hawaii. Honolulu: Hawaiian Service.

Trautman, M. B. 1957. *The fishes of Ohio*. Columbus: Ohio State University Press.

Trewavas, E. 1942. The cichlid fishes of Syria and Palestine. *Ann. Mag. Nat. Hist.*, 11th ser. 9:526–36.

———. 1977. The sciaenid fishes (croakers or drums) of the Indo–west Pacific. *Trans. Zool. Soc. Lond.* 33:253–541.

Tucker, D. W. 1959. A new solution to the Atlantic eel problem. *Nature* 183:495–501.

Turner, C. L. 1946. *A contribution to the taxonomy and zoogeography of the goodeid fishes*. Occ. Pap. Mus. Zool. Univ. Mich.

Vari, R. P. 1978. The terapon perches (Percoidei, Teraponidae): a cladistic analysis and taxonomic revision. *Bull. Amer. Mus. Nat. Hist.* 159, no. 5:175–340.

Vinton, K. W., and Stickler, W. H. 1941. The carnero: A fish parasite of man and possibly of other mammals. *Amer. J. of Surgery* 54:511–19.

Vladykov, V. D. 1963. A review of salmonid genera and their broad geographical distribution. *Trans. Prog. Soc. Can.* 4, no. 1:495–504.

———. 1964. Quest for the true breeding area of the American eel (*Anguilla rostrata* Lesueur). *J. Fish Res. Bd. Can.* 21:1523–30.

Vladykov, V. D., and Greeley, J. R. 1963. Order Acipenseroidei. In *Fishes of the western North Atlantic*, pp. 24–60. Mem. Sears Found. Mar. Res. number 1, part 3. New Haven, Conn.

REFERENCES

Vogt, D. 1973. Catfishes. In *Grzimek's animal life encyclopedia*, 4:361–92. New York: Van Nostrand Reinhold.

Wade, R. A. 1962. The biology of the tarpon, *Megalops atlanticus*, and the ox-eye, *Megalops cyprinoides*, with emphasis on larvae development. *Bull. Mar. Sci. Gulf Caribb.* 12:545–622.

Wallace, A. R. 1860. On the zoological geography of the Malay Archipelago. *J. Proc. Linnean Soc. London* 4:172–84.

———. 1876. *The geographical distribution of animals*. 2 vols. London: Macmillan. Reprint Hafner Publ. Co., 1962.

Weber, M., and De Beaufort, L. F. 1913. *The fishes of the Indo-Australian Archipelago*. Vol. 2. Leiden: Brill. Reprint 1965.

———. 1922. *Fishes of the Indo-Australian Archipelago, IV: Heteromi, Solenichthyes, Synentognathi, Percesoces, Labyrinthici, Microcyprini*. Leiden: Brill.

Wegener, A. 1966. *The origin of continents and oceans*. New York: Dover. Reprint of 4th ed., 1929.

Weitzman, S. H. 1954. The osteology and relationships of the South American characid fishes of the subfamily Gasteropelecinae. *Stanford Ichthyol. Bull.* 4, no. 4:212–63.

———. 1960. Further notes on the relationships and classification of the South American fishes of the subfamily Gasteropelecinae. *Stanford Ichthyol. Bull.* 7, no. 4:217–39.

———. 1962. The osteology of *Brycon meeki*, a generalized characid fish, with an osteological definition of the family. *Stanford Ichthyol. Bull.* 8, no. 1:1–77.

———. 1964. Osteology and relationships of South American characid fishes of subfamily Lebiasininae and Erythrininae with special reference to subtribe Nannostomia. *Proc. U.S. Nat. Mus.* 116, no. 3499:127–70.

———. 1966. Review of South American characid fishes of subtribe Nannostomina. *Proc. U.S. Nat. Mus.* 119, no. 3538.

———. 1967. The origin of the stomiatoid fishes with comments on the classification of salmoniform fishes. *Copeia*, no. 3, pp. 507–40.

———. 1978. *Three new species of fishes of the genus Nanostomus from the Brazilian states of Para and Amazonas (Teleostei: Lebiasinidae)*. Smithsonian Contri. Zool., no. 263, pp. 1–14.

Weitzman, S. H., and Cobb J. S. 1975. *A revision of the South American fishes of the genus Nannostomus Gunther (family Lebiasinidae)*. Smithsonian Contri. Zool. no. 186.

Wheeler, A. 1969. *The fishes of the British Isles and north-west Europe*. East Lansing: Michigan State University Press.

———. 1974. Scorpaeniformes. In *Encyclopaedia Britannica macropaedia*, 16:397–401.

———. 1975. Fishes of the world. New York: Macmillan.

Whitaker, J. O., Jr. 1968. *Keys to the vertebrates of the eastern United States excluding birds*. Minneapolis, Minn.: Burgess Publishing Co.

Whitehead, P. J. 1962. The species of *Elops* (Pisces: Elopidae). *Ann. Mag. Nat. Hist.*, 13th ser. 5:321–29.

———. 1963. A contribution to the classification of clupeoid fishes. *Ann. Mag. Nat. Hist.*, 13th ser. 5:737–50.

Whitley, G. P. 1968. A checklist of the fishes recorded from the New Zealand region. *Aust. Zool.* 15, no. 1:1–102.

Whitley, G. P., and Allan, J. 1958. *The sea-horse and its relatives*. Melbourne: Georgian House.

Wickler, W. 1968. Mimicry in plants and animals. New York: McGraw-Hill.

Wiley, E. O. 1976. The phylogeny and biogeography of fossil and recent gars (Actinopterygii: Lepisosteidae). *Univ. Kans. Mus. Nat. Hist. Misc. Publ.* no. 64, pp. 1–111.

Wiley, M. L., and Collette, B. B. 1970. Breeding tubercles and contact organs in fishes: their occurrence, structure, and significance. *Bull. Amer. Mus. Nat. Hist.* 143, no. 3:143–216.

Williams, J. D. 1975. Systematics of the percid fishes of the subgenus *Ammocrypta*, genus *Ammocrypta*, with descriptions of two new species. *Bull. Alabama Mus. Nat. Hist.*, no. 1, pp. 1–56.

Williams, J. D., and Robins, C. R. 1970. Variation in populations of the fish *Cottus carolinae* in the Alabama river system with description of a new subspecies from below the fall line. *Amer. Midl. Nat.* 83, no. 2:368–81.

Winterbottom, R. 1974. *The familial phylogency of the Tetraodontiformes (Acanthopterygii: Pisces) as evidenced by their comparative myology*. Smithsonian Contri. Zool. no. 155.

Wood, G. L. 1972. *The Guinness book of animal facts and feats*. Middlesex: Guinness.

Woods, C. S. 1963. *Native and introduced freshwater fishes*. Wellington: Reed.

———. 1968. Variation and taxonomic changes in the family Retropinnidae (Salmonoidea). *N.Z. J. Mar. Freshwat. Res.* 2, no. 3:398–425.

Woods, L. P., and Inger, R. F. 1957. The cave, spring, and swamp fishes of the family Amblyopsidae of central and eastern United States. *Amer. Midl. Nat.* 58:232–56.

Wootton, R. J. 1976. *The biology of the sticklebacks*. London: Academic Press.

Yazdani, G. M. 1976. A new family of mastacembeloid fish from India. *J. Bombay Nat. Hist. Soc.* 73:166–70.

Yerger, R. W. 1974. Ostariophysi. In *Encyclopaedia Britannica macropaedia*, 13:757–63.

Young, W. E. 1934. *Shark! Shark!* New York: Gotham House.

Zahl, P. A. 1970. Seeking the truth about the feared piranha. *Nat. Geog. Mag.* 138:715–34 (November).

———. 1978. The four-eyed fish sees all. *Nat. Geog. Mag.* 153:390–94 (March).

Zahl, P. A.; McLaughlin, J. A.; and Gomprecht, R. J. 1977. Visual versatility and feeding of the four-eyed fishes, *Anableps. Copeia*, no. 4, pp. 791–93.

Zander, C. D. 1974. Suborder: Gobies. In *Grzimek's animal life encyclopedia*, 5:176–86. New York: Van Nostrand Reinhold.

Index

194